AF400734

TO COPE *and* TO PREVAIL

Growing up in Germany in 1930-50's

DR. ILSE-ROSE WARG

AuthorHouse™
1663 Liberty Drive
Bloomington, IN 47403
www.authorhouse.com
Phone: 1-800-839-8640

Published by AuthorHouse   11/26/2012

ISBN: 978-1-4772-8566-4 (sc)
ISBN: 978-1-4772-8567-1 (e)

Library of Congress Control Number: 2012920693

Acknowledgments

I'd like to express my appreciation to all the students who have taken my diversity course, "The History and Culture of Modern Germany." Since 2004, students have been asking me to write down my stories. The classes of 2010 and 2011 had the chance to read the drafts of ten chapters. They told me that they liked my proposed book because it reads like a story.

My thanks also to Wolfgang Hamberger and Horst Strohbusch, who kindly gave me permission to quote from their books. They join the many people I was able to consult concerning WWII and the GDR (German Democratic Republic). Hamberger helped to broaden the spectrum of my book by supplying input on the Rhineland.

For my account of the GDR after 1953, I had to rely on interviews with Dr. Strohbusch, Eberhard Fleischer, Horst Bollmann, and my relatives who are still residing in Germany and Switzerland. Special thanks to my three siblings: Ernst W. Höfer, Hildegard M. F. Steinbömer, and Professor Reinhold Höfer, PhD. They refreshed my memory and gave me permission to mention them freely throughout the book.

Especially helpful was my cousin Hermjörg Oemler. He took my husband and me to revisit Klostermansfeld, Eisleben, Edersleben, and Sangerhausen. He also provided valuable photos. I thank my cousin Ingrid Thiel for her information on events that occurred after most of my family members' farms had been confiscated in 1945–46.

I am greatly indebted to my husband, Jamison B. Warg, PG, my son, Ernst Bernhard, and my daughter, Sonja S. M. Chestnut, who supported me throughout the writing process. They read the first drafts and gave valuable suggestions.

Last but not least, I thank Erin M. Kelly, who patiently took on the task of serving as my editor. Her continual encouragement led me to write my story as a history book of a different style.

Ilse-Rose Warg, PhD
Instructor and Lecturer of German
Pennsylvania State University, Altoona

From the Editor

Before I agreed to edit this book in June 2010, I wasn't much for history. I hadn't picked up or even opened a history book since high school. I thought "history" was just that—history—meant to stay stuck in its pages. Roughly a month into the editing process, my eyes were opened.

I found this wasn't a typical historical account like the ones I was forced to read in high school. It was much more than that. With each word, each page I edited, I came to appreciate and understand the way history goes hand-in-hand with people, their lives, and the decisions they make. In this case, the pages of history turn in Germany and trace the author's path to adulthood

There are a lot of adjectives I could use to describe the journey the writer takes you on in this book, but if I listed even one, I would only be speaking for myself—and even if I did, it still wouldn't begin to scratch the surface.

This is a story that needs to be read with no preconceived notions or outside opinions—about history in general or the book itself. The author felt it was important for you to hear her voice in every sentence you're about to read. To that end, I've left most of her words, phrases, and dialogue unedited, per her request, in an attempt to stay true to her German roots and personal writing style.

As her editor, I was amazed at the way she conveys courage and intelligence through words. It only gave me more appreciation for the obstacle course she had to go through to become the person she is today. As a general reader, every page left me wanting more but, at the same time, also left me feeling incredibly humble.

My only hope is that these words will do the same, if not more, for you.

Erin M. Kelly
Editor

Table of Contents

Introduction

My interest in writing this book is threefold. Primarily, I want to give an account of Germany during the rise of the Third Reich, the WWII years, the aftermath of the war, and the division into East and West Germany. I focus not so much on the politics and economics, which are readily available in many history books, but on Germany's people, their customs, and their traditions—in short, their culture. Secondly, I hope to make this phase of German history more enjoyable for readers who are generally interested in these eras of Germany but have no scholarly background. My third reason for this text is to provide students who select the diversity course "Modern German History and Culture" with a supplementary reading. Diversity courses are designed to cover four areas: politics, economics, technology, and culture. Whereas the first two aspects of German history are dealt with in many comprehensive history books, the culture that prevailed or was adopted during these years is neglected. I found the following to be true:

- Most history books about modern Germany written by English or American author, usually depict their point of view.
- Their authors work predominately with abstract data, and in their attempt to include as much detail as possible in a comprehensive manner, they frequently use terms with which the ordinary reader cannot identify.
- Seldom are the emotional reactions of the common everyday people developed, and the influences that led them to make decisions are overlooked.
- German customs and traditions are hardly mentioned.
- Conventional history books rely on complicated sentence structure that too often forfeits enjoyable and easy reading.
- The result is the loss of the "story" element of history.

I agree with the Cambridge historian Geoffrey Elton, who states, "Whatever else history may be, it must at heart be a story, a story of the changing fortunes of men, and political history therefore comes first because, above all the forms for historical study, it wants to, even needs to, tell a story."[1] Yes, history must be a "story." After all, in German, the word for "history" is the same as for "story," namely, *Geschichte*. To me, a story based on historical facts embraces not only the politics of a time period but also the experiences, emotions, and culture of the people who must cope with their political and social circumstances.

The understanding of another nation is exactly what diversity courses should convey to American students whose horizons ought to be broadened by participating in these classes. Therefore, professors must introduce undergraduates not only to the politics, economics, and technology of a nation, but also to its sociological and cultural conditions. For this purpose, they select, in addition to comprehensive history books, literary texts that are usually good translations of a novel or story by well-known German authors of the nineteenth or twentieth century—for example, novels like *Effi Briest* by Theodor Fontane or stories like "Paul the Puppeteer" by Theodor Storm. Both authors are from North Germany and depicted the culture and the rise of the Prussian state as experienced by their fictional characters.

For the early twentieth century, Erich Maria Remarque's novel *All Quiet on the Western Front,* which covers changing attitudes during the WWI years, is a popular choice. There are also excerpts from expressionistic dramas by Kaiser or some from the Dadaism era by Toller and others from the early exil literature by Brecht. They overlap the Weimar Republic era, which can be brought alive through films like *The Blue Angel* or *Metropolis* and a documentary on the Bauhaus movement

When it comes to literary texts for the 1930s, 1940s, and 1950s, there are good translations of German literature describing the Nazi period, the WWII years, the war aftermath, or the *Wirtschaftswunder* (economical miracle years), but for my purpose, these are too confined in their timeframe. In addition, they do not give detailed descriptions of the traditions and customs that survived or were adopted by governments to indoctrinate the youth during the turmoil of the time. Also, these stories are often told from

---

1   Geoffrey Elton, *Political History: Principles and Practice* (New York and Cambridge: Basic Books, 1970), 5.

a limited perspective, missing the experience of the people living in other German regions.

As a child, I lived in the middle of Germany (formerly called its Green Heart) and in West Prussia (previously regarded as East Germany), including the just-recaptured Polish Corridor. I am the eyewitness from those areas. In the twelve chapters of my book, I take readers on a journey. They are given the chance to identify with characters including my friends, relatives, and fictional members of the Stammtisch.[2] They and nonfiction characters[3] talk about personalities in politics, economics, and the cultural scene. Their discussions serve two purposes: to develop the characters as their attitudes change over the course of time, and to give me an opportunity for humorous passages, since traditions and customs of other nations often seem funny to those not raised in them.

To extend the journey into the Rhineland, I draw on experiences brought to life by Wolfgang Hamberger in his book *America—my fascination*[4]. During the Nazi era and the end of WWII, Hamberger lived near the Rhine River, where the bombing of industrial cities and strafing of civilians were more pronounced than in the villages of middle Germany.

My book brings German culture to the forefront. It shows how people responded to ever-changing rules, laws, and regulations. I delve into the emotional aspect of history, into what makes history a "story." Although my account of German culture ends with the 1950s, I give a short glimpse of both the building of the Berlin Wall and its peaceful fall. I draw on archival documents gathered by Dr. Horst Strohbusch in his commemorative book, *Das Licht kam aus der Kirche*[5], published in 1999. He reprinted it in 2009, this time to remind the *Ossis* (East Germans from the former Russian zone) how their outlook toward the *Wessis* (West Germans from the three western zones) had changed and what they had to face in the eitghties.

---

2   To this day, a *Stammtisch* is a group—mainly men—that reserves a table for a designated time and day of the week at an inn, where they play the popular card game Skat and discuss current events. Their *Stammtischpolitik* can be translated as "armchair politics."

3   I chose to modify the names of some nonfictional characters.

4   Wolfgang Hamberger. *America—my fascination: Biography of a friendship from the Nazi era to the present*, trans. Joan Clough-Lamb. Munich and Penzance, Fulda, 2009. The title does not follow the English or American capitalization rules. The translation was published through Impressum (Point Alpha Stiftung) via Hamberger himself.

5   Horst Strohbusch. *Das Licht kam aus der Kirche: Die Wende in Meiningen 1989–1990*, 2nd ed. (Meiningen: Verlag Börner, 2009).

When I asked to have permission to quote from the above books, I had the opportunity to talk to the authors. Dr. Strohbusch, an ophthalmologist, gave me valuable insight into the GDR (German Democratic Republic) regime from his point of view. In addition, I conferred with my relatives and friends still residing in Germany and Switzerland. Since 1948, I was more and more restricted in observing the GDR personally. My family left the Russian zone in 1947. From then on, I had to rely on what I noticed during my visits with my relatives still living in the GDR. So as not to be too one-sided, I interviewed reliable people who stayed in the Russian zone and thus they became *my* eyewitnesses for the 1950s.

I use the lively discussion of the Stammtisch to develop the characters' diverse and wavering attitudes. The group is made up of a farmer, a shopkeeper, a mayor, a pharmacist, a teacher, a minister, and an innkeeper who convey their reactions to the many rules and ever-changing regulations in the thirties and forties. The Stammtisch meets in the Russian zone. I concentrate on this Soviet-occupied area, since it is here one finds the most difficult political and social conditions for Americans to grasp. My book clearly shows what the Cold War meant for individual Germans—not so much economically or politically, as is mentioned in typical history books, but emotionally—and how it influenced their culture, which started to deviate from that of their German relatives and friends in the western zones, for instance capitalism versus Communism (called Socialism in the GDR), the politics and economics of free enterprise (Wirtschaftswunder) versus Kolkhozes politics, and Christian values versus Communist ideology.

In a footnote in Chapter 11, I mention the Berlin Wall that was built by East Germans under Soviet control in 1961. When I debated whether to tell about its construction and its fall in 1989, I realized that there was another "story" in the making. I did not want my book *To Cope and to Prevail* too long. Therefore only a glimpse is given here about a wall dividing Germany. My book was written with the goal of providing supplementary reading for undergraduates. It is intended to be an enjoyable text for students and general readers interested in Germany's culture, keeping political history as a backdrop.

Chapter 1

A New Regime for Germany

Klostermansfeld is a middle-sized village located in the center of Germany. It surrounds a former cloister[6] that Benedictine monks founded around 1140 AD. In the sixteenth century, in the course of the Reformation, the cloister was dissolved. The Count of Mansfeld confiscated its fields, gardens, and buildings, and granted the old cloister buildings and the land to a close friend of Martin Luther.[7] The Mansfeld region stayed Lutheran. The new owners farmed the rich soil. During the following centuries, one of the old cloister buildings, situated in the center of the community, was converted into a majestic farmhouse, flanked by stables and a barn. It was in this surrounding that, about four hundred years later, in December 1930, Mr. Herbert Egmont Gottlob Höfer and Ilse-Paula Oemler married in the Protestant church. They had met while he was an intern at the Domäne.[8] Herbert had been told by his father that he needed to study agriculture in order to farm their land in Thuringia. His father,

---

6   In German, *das Kloster* translates to "cloister."

7   Martin Luther was born in 1483 in Eisleben. His parents moved to Mansfeld when he was seven years old. Although Luther traveled throughout Germany and taught in Wittenberg, he stayed affiliated with Mansfeld throughout his life. He died in 1546 in Eisleben.

8   "Manor," usually a large estate formerly owned by nobility or by the state. Usually men who graduated from a German agriculture academy oversaw these huge farms.

Ernst Höfer Sr., was well known as the leader of the Thüringer Landbund since it was founded in 1919.

The Landbund was originally an association of professional farmers. By 1930, under Ernst Höfer Sr.'s leadership, it had developed into the strongest political party in Thuringia, called the Thuringia Farmers' Party. By now, members included not only owners, renters, and workers of farms but also businessmen, industry workers, artists, craftsmen, pastors, and teachers. The party's strongest support came from the rural areas in Thuringia. Although this political party was mighty, it could not stop the advancement of the National Socialist party and the progress of the Communist party. Those two parties opposed each other on everything except for one common goal: the destruction of the Weimar Republic.[9]

Ilse-Paula was the third daughter of Mr. and Mrs. Oemler. Her father had died not quite a year before. He had suffered from diabetes and succumbed to the disease. He never was a strong man, and farming was not his passion. He would rather work on scientific endeavors, especially chemistry. He liked to create beauty creams based on finely ground almonds and flower fragrances for his three daughters, whom he loved dearly. Paula seemed to have been his favorite. She was intelligent; she loved literature, especially poetry, and music; and she had an open mind for all the arts. She had a gift for teaching and was by far the most athletic member of her family. She helped her considerably younger brother Martin with his schoolwork so he could be accepted into the high school in Halle on the river Saale.

She also attended several years of high school in Halle, but when Germany experienced uncontrollable inflation in 1923, her father, like many middle-class Germans, lost almost all of his money. Now he could not afford a higher education for his daughter. Paula had to decide how and where to finish her education without obtaining a university degree. She chose to go to East Prussia to learn how to manage a big farm household. She stayed with a Mennonite family at their huge estate. She grew especially fond of their beautiful garden and park. She liked their outlook on life, and soon they became dear friends to her. After completing her education, she returned to Klostermansfeld, where she met Herbert. She was a petite, pretty redhead of twenty-four years and he was a very charming, tall young man of twenty-five when they married.

---

9   The Weimar Republic was founded in 1919 as a democratic government to rule over Germany.

Herbert's father owned a smaller estate in St. Bernhard in Thuringia. His mother had brought this farm into the marriage. When her husband, as the first chairman of the Thüringer Landbund, had to be away from home, his wife took care of the farm with the help of her second son, Hans. She hoped her eldest would take over soon since he would inherit the land, but when her husband died in 1931, Herbert revealed that he did not intend to be a farmer.

Ernst Höfer Sr. had succumbed to a severe flu with complications. His doctors ordered him to relax and visit a spa for his rehabilitation. He chose Heiligenberg in the southern part of the Black Forest. On June 13, while on a walk with his wife near the spa, he suddenly stumbled and fell. A doctor was soon at the scene, but although he was transported promptly to a nearby hospital specializing in cardiology, he died the next day. He had suffered a heart attack. His widow and a nurse returned to Thuringia by train. As was customary at that time, they loaded the casket with the deceased's body onto the same train, so Chairman Höfer Sr.'s funeral could be conducted near his farm in Thuringia.

Ernst and his wife, Frieda, had selected a beautiful spot for their graves, located in their own forest. Tall oak trees still stand guard over them.[10] Many people attended his burial. Among his friends were the members of his Thuringia Farmers Party and representatives of all other political parties of Thuringia. Only the National Socialist party did not send members to pay their last respects.

Although Herbert inherited the farm, he preferred to work as an insurance agent and was glad that his brother Hans could continue to take care of the fields and livestock. Sometimes Hans had help from their much younger brother Horst, who was still attending school. Unfortunately, in 1942, Hans had to give up the heavy work because he suffered from epilepsy. When he was a teen, he'd handled his father's pistols carelessly and accidentally shot himself in the eye. He was lucky not to lose his eye, but the bullet traveled between the skull bone and his brain, causing epileptic attacks when he became exhausted. He told Herbert that he was forced to seek employment as a clerk in an office. He actually was very gifted as a painter, but freelancing was out of the question for him. He had married Ida, a woman from St. Bernhard, in 1932. He moved into her house, which was within walking distance from his mother's and Horst's place. Between

---

10   After the farm was confiscated in 1945, the burial place was kept as a culturally historic site.

1933 and 1935, Ida bore two children, a daughter, Marlis, and a son, named after his grandfather Ernst Höfer, although in 1932 Paula and Herbert had already named their son Ernst.

Herbert, not wanting to give up his thriving insurance business, made arrangements to rent the farm and house to Mr. Arno Rassmann. He moved with his large family into the lower rooms. Herbert's mother received legal rights to occupy a small apartment on the upper floor of the two-story farmhouse as long as she lived. Horst stayed with her until he was drafted into the German navy. Hans secured a position as a clerk in the KdF organization.[11] Herbert was pleased with this settlement. Little did he know, his decision to rent the farm would cause him grief later on.

Herbert's mother would visit her two older sons often. To see Herbert, who seemed to move every two years to another town in Thuringia, she needed to take the train—not an easy task, since St. Bernhard did not, and still does not, possess a train station. Often, her oldest would come with his new car to take her to his home.

After Paula and Herbert married, his insurance company moved him first to Stettin,[12] a town at the mouth of the river Oder. He was exceptionally competent and soon received a promotion. As a result, he and Paula moved back to Thuringia. This time, they lived in the little town of Gotha. In December 1932, their first son was born at home. Mrs. Oemler, who had come to help her daughter, thought that she never had seen such an ordeal. Her daughter suffered for over thirty hours because the midwife was too proud to send for a doctor. Finally, Mrs. Oemler called a doctor, who saved the child. The umbilical cord had been wrapped around the baby's neck. The face of the newborn was already a ghastly bluish color, but the doctor was able to get the baby to breathe. He saved the young mother as well, although Paula needed quite some time to recuperate.

In 1932, the German political scene was not quiet. President Hindenburg's term in office expired on May 5, 1932. The attempt to have Hindenburg stay on for another year without an election was spoiled by the National Socialists as well as by the Communists. Hindenburg was a revered Prussian soldier, well-known for his military accomplishments. For most Germans, he symbolized the Weimar Republic.

---

11   *Kraft durch Freude* (Strength through Joy) was a state-controlled organization in Nazi Germany, connected to the worker organization Deutsche Arbeitsfront. Workers could take paid vacations away from home.

12   Stettin/Szczecin, since 1945 in Poland, just across the Polish/German border.

At Stammtisches all over Germany, hot debates could be heard among the members. The group would consist of regulars including a pastor, one or two farmers, a pharmacist, sometimes a teacher, the mayor, a shopkeeper, and any other person of a respectable profession. They would gather over a beer and play a round of cards. Often, they debated everything of interest, and in 1932 their interests were especially political. As occurs everywhere else in the world, the media altered the news; reporters voiced their opinion and often tainted their statements, thinking they made it more dramatic and exciting. At a Stammtisch, these reports would be speculated on, considered, and talked over among the members.

In one of the villages in the middle of Germany, as the Stammtisch gathered at their customary inn, the pharmacist said, "Our trouble started with the uncontrolled inflation in 1923." He paused, remembering the effect it had on everybody. "Even here in our village, a few people committed suicide because of the inflation."

The teacher agreed. "Yes, that's when we had all of these foreigners come and buy our cultural heritage. Even our old castle was bought up by somebody who wanted to pretend he belongs to the old aristocrat class."

A farmer chimed in, "We should have kept our old castle."

"How could we?" the teacher replied. "I went with a basketful of money to buy some rolls, and while I was at the bakery, the inflation reduced my money to half its buying power. I needed one more basketful of paper money to pay for a few rolls."

"We, at the farm, had it better when it came to food," the farmer nodded. "But we could not afford to repair our machines or pay for seeds, let alone keep up with salaries for our workers."

The mayor sighed. "Whoever had foreign currency could buy anything. They came and wanted to purchase our Romanesque church, and when I declined to sell it, they behaved like big shots."

Members of another group at the inn entered the debate. "Foreigners and Jews are to blame for our blight."

Somebody suggested, "But don't forget Chancellor Gustav Stresemann; he got us out of the trouble."

A shopkeeper moaned, "Too bad he had to die three years ago."

Their debate continued, with one member exclaiming, "Oh, well, that's quite some time ago! What about now? The election is coming up. What about President Hindenburg? Did you hear they could not extend his term for another year? Now we must have an election."

"What do you think about that new guy, Adolf Hitler?"

"Wait a moment, he's not so new."

"Isn't he the one who was in prison?"

"Yes! He wrote a book there."

"I read *Mein Kampf*,[13] as he called it," the teacher said, and he went on to voice his opinion. "Everybody needs to read it. It gives you an idea of why he is the leader of the National Socialists."

"Bah, he is not a candidate. You might quite as well say Thälmann of the Communists is one too."

"I, for one, hope they vote for Colonel Düsterberg, the candidate of the German Nationals and the Stahlhelm. After all, I was a soldier in the Great War!"[14]

"So was Hitler!"

"But he lost his Austrian citizenship because he joined the Bavarian army. Can you imagine? He even is not a German citizen."

"Not so! My sister, who lives in Brandenburg, told me that the National Socialist government of Brandenburg naturalized him."

"So this upstart is German now?!" exclaimed the pharmacist in disbelief.

A week later, our Stammtisch met at the same time and place, but something was different. They barely opened a deck of cards. They started their discussion right away about the outcome of the election that had taken place on April 10. The mayor pointed out triumphantly, "Hindenburg got elected after all; he collected 19 million votes. That is the absolute majority. Your candidate, Hitler, only received 13 million and Thälmann 3 million."

"Hitler only acquired so many votes because Düsterberg from the German Nationals and the Stahlhelm withdrew his candidacy," the pharmacist interrupted.

Still a few months later, in the beginning of June, the mayor thought he had good reason to shake his head. "I don't know what is wrong with President Hindenburg. He dismissed Chancellor Brüning at the end of May. And that aristocrat Franz von Papen replaces him."

As one can tell by the rapid changes of leadership in such a short time, the Weimar Republic was particularly unstable in the year 1932.

Von Papen only "reigned" until November, when he was replaced by General Kurt von Schleicher, who in turn was ousted on January 28,

---

13 German title of Adolf Hitler's book *My Struggle*.

14 W WI was called the Great War before W WII.

1933. Two days later, in the evening, Hitler celebrated his appointment as chancellor with Hindenburg by his side. They stood in the reviewing stand, looking at the spectacular torchlight parade of his SA[15] troops marching through the Brandenburg Gate in Berlin. Hitler was always able to impress the masses by staging dazzling events. Later, one of his many theatrical, dramatic showcases was the 1936 Olympics in Berlin.

In February 1933, Herbert and his wife recalled the events of the previous year. Paula, holding her baby in her arms, sighed, "How things changed! First Brüning, then von Papen, and then von Schleicher, and now Hitler. How did this all come about? I am glad you never were in the SA or SS[16] when it was an illegal group."

Herbert looked with pride at his little son, who enjoyed his mother's milk. "He is quite a little drinker; he will become strong. I'll make sure that he has a good future under the new regime," Herbert said. He continued, "I don't believe I ever will enter the SA or SS. My father did not like them—and I really have no time for their meetings and events, as fantastic as they may be."

"How did everything come about so quickly?" Paula wondered. "After von Papen was elected, the Reichstag was dissolved already in June. So much for the Weimar Republic! And just two weeks later, still in June, the SA and SS were declared legal. I always agreed with your father in that respect; they behave so boisterously. No, you are not like them."

Herbert took his son from his wife's arms and gently tapped the baby's back to burp him. It worked almost too well. "That was a good one, Ernst!" He turned back to their political discussion. "In July, von Papen had already filled all posts in the administration of Prussia with rightist officials, and he became the Reichskommissar for Prussia."[17]

Paula smiled, "He and his Baron's Cabinet." She used a nickname she

---

15 SA stands for Sturm Abteilung. 1921 Hitler initiated his own army for his protection and political advancement. They are also called brownshirts or stormtroopers.

16 SS stands for Schutz Staffel. It was formed in 1925 as part of the SA. It became the personal guard for Hitler. They wore black uniforms. Like the SA they initially were illegal during the Weimar Republic.

17 Since Prussia was the largest state in the Weimar Republic, the person who gained the position as commissioner over Prussia had the greatest influence on the government.

had heard for the von Papen cabinet. "After all, as far as I know, von Papen appointed mainly aristocrats to his cabinet."

Herbert pointed out, "His cabinet represented the moderate right.[18] That could have been good for my job. Except von Papen resigned in November."

"Yes, after the Stahlhelm staged the biggest parade Berlin ever saw. I heard they had 150,000 war veterans marching and pledging allegiance to the black-white-red flag of old Prussia."

Herbert laughed after Ernst burped a second time. "Maybe we should have named Ernst not after my father, but after the Old Fritz, Frederick the Great."[19] He chuckled, and Paula laughed with him.

She returned to their discussion of the demise of the Weimar Republic. "After von Papen, we had von Schleicher,[20] another of the aristocrats in control, as the Reichskommissar for Prussia. I think he might have been better suited to reconstruct all of Germany, not just Prussia."

Little did they know that, although von Papen resigned, he had met with Hitler and the banker von Schröder in Cologne to discuss a corporative order similar to the one outlined in Pope Pius XI's encyclical *Quadragesimo Anno* (1931). Von Papen and Schröder assumed that the encyclical could correspond with the corporatism of Mussolini's Italy and the demands of the National Socialists. However, this was rather naïve, since "solidarism," as foreseen by the papal encyclical, was based on the free development of human personality. It envisioned free service, voluntary association, and the acceptance of sanctions of divine, natural, and moral law, whereas the Italian Fascists' and German National Socialists' "corporatism" was centered in the absolute power of the state or the race. There was nothing voluntary or free, but instead the so-called coordination[21] of individuals and

---

18 In the Reichstag election of July 31, the National Socialists acquired 230 seats and the Communists 89, with the parties of the middle losing considerably.

19 Frederick the Great (1712–1786) reigned as king of Prussia from 1740 until his death. He is very much loved in northern Germany, but a controversial figure in history books.

20 Schleicher's cabinet tried to establish a broad front for the task of reconstruction. He believed that the Reichswehr (German state army) should be transformed into a democratic people's army with the support of the trade unions and anybody who wanted Germany to succeed as a whole state. The Social Democrats did not go along with this proposal, because they distrusted von Schleicher as merely a representative of the hated military caste, while the centrists begrudged von Schleicher for his part in overthrowing Brüning's cabinet.

21 Called *Gleichschaltung* under the Nazi regime.

groups by means of physical and spiritual browbeating, threatening, and violence. Von Papen only chose Hitler to be part of their plans because he was aware of Hitler's oratorical skills. He wanted to make Hitler chancellor as a mock figurehead—as von Papen's mouthpiece. However, Hitler took another course of action.

When Adolf Hitler became chancellor, he called only two National Socialists into his first cabinet: Joseph Goebbels as minister of propaganda and enlightenment, and Hermann Göring as minister without a designated agenda. Two other commoners were appointed for agriculture and labor. Von Papen became vice-chancellor and Reichskommissar for Prussia. He and three other aristocrats filled the rest of the positions.[22]

In April 1933, the weekly Stammtisch met as always at the inn. The mayor brought up a political discussion by asking all of them, "Do you think it was really that feebleminded Dutch Communist who burned the Reichstag's building in February?"

"Maybe …" mused the pharmacist.

"Why not? The Communists are always violent!" the shopkeeper stated.

"Well, not all of them are violent, I think," the minister added. "They needed a scapegoat, and this Dutch man was seen near the burning building. They want to get rid of the Communists, and now, they can claim that the reason why they're arresting all these Communists is to protect the people from communistic vandalism."

"Who do you mean by *they*, Pastor?" asked the teacher, frowning.

The minister was not slow to reply. "Well, *they* are the whole Hitler cabinet, Hindenburg included. He is really getting too old to be our president. He signed the decree 'for the Protection of the People and the State.'" This decree will haunt us, I tell you. *For the protection of the people and the state* can be interpreted many different ways. From now on, we have to watch what we say and who is listening. Better just keep to our card game."

"Hindenburg has become von Papen's and Hitler's puppet," the farmer grunted. "Did you know that the SA and SS are now part of the military

---

22 The commoners were Alfred Franz Maria Hugenberg, minister of agriculture, and Franz Seldte, minister of labor. Hitler reached out to the aristocrats under von Papen's influence. General von Blomberg was named minister of defense, Baron von Neurath retained his position as minister of foreign affairs, and Count Schwerin of Krosgk became minister of finance.

police? I agree with you, Pastor; I predict bad times ahead—maybe even censorship again."

The pharmacist leaned back in his chair and pondered, "Many of my clients are Communists."

"You have to report them," the teacher insisted.

"And lose my clients? No, they are decent workers. Most of them are miners and farmhands," the pharmacist replied. "Anyway, I don't think they'll be arrested, even if someone reports them. The state needs them. *We* need them. Yes, they may go to jail for a short time, but who would want to replace them in the deep mines?"

"Certainly not me," said the farmer. "I need fresh air—can't stand the darkness down there." He paused, considering all the tasks waiting for him to do in the spring. "And my farmhands, who have communistic notions—I choose not to notice political affiliations. Let them arrest the Communists who staged the uprisings after the Great War, not our diligent workers."

"I don't trust the news reports on the radio. They sound biased to me," the shopkeeper noted. He looked at the teacher, who had pulled a pamphlet out of his jacket, and asked, "What do you have there, Teach?"

"It's the Versailles treaty—actually, excerpts of it. Just the articles that are most relevant to the German people[23]."

The minister fell in. "I received it too. Look at the subtitle. It says: 'The reason for Germany's blight,' and in smaller letters 'with 18 drawings, maps, and a foreword by Dr. PhD Hans Draeger, in connection with German organizations published for the folk and youth.' Why do they separate folk and youth, I wonder?"

"It was published in Berlin in connection with the weekly paper *Der Türmer*,"[24] the teacher explained.

The minister had read the pamphlet and felt he had to tell them about it. "It is very biased, just like our newspapers. In the footnotes to various quoted articles, you read such adjectives as *vicious, vile, wicked,* and *unjust*. With these words they tried to underscore the unwarranted points of the treaty. And here on page 32, they marked article 231 in red."

"Ah, *ja!*" the pharmacist remembered, "The infamous article 231! We

---

23   The German people were informed about the unfair conditions of the Versailles peace treaty by selecting articles of the treaty and printing them in a pamphlet for "folk and youth." The Heinrich Beeken *Verlag* (publisher) in 1933 marked article 231 on page 32 of its booklet in red.

24   This weekly journal had been in circulation since 1898.

supposedly started the war, and now Germany agrees to be responsible for all repairs of war damages."

The farmer listened to his friend, but he wanted to go back to their discussion about newspaper and radio reports. He interjected, "Words, words! They lose their meaning as everything and everybody seems to be watched. Soon, free press or speech is merely a dream."

The farmer predicted correctly. By the end of 1933, many political parties in Germany had been outlawed or dissolved. Only the NSDAP[25] became "insolubly tied" to the state. Many Communists were arrested. They were not the only ones. Liberals, Catholics, pacifists, and even socialists were seized, beaten, tortured, murdered, or sent to prison camps, where the inmates could "concentrate" on their attitudes and change their convictions. The Communist parties were represented in the parliament in too huge a number to be banished easily. For them to vanish from the political scene in Germany, the constitution needed to be changed. To alter the constitution, a meeting was necessary to vote on the proposal for the *Ermächtigungsgesetz* (Enabling Act). Hitler, with the support of the right-wing parties and the centrists, was able to get the necessary votes to change the constitution. Now, with the dictatorial powers obtained by Hitler, state and municipal governments were "cleansed" of all politically undesirable administrators. That meant they were ousted and replaced by National Socialists.

When the Stammtisch met in July 1934, they were more cautious about what and with whom they might discuss their opinions.

"So, Röhm is dead," the pharmacist declared.

"What was wrong with the SA chief?" the farmer asked.

"You have no idea, do you?" smirked the teacher. "Röhm and his SA wanted to destroy our Hitler regime. He wanted to stage a coup d'état. Yes, that surprises you, doesn't it? He wanted to take over. Luckily, Hitler already had dictatorial power, so he could gain control of the situation before it became a problem. The police secretly set a date for the arrest. I was aware of their password *Kolibri* (hummingbird). When the assigned policemen met and whispered it, the arrest of Röhm was at hand. It turned out to be a deadly brawl. It was the 'Night of the Long Knives.'"

"Were you harassed too? I mean, you being in the SA and affiliated with Röhm ..." the farmer asked.

---

25 *National Sozialistische Demokratische Arbeiter Partei* is the National Socialist Democratic Worker's Party, comprised of the former Nationalist Democratic Party and National Socialist Party.

The teacher answered him by pointing out that he was smart enough to change his pledge. "I handed in my dagger," he told them. "Röhm's name on it was erased. Now, our decorative SA blades will have the inscription, 'Everything for Germany.' That is more to my liking."

Before a heated debate could start between the farmer and the teacher, the minister noted, "So many of Hitler's close associates were killed too. Father Bernhard Stempfle, who did editorial work on Hitler's book *My Struggle*, and the head of Catholic Action in Berlin, and even von Schleicher and his wife were killed. I heard von Papen has been arrested as well. But I guess he is too close to Hindenburg to be murdered."

"Hindenburg praised Hitler for his action," the teacher interjected.

"We all heard Hitler's speech over the radio. Interesting, very interesting," the farmer said, giving the teacher a short glance. "I made sure all of my workers and I heard Hitler. We left the hay wagon on the field and headed home to listen to the radio." In reality, he and his workers only heard the excerpts of the speech during the evening news. By now, the farmer wanted to be on his guard. He had started to mistrust the teacher, who could report him to the police for who knows what!

The teacher was only too happy to approve. "That is the way it should be. We have to pay attention when Hitler, our chancellor and leader, addresses the German nation. He will tell us the real reason behind sentencing the convicted."

The shopkeeper shrugged his shoulders. "You call this 'sentence'? There was no trial. They were arrested, put in jail, and killed, or even not that …"

"Shush!!!" the pharmacist stopped him. Changing the subject, he asked, "Whose turn is it to deal the cards?"

"Not mine," the shopkeeper said, and he left.

In 1934, the year of the "Long Knives" and Hindenburg's death, Hitler abolished the title of Reichspräsident. Instead, he assumed the title and office of Führer and Reichskanzler.[26]

The same year, Herbert and Paula moved from Gotha to Jena's outskirts. Here, their daughter was born three days after Hindenburg's death. This time, giving birth was easy for Paula. Hildegard was a beautiful little baby. Mr. Höfer loved her dearly. She was so dainty—healthy, but fragile. Paula

---

26 *Führer* means "leader" or "guide," and *Reichskanzler* is best translated as "chancellor of the realm," the Third Reich.

had grown up with many servants in her parent's household. She decided it was time to hire at least one helper as nanny for the children.

Later in 1934, the Stammtisch continued to meet as always. This time, the mayor's son was present. He had just enlisted in the armed forces of Germany (the Reichswehr).

The teacher's face showed clearly that he was very pleased with the young man's choice to join the army. He greeted him with, "So nice of you to mingle with us old folks. I am proud of you. We need young, strong men like you to protect our country. Did you recite the oath yet? I remember when I swore 'obedience to the constitution and the fatherland.'"

"Yes, but with a different meaning; the wording of the oath has changed."

The teacher, surprised, asked, "To what do you commit yourself to now?"

"Not *what*, but *who!*" corrected the son. "We swear, 'under God, to give unconditional obedience to the Führer of the German Reich and people, Adolf Hitler.'"

The minister remarked, "Well, at least God is part of your oath."

"You would notice that, Pastor! What I like about the Reichswehr is that from now on, we are the only ones who may have arms," the son informed them.

The pharmacist interjected, "Except for the police, the SS, and the Secret Police."

The son was quick to react. "But they have nothing to do with us soldiers. They are to protect the Führer, the constitution, and the homeland. Party militias are forbidden now." Proudly, he declared, "I tell you, we will fight to get back the areas that belonged to Germany before the Great War."

The farmer, who liked to participate in kettle-hunts every January, when they shot hares and foxes, wondered, "Do we hunters have to give up our guns now?"

The mayor shook his head. "Of course not! How can they abolish all of our hunting clubs and our competitions in target shooting? They only want to stop all those bloody fights between the parties."

In the meantime, the teacher invited the young soldier to join them for a drink. "Be my guest," he said and called the waiter. "Oskar, a beer and schnapps[27] for our young hero-to-be."

---

27 A strong clear alcoholic drink made from grain or fruit. Now and then, people drink it with beer.

One year later, in March 1935, Germany recovered the highly industrialized Saar Basin by negotiations. It was the first area to be brought back under German control after it had been lost as a result of the Versailles treaty. In the same year, Hitler installed the draft into the military for all able-bodied young German men. Twelve months later, he ordered his enlarged military to enter the Rhineland, which, according to the Versailles treaty, should have remained permanently demilitarized. When negotiating with European governments, Hitler pointed out that the unfair terms of the Versailles treaty could lead to uprisings, even another war. Hitler reiterated that he wanted peace and all Germans did not want another war.

In 1936, Mr. Höfer received another promotion. He had covered practically the whole state of Thuringia for multiple insurance companies. One day, he came home and announced, "We are moving!"

Paula sighed, "Not again! I am pregnant, as you know, and every time we move, you are busy relocating your office, so I have to do the packing all by myself."

Herbert reassured her, "The movers will help you."

Paula refused to be consoled. She pointed out, "The last time they helped, expensive dishes we had gotten for our wedding were chipped or even broken."

"With the money I earn in my new position, we can afford new ones," Herbert said proudly, trying to cheer her up.

This time, they moved to Gera, east of Jena, where Mr. Höfer rented a house for his family. Grete, their household help and nanny, moved with them. She slept in the servant's bedroom upstairs. It was the first time they did not live in an apartment, where the children had to be kept quiet and Grete had to take them to a park for outdoor play. Since both parents grew up on farms, they wanted their children to have the same opportunity to strengthen their little bodies in the fresh air as they had. They liked living in a house that was surrounded by a nice garden with a big cherry tree and other fruit trees. There was a sandbox for the children, a swing set, and a good pathway on which they could try out their tricycles.

For Germans, physical fitness had become a virtue, ever since the father of gymnastics, Turnvater Jahn,[28] established the first open-air sport site

---

28 Turnvater's real name was Ludwig Jahn (1778–1852). A teacher at a Berlin secondary school, he started gymnastic training for his pupils on the *Hasenheide,* a meadow near Berlin.

on the outskirts of Berlin, as early as 1811. Soon his students started a nationwide organization of young athletes. They frequently traveled across the country to meet other athletes in competitions, games, athletic drills, and gymnastic festivals. The members came from every class in society. As is typical for German people, who seem to love their uniforms, all wore the same outfit and had standard equipment in all clubs throughout Germany. Eventually, they extended their competitions to track and field events and added team sports.

Nowadays, soccer has become the national team sport, followed by handball, water polo, hockey, and ice hockey. All other sporting events, such as rowing competitions, are designed for individuals or small teams of two to eight athletes. These teams may compete in gymnastics, track and field, and relay races.[29] In order to be selected for the Olympics, athletes practice at the Sport-and-Turnvereine.[30] Since so many Germans participate in a variety of physical exercises, they know how hard an athlete has to work to be selected for the Olympic games. Therefore, they admire not only German athletes, but also athletes from different nationalities and races who achieve outstanding results.

By 1936, Hitler was residing in Berlin, the capital of Germany, which had been selected for the Olympic games. Hitler felt that he now had the best opportunity to show the world the superiority of the German race—the Aryan race. He was confident that German athletes would reap most of the medals.

When Jesse Owens,[31] a young student from Ohio, received four gold medals, the German public adored him. He is still a legend for many. Hitler did not like it that somebody who obviously was not of the Aryan race could outdo German athletes. After the first day of the Olympics, when he extended a handshake only to some Finnish and German participants who received medals, the Olympic Committee told him that to keep the

---

29 Naturally, associations for motor sports are separate from local sport clubs, since they require much more money, and often an individual is sponsored by a car or motorbike factory. Horse races, jumping competitions, and *haute école* or *Hohe Schule* (dressage horse training) are separate as well, as are the many gun clubs. Winter sport and water sport are confined to suitable locations.

30 *Verein* is a term used for club-like associations. *Turnverein* means a gymnastic and track-and-field club.

31 Owens, an African American, has become a legend. In every Summer Olympics since 1936, his name is mentioned in reference to the 100-meter dash, the 200-meter run, the long jump, and the 400-meter relay.

Olympic Games neutral, he would have to shake hands with everyone or no one. So, claiming that congratulating everybody was too tedious for him, he chose to honor no one with his personal handshake, thus avoiding the public recognition of medalists of a different race.

Chapter 2

Gera and Erfurt

In 1936, the Stammtisch became adventurous. The minister made a proposal: "Because of the Olympic games, they have an exhibition of modern art in Munich," he said. "Who can join me to go to Munich? That might be the only time we can see the works of our Expressionists, Impressionists, Cubists, and Dadaists."

The farmer looked at the minister with amazement. "I never knew modern art was a favorite of yours. I don't understand it; don't like it. Anyway, hay has to be brought in. The weather is just perfect for it."

The teacher, who had been promoted to headmaster of the elementary school in their village, was obviously uneasy when he spoke. "I used to teach modern art in school, but now, our Führer declared it Degenerate Art.[32] Therefore, I have to stick to the artists of the nineteenth century and earlier, no more Bauhaus. I must confess, I am not very familiar with the painters and sculptors, let alone architects, of the NSDAP."

"Hey, Teach!" called the pharmacist. "You and I could go with the pastor. It could be fun. We don't have to publicly approve of the art pieces shown. I always wanted to go to the Hofbräuhaus[33] and taste their beer."

---

32 Practically all of the modern art (late nineteenth to early twentieth century) was designated as "Degenerate Art"—*Entartete Kunst* by the Nazi regime.

33 Famous beer hall in Munich. It used to be the royal court's brewery. Any shop that was a court deliverer earned the by-name "Hof," i.e. *Hofbäckerei* (court bakery) or *Hofschneider* (court tailor).

"It is not better than the local brew!" the innkeeper chimed in. "My motto is: 'Stay at home and earn your bread with honesty.'"

The mayor sighed. "Since when are you part of our discussions, Innkeeper?" He turned to the others. "My son is in the Ruhr district. He wrote a letter, told me that they built all kinds of …" He stopped, looking at the headmaster. After a short pause, he continued. "It looked like his letter had been opened."

The pharmacist explained, tongue in cheek, "Nowadays, they have to know what our soldiers think and write. They have to make sure that there are no traitors in the military. The military police checks on the correspondence." He bent over toward the farmer and said under his breath, "Actually, the Gestapo[34] reads those letters."

The headmaster left for a short time. That was the moment when the pastor, the pharmacist, and the farmer put their heads together, speaking softly. "We have to be on our guard with Teach," the minister whispered.

"And with the innkeeper," added the pharmacist. "I saw some suspicious strangers staying overnight here. They are snooping around, I'm sure. Better forget going to the art exhibit in Munich."

When the headmaster came back, the minister said to him, "We discussed our trip to Munich and decided not to go. We have too much to do here."

The headmaster nodded approvingly. "It is better so."

The exhibit of so-called Degenerate Art didn't just take place in Munich, it traveled to other large cities in Germany. It did not come to Gera, a town in Thuringia. Here, my father received a phone call from the hospital.

"Mr. Höfer, your wife gave birth to a little lady, but …"

"Thank you, nurse!"

My father put the receiver down quickly and rushed off to send telegrams to his mother, mother-in-law, friends, and all the other relatives.

Mother and third child, a son, fine. Stop. Born June 30. Name. Reinhold. Stop.

In the meantime, his wife lay in the hospital, pale and exhausted after the long, strenuous birth. Nurse Erika entered with the baby.

"How is my little girl?" my mother inquired.

---

34 *Geheime Staatspolizei* was the secret police of Nazi Germany. They were notorious for their use of underhanded and terrorist methods against persons suspected of showing disloyalty to the Hitler regime.

"She is a fine lady, madam—weighs almost eleven pounds. How did she ever fit in that small body of yours?"

She laid me close to my mother. "Try to breastfeed her now."

My mother opened her gown and hugged her third child closely. Eagerly, the little mouth searched and found the food source, drinking immediately. My mother had nursed her other two; she knew what to do, and this little one needed no coercing.

The doctor entered. Raising his eyebrows, he instructed the nurse, "Take the baby away. Mrs. Höfer needs to rest a few days before she nurses. She is highly anemic." Turning to his patient, he said, "Mrs. Höfer, you will have to get your strength back before we can let you go home, where the two other toddlers and the baby will demand your attention and care. You have lost a lot of blood. I ordered finely chopped raw liver for you. You have to eat it once a day for the next six weeks[35]. That will bring your red blood cell count back to normal."

My mother tried to smile at him. The few moments of nursing had exhausted her already. She closed her eyes and drifted off into a deep sleep. The doctor nodded at the nurse. "The medication is working; keep her sedated. Her milk is not worth much anyway. The child has to be fed by a formula."

The next day, my father came to see his baby. "Nurse Erika, where is my son, 'the little laddy,' as you called him."

She looked at him questioningly. "Excuse me, you are Mr. Höfer, right? You do not have a son; you have a daughter."

"Oh no, you must be mistaken. You told me we had a little laddy!"

"Mr. Höfer, I speak the regional dialect. 'Lady' might have sounded to you like 'laddy,' but we refer to all babies as either little ladies or little gents. You have a daughter."

My father turned away abruptly, very upset. Now he had to send new telegram messages to everyone again and tell them that they had only a daughter, not a son. How could Paula have done that to him? *She* should have called him, not the nurse. He'd had it all planned in his mind. First, they had a son, the heir. Then came the second child, a beautiful dark-eyed girl, so smooth and lovely that he sometimes called her his little kitten. The third child should have been a son again. After all, Paula and he had agreed on a good Germanic name already.

---

35 My mother almost died. For six weeks, she needed therapy and intensive care that could not be provided at home.

He was angry when the doctor saw him. The doctor said, "You know, your wife had a very hard time with this baby. She lost a lot of blood. Her red blood cell count is terribly low. We have to keep her here beyond the regular ten days. She needs more strength. We hope there will be no other complications. We are even not sure if she'll survive this ordeal."

The door to my mother's room was slightly open, and she heard the doctor's remarks. She thought, *My God, you know I have three children. I have to survive. I may not die; no, I will not leave them alone. As surely as I lay here, God, you have to help me!* She had been waiting for her husband to come. She wondered, *Why is he so concerned about the baby's gender? It's a healthy child, right? No, Doctor, I have three children. God will not permit me to die. I'll get my strength back.* She was too weak to call for her husband.

He thought, *How can I face her, tell her what an idiot I made of myself? I have to make those phone calls, send telegrams, find another nanny for the children, if Paula needs to stay in the hospital.* To make it even more complicated for him, he knew that Nanny Grete had to leave; she was pregnant and would be due to give birth before Paula was released from the hospital.

Thinking my mother was asleep, he left the hospital without seeing her this time. When he arrived at home, he saw a strong, healthy, blue-eyed woman in front of the garden gate, talking with Ernst and Hildegard. All three laughed. Seeing her father, the little girl screeched happily and stretched out her arms. He picked her up gently and asked the woman, "Who are you?"

"I am answering your ad for a nanny. I am Elisabeth Braun," she replied with a slight local accent.

Herbert looked at Ernst. "Where is Grete?" Ernst pointed to the big cherry tree in the garden, where Grete sat knitting a baby outfit.

"Grete, why do you let the children speak to a stranger?"

"She ain't no stranger, I know her from the garden festivals. She is a good nanny, worked for a family. Them left for France or so."

My father always winced when he heard her local dialect and the many grammar mistakes she made. He only hoped his children would not imitate her.

"They had three kids; you'd seen them love her," Grete answered, ready to give more information.

Elisabeth had entered the garden. She picked up the toys strewn over the path and on the lawn while approaching Grete and my father. "Mr. Höfer, I could start soon. I lost my job with the family I worked for. They had to move and could not take me with them. They moved to southern

France, I think. They had three children; I took care of them. I surely can take care of two now."

"Three," my father corrected her. "My wife just had a little girl and is very sick. She has to stay in the hospital for quite some time. Can you take care of the household as well? Do we need to hire a cleaning woman? We just moved here, rented this house from Dr. Goldstein. Well, his household staff left. They did not want to work for somebody with youngsters. His daughters were already in their teens. They surely did not need a nanny. I have no idea how to get a good cleaning woman. My wife usually does the hiring of our household help."

Elisabeth noticed his despair. She took her jacket off and said, "Mr. Höfer, let me give you a practical example of my work. Let me start right now, and then decide if you want to hire me." She turned to Ernst and Hildegard, who had been watching their father's attempt to interview Elisabeth with interest. "Both of you, help me find the kitchen, yes?"

The four-year-old proudly took his little sister by one hand and Elisabeth by the other and went into the house. "Here you hang your jacket, there's the umbrella stand … this is the dining room … here is the kitchen." Elisabeth set her oversized handbag down, pulled out an apron, put it on, rolled her sleeves up, and started to prepare the evening meal. Ernst brought things from the icebox and Hildegard even helped, trying to wipe the kitchen table and bringing a tablecloth. Elisabeth set the table, put Hildegard in a highchair, cut an open sandwich into small pieces, and placed it in front of the girl. "She won't eat it!" Ernst informed her. "She only drinks and eats spaghetti."

"She looks it—the skinniest little girl I ever saw," replied Elisabeth. "Sit down, Ernst. She might eat when you do."

"I am big. I don't need my sandwich cut."

"Now, just have the same as she has. When she sees how you eat it and what you eat, she might want to try it. Okay?"

"Okay," he sighed and started eating his food.

Hildegard played with her bread cubes. Elisabeth took one of them. "Oh, look, this little sheep says 'bah.'" All had to laugh at the funny face and sound Elisabeth made. "It wants to be in Hildegard's stomach where it is nice and warm." Hildegard opened her mouth and ate the cube. Elisabeth bleated again and Hildegard munched the next piece. She started to feed herself, continuing what looked like a game to her, until the sandwich was gone. At the same time, Elisabeth had prepared a light evening meal for my father. She set a place in the dining room for him and sent Ernst to pick a few pansies in the garden. Ernst knew were the vases were and brought one. Water in the vase, flowers arranged, set on the table, wine bottle opened, one glass poured, and the children all the time with her.

My father had made his phone calls, saw an appetizing meal on the dining-room table, and sat down to enjoy it. Meanwhile, Elisabeth took the children for their bath and then let them show her their bedroom and beds. She played with them, always with one ear toward the dining room in case my father would need anything, but he did not call. The children were well-behaved and soon nestled in their beds. My father came upstairs to say goodnight to both of them. He finally told them about their new little sister, and that Mom would have to stay away a little longer.

During that time, Elisabeth had set the kitchen table for herself and Grete. She opened their conversation with a question. "How long, do you think, before your baby is due?"

"Six to eight weeks! I am often so worn out. The kids are good ones. The Höfers are nice people. I came with them from Jena when Mr. Höfer was promoted to district manager of his firm. Him is a very successful man. The wife has a heart good as gold. They took myself along when they visited with her mom. What a lovely place! Lots of servants, I didn't need to do nothing, just played with the kids. Then they moved here. They don't know nobody here. First, Mrs. Höfer's mom came for some weeks to help her and then his mom came. Those two ladies are sure different. Mrs. Oemler—Oma, as they call her—is Ernst's favorite. Mr. Höfer's mother is a little too harsh with the kids, more work than play. You know, but the little dress Hildegard had on, got crocheted by Grandma. She does the prettiest things. Not so Oma Oemler, but she is the one who knows how to treat the little ones. She takes them to festivals, carnivals, circuses, lets them touch the farm animals." Grete sighed. "I hate to leave. I'm not married, you know. I have to go to my grandparents. They said they'll take me with the baby in … maybe raise it too. I can't stay here and help with three little ones when I have my own baby."

"Aren't you getting married to the father of your child?"

"Well, I really do not know who the father is. There were several who took me out to eat and danced with me. I wanted to repay their kindness, but what do I have to give them, 'cept for a little fun in the bushes or meadow?"

Elisabeth glanced at her with pity. Poor thing did not know that she was taken advantage of. Getting up, she said, "Well, I will do the dishes now. I think you can go upstairs and pack your things, so that I can move in. I am pretty sure Mr. Höfer will hire me. Do you need any help?"

"The stairs up to my room under the roof are steep. Maybe you'd help me with my suitcase tomorrow? I would have left a week ago, but then Mrs. Höfer went into labor early, right after they moved here. She and me had packed all the things for the movers, 'cause Mr. Höfer was here already. Mrs. Höfer is quite an organizer; I'll tell you, she's efficient. When I suspected I was pregnant, I wanted to lose the baby. I started to carry heavy loads of wet laundry. Mrs. Höfer saw it right away and asked me why I would load up like that. I told her that I hoped to have a miscarriage, but with us simple folks, what sits, sits tight. She, of course, forbade me to haul big loads anymore."

Elisabeth interrupted Grete's rambling. She nodded over the sink. "I noticed this household is in good order. Even the children know already where things belong. Did you put their toys away? I mean outside?"

"Yes, I did, and thank you for helping right away. This morning, I did the laundry, hung it on the line in the cellar. Well, goodnight! When do you come tomorrow?"

"I'll ask Mr. Höfer. You know, he hasn't hired me yet. Maybe his wife does not want me."

"Oh, don't be silly! She needs you, so do the little ones, and so does he … he—you get my drift." Grete's pretty face showed a sly smile.

"Hogwash!" said Elisabeth and rubbed her hands more than needed on the kitchen towel. "You might feel obligated to men who take you out, not me. I have my Heinz. We'll get engaged as soon as I am twenty-one, and when I have saved enough money, we'll get married too, before we make children."

Grete bent her head; her shining blond hair fell in cascades over her face and shoulders. She cried softly.

"Now, now, Grete, sobbing is not good for your baby," Elisabeth comforted her. "Be glad you have grandparents to help you. I was raised by my grandparents too. My mother gave me to them shortly after I was born. She later married a man who never knew that I wasn't her younger sister. You see, it can work out all right, especially if you have a boy. Our government rewards us when we have strong boys. With your blue eyes and blond hair, you are the image of the Germanic race. How do they call it? Aryan or so."

"I never bother with all them fandangle words," Grete replied.

Elisabeth reassured her. "You know, the welfare agency will take care of you and your child, if your grandparents won't. Get to bed now. I'll sweep the kitchen."

My father tucked my siblings in for the night. He entered the kitchen. "Miss Braun, I think you are a godsend. Please stay with us. The pay is good. You'll get hospitalization, of course—and life insurance, paid vacation, one day a week off at our convenience, room and board, and a nanny uniform."

"All acceptable, Mr. Höfer, except for the uniform. I think Ernst and Hildegard like me as I am. And call me Elisabeth, please."

"All right, but let us supply you with a skirt, blouse, aprons, and a pair of shoes once a year."

"Fine," Elisabeth agreed. She pulled a few papers out of her handbag. "Here are my recommendations, my medical records, and my family tree. You see, I don't have any Jewish ancestry. Grete told me that, although you rent this house from a Jewish doctor, you are not Jewish, so I may apply for a job with you."

"Was your family tree approved by the authorities here in Gera?" my father inquired.

"Yes! Last year, I went right away to have my ancestry researched and my papers for hiring authorized. I did it as soon as the new laws were set up in Nürnberg."

My father looked at her approvingly and said, "So, you are aware that German families with small children may not hire any Jewish persons to help in their households anymore, let alone with their children. You seem to be familiar with the Nürnberg Laws."[36] My father looked at the seal with the swastika and its date, and then he read her recommendation letter.

Elisabeth continued, "Even if the family whose recommendation you read did not move away, I would have been forced to leave them, because they were Jewish.[37] I liked them a lot."

My father finished reading her papers and said confidently, "I am

---

36   The Nürnberg laws formalized the action taken by the Nazis against the Jews before 1935. The first law aimed to protect the "German Blood and Honor," prohibiting marriages and extramarital intercourse between "Jews" and "Germans." German (Aryan) females under forty-five were not allowed to work in Jewish households. The second law stripped Jews of their German citizenship. Between 1937 and 1938, new laws were added to further segregate Jews from the German population.

37   In 1978, Elisabeth showed me pictures of that Jewish family. She told me that she was in loose contact with them; she even had a letter from them, but I had to promise not to tell anybody about this. She lived still in Gera in the Soviet zone of divided Germany. Elisabeth, like many in the Soviet occupied zone, was watched by the *Stasi* (secret police in the GDR) ever since she had connection to us in West Germany.

positive my wife will like you. Maybe when she feels better, you can go to the hospital and introduce yourself to her."

"Fine, I'll go tomorrow on an outing with the children. We'll take the bus to the clinic. Maybe she can see us from her window, and we can wave to her. She must be longing for her darlings."

"Good, then you'll start tomorrow morning at seven a.m."

"Yes! May I ask you a question? What is the name of the baby?"

"I don't know, and right now, I do not care. We expected a boy, not a girl." Elisabeth was taken aback. How could this man be so uncaring? Was something wrong with his third child? She had been told by Grete that the baby weight over eleven pounds and was healthy as far as she knew. Didn't that child deserve a name?

Soon, my father had to register his third child with the town's authorities. He had to find a name. He went to visit my mother.

"Let's discuss a name for the girl."

"Your daughter!"

"I was thinking of your mother's or my mother's name."

"But we gave both names to Hildegard as her middle names, Minna and Frieda," she replied.

"Well, Hildegard is named after your oldest sister, what about your other sister's name then?"

"You really would not want us to call her Magdalena, would you? It is a Hebrew name; that might mark her as of Jewish ancestry.[38] It will give her problems in school later on. The Gera authorities already think we are affiliated with Jews since we rent from Dr. Goldstein. Maybe we should have bought the house from him. He begged us to do so, and we would have paid much less than it is actually worth."

"You are right, but I do not like a big mortgage. I might get promoted again, and we might have to move. In this case, we would own a property to be concerned about."

"Please, Herbert, don't even mention moving again. We are not even settled here. Right now, we need a name for our daughter."

Their discussion developed and finally led to a name that would cause

---

38　People of Jewish background who had German names had to add a Jewish name in front of their name. Their passports were marked with a big *J* extending over the information on the passport.

the raising of eyebrows, inquiring looks, mispronunciation, and modulation throughout their daughter's life.

"Let's name her after you, Ilse-Paula," my father suggested.

My mother looked at him, smiling. "Not Paula, you know, Hebrew derivative! But Ilse, yes. You see, near my birthplace, there is a brook called Ilse. The legend has it that once there was a strong beautiful princess named Ilse who jumped over a huge crevice to escape a giant. She landed so fiercely that her foot crushed the stone beneath her, striking water. It gushed out of the rock and formed the spring named after her, Princess Ilse."

Looking at his daughter, who was drinking from a bottle, he said, "Yes, that little river might murmur and gurgle just like her when she drinks from her bottle."

"What about a middle name?" Paula asked.

"Why? You don't have one either."

"But you have two, and the last means 'Praise to God.'"

"Well, I never liked it too much."

"Maybe we could give her a hyphenated name; it's very fashionable now."

At that moment, a gentle morning breeze swept through the open window, bringing with it a scent of blooming rosebushes, concealing the odor of the hospital. My mother took a deep breath and said, "Let's call her Ilse-Rose." And that is how I was registered under the National Socialist's regime in the books of Gera, the town of flowers … only the town clerk spelled my name Ilse-Rosa, and it took some persuasion from my father to change the *a* to an *e*.

Soon, I joined the rest of the family at home. Why keep me at the hospital, where my sick mother could not nurse me anyway? Elisabeth had made up her mind to take me to her heart. She fed me with homemade formulas and cared for me like I was her own. No matter which formula she tried, I would respond to it well. When I was six months old, I became too chubby. The pediatrician ordered malt coffee instead of full milk for me. My Uncle Martin, typically for a farmer raising livestock, noted, "Ilse-Rose's body surely utilizes her food well!"

I grew up well and gained enough to be called "Fatty" by my brother and sister—or, jokingly, "Stinky Rose" by my Aunt Ursel. Before I received these less favorable names, my father learned to appreciate and love me, naming me "Little Rosebud" or Roselett. I was a quiet child. I loved to stand in my playpen and stare into the big cherry tree, watching the leaves and the birds. Later, when I started to walk, I scrutinized night crawlers twisting out of their holes, the aphids clinging to the roses, the flies circling under the bedroom lamp. I loved animals. I observed much and said little, hardly spoke at the age of two. My parents were concerned about their little daughter, so different from their two inquisitive, talkative older children. *Maybe she is slow-witted*, they feared.

One day, their anxious thoughts about the intelligence of their third child vanished. My father was in a hurry for work. He dashed out of the door, ran to the garage, and started the car. When he looked in the rearview mirror, he noticed me dragging his briefcase over the back steps, muttering something, and pointing my chubby little finger at him. My mother appeared at the door, caught me, and called out, "Herbert, don't you ever think this child is dumb! She saw that you left your briefcase. She wanted to bring it to you before anybody else noticed that you left without it."

My father was grateful and hugged his little plump girl for the first time with fatherly love. He whispered "Little Rosebud" and off he went, beaming with pride and happiness about his three children.

It seemed like his embrace released my tongue. I suddenly spoke better and tried to express myself in whole sentences, although I still spoke seldom. I liked to be alone, even if my brother and sister let me be part of their games. They always wanted me to mimic a baby who had to sit in the backseat of the sandbox car, or I had to pretend to be the servant who cleaned or the errand boy. I could not master the tricycle. My legs were too short. I did not know how to use the scooter. I could not get on the swing without help. It sometimes was frustrating for my older siblings to let me play along. I would rather observe all the life around me, especially animals.

I whispered while climbing up the back steps of the apartment house in Erfurt, "Poor, poor, an'mal," holding a rather stiff grayish thing to my rosy cheek, its tail fairly passing my mouth.

We had moved to the capital of Thuringia when I was two years old. Ernst had remarked, "Oh, good, now we get another baby. When you move, you get kids." The knowledge of this five-year-old was great. But my mother, for once, moved with the help of competent Elisabeth and was not pregnant as she had been when they moved from Gotha, where Ernst had been born, to Jena, Hildegard's birthplace, and Gera, where I appeared.

That day on the back steps, my mother spotted me and said, "What is that she holds so tenderly to her face?"

Elisabeth answered in horror, "My gosh! That is the dead rat I saw in the gutter the other day. I forgot to tell you about it." Both women dashed to pry the worm-eaten animal out of my fingers. Elisabeth was telling me, "Honey, dear, give it to me. This animal is dead." Reluctantly, I released my grip on the carcass. "Let's have a funeral," Elisabeth suggested while they were cleaning me with soap and water until my face resembled a tomato from scrubbing and rubbing. That was the day I learned to brush my teeth and gargle with mouthwash.

A cigar box served as the casket. The rat was laid on a bed of rose petals and covered with a small rhubarb leaf. We formed a procession down the garden path to the honeysuckle bush, where Elisabeth had dug a little grave. Ernst acted as pastor and Hildegard as funeral director. I carried the casket. Elisabeth was the undertaker, and my mother prepared the funeral feast, to be enjoyed by the mourners after the burial. We sang a children's song, and then Ernst spoke solemnly as the clergyman:

Ein Huhn und ein Hahn,	A hen and a chick
die Predigt geht an.	the sermon is quick.
Eine Kuh und ein Kalb,	A cow and a calf,
die Predigt ist halb.	the sermon is half.
Eine Katz und eine Maus,	Kitty and Rover,
die Predigt ist aus.	the sermon is over.
Ich bin der Herr Pastor,	I am your pastor dear,
ich pred'ge Euch was vor,	I preach without a fear,
und wenn ich nicht mehr weiter kann,	and when I am lost for words
dann fang ich wieder von vorne an	I start from the beginning, of course.

Then, he added, although it was not suitable for our funeral:

Ich taufe dich mit Kaffeesatz,	I baptize you with coffee ground
du bist ein alter Schweinematz.	you are an old piggy-hound.

I paid little attention, although I remembered these verses for the rest of my life. I was unfailing in learning rhymes as fast as I heard and comprehended them. That was one reason Grandma had introduced me to an additional prayer we would say every night:

Ich bin klein,	I am small,
mein Herz ist rein,	my heart is pure,
Soll niemand drin wohnen,	Nobody shall live in it
als Jesus allein.	but Jesus alone.

Grandma taught me the following verses:

Müde bin ich geh' zur Ruh,	Tired now I lay me down
schließe beide Äuglein zu.	closing both of my eyes.
Vater, lass die Augen Dein	Father, keep your eyes on me
über meinem Bette sein.	watching over my bed.
Hab' ich Unrecht heut' getan,	Did I commit sins today?
sieh es mir nicht böse an.	look unto me with favor.
Deine Gnad' und Jesu Blut	Your grace and Jesus's blood
machen allen Schaden gut.	will repair all harm and damage.

Stories of the Bible made a big impression on me, just as much as fairy tales and legends did. Early on, I started to imagine how the stories would end. I identified with princesses, but even more with the poor little girls in the tales, like Sterntaler,[39] who was so poor but still gave her last shirt away. However, God rewarded her. In my mind, my belief in God and the themes of the legends would get combined to form my own fairy tales. Later, I would tell them to my younger brother and to the many children for whom I babysat. Even grown-ups liked to listen to my stories. I had a knack for dramatizing them. I spoke with different intonations to characterize my heroes, villains, animals, insects, flowers, trees, bushes, even furniture, just everything. I loved Grimm's fairy tales, but adored Christian Anderson's stories, where even a needle could have fellowship with a broken pin.

One day, my father said, "Paula, we are moving to West Prussia."

"Oh no, not again! I just got used to Erfurt, the capital of Thuringia, the shops, the entertainment, the theater, and Ernst is in school now. He started first grade at Easter a year ago. Must we go to the east, and so far away from your mother and my mother, our friends, our relatives?" You could tell she was not happy about having to relocate, especially after she found out that Elisabeth would not move with us. She had been engaged for quite some time to Heinz, and now they wanted to marry and move back to Gera.

My mother wondered about a new nanny, and new servants, but especially about how the Poles would treat her and the children. She surely was anxious about a move to the Polish Corridor newly reclaimed by Hitler's Blitzkrieg,[40] but my father felt that West Prussia had belonged to Germany

---

39   From "The Star Coins," a fairy tale among the collection of the Brothers Grimm.

40   A war as fast as lightning or as a flash. On September 1, 1939 the German army took Poland from the west; on September 17, Russia invaded it from the east. Stalin and Hitler concluded the Nazi-Soviet pact on the eve of the attack on Poland.

before, and it had been a disgrace that East Prussia was separated from the Fatherland by this strip of land. That was one more ignominy left over from the Versailles treaty after World War I. Now, in 1939, Hitler, with a Blitzkrieg, had overrun Poland and just took the strip of land back, thus uniting East Prussia with West Prussia, and therefore with the rest of Germany. Poland did not exist anymore. After the Blitzkrieg, it was divided between Russia and Germany, with its bigger part belonging to Russia.

The Stammtisch members had their own ideas about the Blitzkrieg. The headmaster proudly wore the NSDAP button on his lapel when they met in 1939. He smiled. "Now, Adolf, our Führer, has united Germany again." The former teacher was a member of the Nazi party, and so was the mayor—reluctantly. He would have lost his job, might even have been arrested, if he did not join the NSDAP.

The pharmacist sighed. "Well, it is nice to have Posen, Thorn, and Danzig back; now the Deutschlandlied has its true meaning again. 'Von der Maas bis an die Memel, von der Etch bis an den Belt.'"[41]

"Yes, yes, Germany above everything else!" the farmer nodded. He changed the subject, saying, "Somehow, our Stammtisch is not anymore what it used to be. Schumann, our shopkeeper, left soon after the Nürnberg Laws. I never knew he was Jewish."

The minister added, "You would not think so. His children were baptized in the Catholic Church."

The mayor knew from his files why the Schumann family had to move. He informed them, "His wife is a Jewish descendant; that is the reason he moved away. He could have filed a divorce, and then he could have stayed. But he did not want to do that to his wife and children, who might have been transported to England or France anyway."

The farmer, missing them the most, noted, "Old Schumann had a good business here, always had the best quality material for dresses and suits." He stopped and scratched his head, saying, "You know, come to think of it, what happened to all his stock? He was too thrifty to give all of his goods away. Hmm, I wonder … I never saw trucks or even wagons pulled in front of his shop. I never saw him load up anything."

The mayor added, "I had to let the police in to check their premises after they did not come back from their so-called vacation. All the shelves

---

41 Germany's national anthem. The first verse mentions the four waterways as borders for Germany. This verse was abolished after WWII.

in the shop were empty; no material, no yarn, no sewing thread, needles, scissors ... in short, nothing was left."

"They could not have taken all of it with them when they claimed to take a vacation in France," the farmer said ponderingly. He started to shuffle the cards, ordered a beer, and invited the rest of their dwindling group to join him.

Political discussions became dangerous,[42] unless people praised Hitler and his cabinet for having Germany delivered from the many uncertainties brought about by the Versailles treaty.[43] Hitler had promised early on to lead Germany out of its difficulties created by that notorious treaty. In 1936, Hitler seemed to have kept his promises to the German people. Germans prospered. The Rhineland was under German control again. Social institutions were established. Mothers could have vacations in retreats called "homes for mothers." Children were sent to camps, and even babies were taken care of in well-run "social homes." Already, before the draft into the military was installed, the metal industry was stimulated. Airplanes were developed, along with panzers and cannons. Germany's infrastructure on rivers and canals supplemented the street and railroad networks. Transport of raw goods and finished products functioned well. The draft into the military helped to keep unemployment down, and many people also found employment in social work, factories, and transportation. Politically, Germany had again gained respect in the eyes of the world.

---

42 Germany became increasingly a police state, where the Gestapo shadowed everybody, using neighbors, teachers, even children to get information about anybody living in Germany.

43 On June 28, 1919, the signing of the treaty by Germans took place in the same Hall of Mirrors in Versailles Palace where the German empire had been proclaimed on January 18, 1871.

Chapter 3

Klostermansfeld

At night, Uncle Martin listened to the news. One evening, in October 1938, he called Oma and his friend. "Mother, Fritz, come quick! Listen to this …" he shouted. The announcer reported with enthusiasm how the German people living in Sudetenland[44] greeted German soldiers with feverish excitement. He prophesied that a new era of expansion toward the east would start for Germany.

"Well," Fritz reflected, "in March, Hitler annexed Austria, apparently with the same enthusiasm. Now Sudetenland. Where will it end? The Czechs will not tolerate this. We might have a war."

Oma continued to listen to the radio. At the end, she concluded, "And to think the British are on our side. This Sudetenland thing was decided without the Czech government. Hitler only met with Neville Chamberlain from Great Britain, Daladier of France, and, of course, with this Fascist dictator, Mussolini of Italy."[45]

Uncle Martin's fiancée, Ursel, who had come to discuss wedding plans with Oma, mentioned, "I wonder what my brother, Günther, thinks. He joined the panzer division, you know."

---

44 An area in northern and western Czechoslovakia. Czechoslovakia was created by the Versailles treaty. It used to be Bohemia. Many ethnic Germans lived in Sudetenland, which formerly belonged to Silesia.

45 The conference between Hitler, Neville Chamberlain of Great Britain, Édouard Daladier of France, and Benito Mussolini took place in Munich on September 29, 1938. Later, this meeting was known as the Munich Conference.

Oma, always ready to console, pointed out, "Chamberlain wants peace, and Hitler reiterates he does not want war. At least, when we are friends with England, Günther does not have to fight the British."

Fritz was concerned. He had been drafted and went through military training before being released to pursue his studies in agriculture. He voiced his opinion. "I am afraid the Czechs are not without support. France is their ally. It smacks of the Great War of 1914–18, when we Germans had to fight on two fronts. We faced France in the west and Russia in the east. Now, it will be France and Czechoslovakia."

Uncle Martin shook his head. "I am sorry to have called you. We can't change anything. It looks like a war has been avoided again due to this conference." Turning to upcoming events, he continued, "Right now, it's more important for us to make preparations for Thanksgiving. We just have a few more potatoes and sugar beets to bring in, and then we will celebrate. I reserved the big hall of my Stammtisch inn. We will have the village band for dancing later on."

Oma asked, "Who is going to cook the meal for all of your farmworkers, their spouses and children, and our friends?"

Uncle Martin chuckled, "You, of course!"

Oma knew better. She might bake cakes for all of them, but the meal had to be cooked by the chef of the inn.

In six years, Hitler had brought Germany back into serious negotiations with European countries. England realized the injustice done to Germany at Versailles. Chamberlain appreciated the role a conservative Germany could play as a bulwark against Communism. Therefore, the British government agreed to let Hitler annex the Sudetenland as long as Hitler promised not to further pursue any lands beyond the established eastern borders of Germany.

Not quite a month later, on November 9, 1938, a nationwide pogrom[46] was staged in Germany, to the dismay of the civilized world. During the night of the ninth to the tenth, over one thousand Jewish establishments were destroyed. The Gestapo chief, Heydrich, reported that 7,500 businesses were demolished, 250 synagogues were burned, Jewish cemeteries were desecrated, and thousands of houses or apartments were vandalized. Many

---

46 Etymologically, the word *pogrom* is Yiddish from Russia and means "devastation." It was most likely coined in 1903. It refers to an organized massacre of defenseless people, especially the massacre of Jews.

Jews were beaten, killed, or thrown into concentration camps. The people in villages like Klostermansfeld experienced little of this, but they heard rumors about the pogrom. I only know of one store near us that might have belonged to Jews, but the family had left Germany long before the Kristallnacht,[47] as Hermann Goering termed the massacre. The pogrom happened mainly in big cities and in the south of Germany. The Nazi plan for administrative murder was a guarded secret. Freedom of information did not exist during Hitler's regime. Therefore, it is true that many Germans did not know of the atrocities committed in concentration camps, although rumors were abundant. The German people were cautious not to talk about it, especially not in front of children. I knew about prisons where criminals were kept in single cells, but I had no idea about concentration camps until 1945, and then I did not believe that Germans could have committed such outrageous terror and horrible treatment of defenseless people in these camps.

Censorship of the newspaper, radio, cinema, and theater was enforced under the strict control of Joseph Goebbels, Hitler's minister of popular enlightenment and propaganda. Looking back, one might ask, "What was the Nazis' concept of *enlightenment?*" It was not light Goebbels shed on the German population, it was darkness. Two years later, the blackout followed, literally and symbolically. Soon the German people had to make sure that all of their windows had shutters or shades that did not let any light through, so the streets would be in absolute darkness during the night. It would protect people and their houses during bombing raids. The blackout was strictly enforced by the police. Symbolically, Germans were kept in the dark about jail sentences for high officials, administrative murders, euthanasia of mentally retarded or physically deformed people, and the atrocities committed in concentration camps.

Most Germans hid behind the saying, "Was ich nicht weiß, macht mich nicht heiß," which, when translated literally, means, "What I do not know can't make me hot." In other words, if I do not know about something, I will not be concerned or get anxious about it.

My father had opened up the whole Thuringian section of Germany for his insurance company. Now, after the Blitzkrieg in Poland in 1939 and the annexation of the western part of Poland to Germany, he followed the

---

47 *Kristallnacht* means "crystal night." The Nazis camouflaged their cruel actions by coining "pretty" words for them.

call to the East. Soon, he had an office established in Thorn (Torun), the birthplace of Nicholas Copernicus.[48]

Before we moved to Thorn in West Prussia, we stayed with Oma in Klostermansfeld. There, they were making big preparations for Uncle Martin's wedding. He had courted a beautiful woman from a nearby village. It had been a considerably long courtship. Already in 1936, they knew each other well enough that my parents decided to ask his fiancée to become my godmother. Now I was three years old and taking part in the wedding festivities. Hildegard and I scattered flowers and petals in front of the bride. Ernst carried her veil and train. Mother had taken a popular sailors' song with a refrain that everybody knew and wrote her own verses for Uncle Martin and Aunt Ursel. We were dressed in sailor suits. We had to march around the dinner table and salute while everybody sang the refrain. I am told that I was rather stubborn when it came to practicing for the little parade. My mother talked to Oma and sighed, "I don't know if this little skit will go over well with Ilse-Rose not cooperating at all."

"Just don't worry, Paula, Roselett is cute no matter what she does, and the older ones sing very nicely. You will lead them. Everyone will enjoy it," replied Oma, defending her favorite little granddaughter.

I only remember a few things about our performance. My sister told me that, when we presented our skit, my mother walked into the dining room where the guests were waiting for their desserts. She acted as the head sailor, followed by my brother and then my sister. All three were singing, and I was at the end. I was not singing, but when the refrain came, I repeated the verses solo to the delight of all the guests and pointed to myself at the line, "down to the smallest mate." Nobody suspected that my performance had not been planned. My mother reaped the compliments on having trained a three-year-old so well.

Let me tell you about todays German marriage rites, especially ones in the country. They are quite different from American weddings. First, the engagement ring: in my grandmother's time, it could have a stone, but in the twentieth century two simple gold rings suffice for the couple. To this day it is common that they are worn on the left hand to show engagement until the minister slipps them onto the right ring fingers at the wedding ceremony.

---

48 Nicholas Copernicus, the Latin version of Mikolaj Kopernik (also known under his German name Nikolaus Kopernikus), was born in 1473 in Torun and died in 1543 in East Prussia. He was a famous astronomer whose theory on the heliocentric system revolutionized the Christian outlook for man in the cosmos.

Secondly, the church service cannot not take place until the couple has gone to the courthouse to receive their civil wedding papers. They usually go to the administrative office on the morning of the wedding day. For this occasion, the bride wears a pretty Sunday dress and the groom a suit. When they come home from the registry office, everybody welcomes them with a glass of champagne. Then the bride and groom change into their wedding outfits. The wedding dress, worn for the rest of the day, is white. The bride does wear a veil, and they do have flower children—mostly girls—who scattere petals in front of the bride and groom when they enter the church together. Most of the time, there is no "giving away" of the bride[49] by the father like in America. That eliminates a lot of embarrassment when the parents of the bride are divorced, or her father is deceased.

After the ceremony, the new couple leaves the church first, but at the church door, children from the village stop them. They stand facing each other, holding ribbons or flower garlands in their hands, forming a boundary. The groom reaches into the pocket of his tuxedo or suit. He pulls out hard candy and pennies and throws them in the midst of the children. They drop their ribbons and dash for the money and sweets. Now everybody can step out of the church and continue to the place where the festivities will be held. A table is provided for the gifts, which are not wrapped so that everybody can see them, talk about them, and point them out to the couple and each other.

Usually, the wedding guests are relatives and best friends. There are no bridesmaids or best man. At noon or early afternoon, the guests take a huge meal, preferably all sitting at the same table. The bride and groom sit at the head of the table, flanked by their parents. Couples do not sit with their spouses; therefore, the mother-in-law of the groom sits beside him with his father as her dinner partner. The grandparents are next in line, and then the siblings of the bride and groom, godparents, friends, and often the minister with his wife. This arrangement lets the two families get acquainted better. Children under ten years of age usually sit together at an extra table, where they are taken care of by an adult. Sometimes their table is even not in the same room, so the children may get up early and play. They do not need to sit through the long, drawn-out meal. Between the traditional five to seven courses of the meal, speeches are made, skits are performed, wedding

---

49 Except for weddings of the nobility, in which the father, or a politically important man, would lead the bride to the altar.

papers[50] are handed out, and everybody sings songs or recites poems. For the many toasts, which are brought to the couple or to their parents and relatives, they serve several wines. The groom will thank the guests for their attendance and the gifts. After the meal, which takes hours, everybody will rest or walk around the premises. In the evening they have a meal, served banquet-style, that will be open for helping oneself during the whole evening. Meanwhile, they dance to modern and old music from discs, tapes, records, or even a band. Usually the new couple leaves the wedding guests by midnight. They start on a short honeymoon the next morning. Both families share the cost of the feast. Relatives make pictures of the event. Only lately have some Germans started to imitate American customs by taking on a few of their traditions, such as bridesmaids, diamond rings, professional photographers, and tiered wedding cakes.

After Uncle Martin's wedding, we stayed with Oma. Father was already in Thorn, looking for a suitable place to rent. He found a spacious apartment near the garrison barracks and its church. Our new living quarters were located on the third floor of a big apartment building, adjacent to the former high school that was now converted into a veteran's hospital. In the years to come, many injured soldiers were treated there and healed, just to be sent back to war, mostly to the eastern front.

Before we settled in our new home, my father took all of us to Hermannsbad, formerly the Polish spa Ciechocinek. It belonged to an area named after Hermann Göring. After our vacation, Mother, Ernst, and Hildegard moved to Thorn, and a relative brought me back to Klostermansfeld. In the summer of 1940, Hildegard entered first grade and Ernst had to prepare to be accepted into high school, which began after the fourth grade.[51] He was an excellent student and enjoyed school. My parents had no doubt that he would be admitted into the Sexta. The high school started its classes with Latin numbers for the grades and counted backward to Prima,[52] the last grade, after which students still have to take a difficult

---

50 A humorous pamphlet usually written and drawn up by the siblings of the couple. It often included poems and songs about the couple.

51 In some German school districts, the high-school years still begin after fourth grade.

52 During the development of the high schools in Germany, it became necessary to add classes. They kept the Latin numbers but divided them into lower and upper Tertia, Secunda, and Prima, thus adding three more upper classes before schooling was finished.

examination called *Abitur*. After passing all of the many exams, students receive a diploma that openes practically all university doors in the world.

I visited often with Oma. She still lived with her son, Uncle Martin, and his wife, Aunt Ursel. It was understood that Oma should not move out of the house when her son married. The house was big. There was enough room for Oma's bedroom, her living room, and her formal dining room. She used it seldom—usually for her birthday celebration, when she invited the many friends she had in the village.

She helped in the household. I enjoyed being the only child, but I was not spoiled. I was only four years old when my uncle asked me to get him a freshly drafted beer from the nearby pub, where he met weekly with his Stammtisch to play cards and discuss the weather, the field preparations, or the harvest. When I turned six, Oma taught me how to run errands for her and not talk about them to anybody. The grown-ups stopped talking about politics in front of children. There was always the possibility that somebody might misinterpret things children said. The attitude toward the Nazi government had to be favorable; criticism was not tolerated. Informers targeted children, asking questions about what their parents and relatives did and what the grown-ups talked about. Often there were arrests, prison terms, and sometimes torture and death, just based on what one child told an informer.

I loved my Oma. I slept in her bedroom. Our window overlooked the enclosed courtyard. Buildings surrounded it on all four sides. Only a huge gate, which stood perpendicular to the two adjacent buildings and was covered by a roof, led to the outside. Most of the time, two gigantic doors kept the gate closed. The covered gateway was roomy enough for a hay wagon to be stored in it during a thunderstorm. Here was the doghouse, with a German shepherd to guard the premises. He was chained at daytime but let loose to roam the courtyard during the night. A door alongside of the big gate was used by people entering or leaving the courtyard. If a stranger crossed its threshold, a loud bark from the watchdog announced him.

Every morning at five a.m., Oma got up. She threw her shawl over her shoulders and walked downstairs to open the big oak door of the main house. She let in the faithful elderly maid and cleaning lady, Mrs. Münch., who had been with Oma for many years. Except in the warm summer days, Mrs. Münch. started the fire in the tile stoves of the house. One warmed the gentlemen's room and another the Wirtschaftsstube[53], a room near the kitchen. We took most of our meals there. It had two windows. One faced the street and the other one, across from it, opened to the courtyard. Both windows could be sealed off from the outside by thick oaken shutters so no light penetrated them. In this room stood a washstand, where I had to wash my hands before each meal. A table that could be extended to seat twelve people comfortably stood in front of a sofa. Near the street window hung a bookshelf stocked with books about domestic animals and a few children's books. It overlooked the big roll-top desk at which Oma did the weekly payroll for the household helpers and the farmworkers. Later, the male workers were drafted and had to fight in the war. My uncle had no choice when it came to replacing his farm help; he had to take prisoners of war, most of whom needed training in farming and domestic animal care.

While Mrs. Münch started the fires in the various stoves, Oma came back upstairs with a can of hot water she had drawn from the water basin mounted alongside the huge kitchen stove. I would lie in my bed with my eyes closed, pretending to still be asleep. I watched Oma, who had her back to me, face the washstand. It was not an ordinary small one but a big dresser with a marble top. Its enormous mirror reflected the sky through the open window. A shelf on either side of the looking glass served to store combs, hairpins, and other utensils necessary for Oma's morning toilette. First, she poured some warm water into a cup for brushing her teeth. She filled a big porcelain bowl with half of the water from the can and mixed it with the cold water from the matching pitcher. She washed her face, neck, and arms and proceeded down to her feet. Then she dried herself. She still wore an old-fashioned bodice—without staffs, but starched to the hilt. She put on an embroidered linen shirt with lace at the top, followed by two snow-white long cotton underskirts, covering black stockings that she had fastened onto her corset. She folded a square flannel cloth into a triangle and draped it over her shoulders, crossing its ends over her chest. Finally, she slipped her dress over her head, buttoned it in the front, added a woolen knitted jacket, and topped the outfit off by fastening a little black embroidered choker around her neck.

Now she combed her long white hair, braided it, and arranged it into a flat bun on the back of her head, tying it together with beautiful horned hair needles and pinning a very sheer net over her hairdo. Last of all, she pulled on high-buttoned black shoes. She was rather plump and had some

---

53   Wirtschaftsstube is vernacular for a room serving multiple functions.

difficulty reaching down to tie the long shoelaces. That was the moment for me to pretend to wake up, slip out from under my warm feather covers, and lace the shoes for her, being careful to get the leather tongue just right so it did not hurt her feet.

Oma emptied the washbowl into a shiny enameled pail, poured the rest of the warm water into the washbasin, and started to wash my face, hands, arms, and the rest of my body. She dried me off with a soft cotton towel. Then she helped me to fasten the buttons on the back of my little bodice, which I had pulled over my undershirt. Two elastic bands with clasps on each end hung from this vest. The long knitted woolen stockings were fastened with these. Oma had laid out a pretty blouse and an artfully knitted jumper for me, which my father's mother had made. Grandma Höfer had an eye for beauty. She made sure my sister and I had enough of her color-coordinated, beautifully knitted or crocheted garments.

I had to wear brown high-laced shoes. I protested every morning. "Oma, do I have to wear those ugly insoles today?"

All my pleading was to no avail. "Well, child," the old lady encouraged me, "try it, just for a short time. If it gets too painful, you may wear your house shoes, but you have to do your foot exercises faithfully." With a sigh, I agreed, leaning forward so my head touched Oma's. I embraced her. She, in return, drew me to her chest and kissed me gently. I like to think she might have silently prayed, "My Darling, may God guard you always."

Now, it was time to get downstairs for breakfast. Mrs. Münch had set the table for Uncle Martin, Aunt Ursel, Oma, me, and usually one or two visitors. It seemed there were always visitors. There was skinny Great-Aunt Bohne from the outskirts of Berlin, with her slender, long fingers; or Aunt Magda, my mother's sister; or my older cousins, Ingrid and Klaus; or Aunt Mertens, Aunt Ursel's mom; or friends of Aunt Ursel; or my great-grandmother, Oma's mother. I was always a little afraid of that stern-looking, slender, small, and energetic woman, but I loved her baked goods. She made soft sponge cakes, crisp cookies, lid-cookies, spiced tarts—all of them in delightful shapes and delicious.

She lived about twenty-four kilometers[54] away from Klostermansfeld, in Edersleben. When we visited her occasionally, two horses were hitched to a carriage. Oma took the reins and off we went. She seldom urged the horses to trot and never to gallop, as Uncle Martin did, but let them go at

---

54   One kilometer equals 0.621371192 miles. Twenty-four kilometers is approximately
    fifteen miles.

their preferred pace. That meant hours of travel sitting behind the horses. I looked all around me, except when it was winter and the horses were hitched in front of the big sleigh. Then, Oma had a foot warmer for herself, in which two big heated stones were laid. She and I were wrapped up in a huge bearskin. The fur obscured my view. I never was cold on these outings, or hot when we visited Great-Grandmother in summer. The fresh breeze from the open carriage kept us cool. If we had to stop so the horses could let water, I would climb out and look for a suitable place in the woods or bushes to do the same.

Often, we returned late, under a moonlit sky, from our visit with Great-Grandmother and Aunt Klara, my oldest godmother. She lived just a short walk away from Great-Grandmother. Aunt Klara had married Oma's brother. He was soon drafted. After he was killed early on in the war, she—like her mother-in-law—worked the large estate with the help of a man put in charge of the everyday tasks. She had a daughter, Aunt Lisbeth, and three sons: Uncle Fritz, Uncle Hugo, and Uncle Wolfgang. They were the younger cousins of my mother. Aunt Klara liked to play cards. When she was alone, she amused herself with Solitaire. She taught this game to me. It is remarkable how she was accepted and welcomed at the usually male-dominated circles of various Stammtisches. The men invited her to play Skat[55] with them, because she played this popular game with intelligence. Later, when I knew the times tables, my brother taught the game to me since sometimes he and his friend needed a third "man."

Great-Grandmother had an apartment above the living quarters of the farmer's family who oversaw her large estate. Her husband had died when she was only twenty-four years old and left her with two young children. Great-Grandmother sent Oma as a young girl to the Frankische Stiftung in Halle on the Saale. This school, affiliated with the university in Halle, was founded by August Hermann Franke in 1698. Its goal was to give children a well-rounded education, with special emphasis on education for orphans and half-orphans. In the nineteenth century, the tradition of caring for orphans was continued. Oma's education was enhanced at this

---

55 A very popular card game in Germany. At least three players are needed. One player plays against the other two; his position is determined through bidding. Each of the four suits has a number from nine to twelve. The bidding depends on which Jack one has and which suit one would like to announce as trump. Multiplying the suit-number by the "Jack situation" determines how high one can bid. The one with the highest bid announces the trump and plays against the other two. You may not outbid yourself.

institute. She had learned the usual writing, reading, and arithmetic at the public school. When she entered the Frankische Stiftung, she took courses in French and some Latin, mathematics (including bookkeeping), and subjects that covered household and garden chores. In addition to that, she had music and art lessons.

Back in Klostermanfeld, it was always a special treat for me when Oma unlocked the formal dining room downstairs, where the piano stood, and played some songs for me. This dining room had a vaulted ceiling reminiscent of the cloister that our farmhouse and buildings once had been. We lived in the main building of the former cloister. Later, toward the end of World War II, when bombing raids were even possible in the countryside, I was told that those vaulted ceilings were supposed to give special protection. "Bombs cannot penetrate this type of ceiling; they slip off the vaulted center," the adults said, and I thought, *Even if they get through the first vaulted ceiling, they certainly would not have enough power to get through the second vault under which we sit in the cellar, waiting for the Entwarnung* (sounding of all clear).

Almost every morning, Oma prepared for me warm rolls, which the baker across the street baked each weekday. She spread butter and honey on them and poured hot milk in a cup. I ate, and I drank all of the milk, even if an unappetizing skin formed on top of it. The milk was fresh from Uncle Martin's stable, where twenty to thirty cows stood alongside one big bull with a ring through his nose. After breakfast, I went to cluck for the chickens and feed them. Usually a flock of pigeons fluttered by to get their share of grain. At the same time, Uncle Martin gave his farm helpers instructions for the day. They had gathered in front of the horse stable, waiting for him. I listened, observing everything, and hoped to be allowed to go with one group of workers into the fields, preferably the crew in which Hans, my favorite horse, was employed. He was the gentlest old farm horse. Usually I was allowed to ride him, even when he was hitched alongside his partner, Max, to pull a wagon.

When it was plowing time, the birds and I followed the dark furrows. I watched them picking worms, larvae, or unearthed kernels. Once in a while, the plow destroyed a mouse nest, and then I watched attentively how the little pink, naked mice with slits for ears constantly opened their mouths in a sucking motion. I had mixed feelings about these babies. Should I rescue them? Should I let them starve or be eaten by a crow? I had heard how much damage these mice did to Uncle Martin's harvest.

At lunchtime, one of the servants brought food into the fields, mostly hot pea, lentil, or bean soup and a big doubled-over sandwich with liver or blood sausage. Oma always asked me what I liked for lunch. In the evening, after work, I seldom rode sweaty old Hans, but sat on the wagon with all the women who had helped to plant potatoes. I did not like this very much. They talked with each other like I was not there. Their conversations did not interest me, either—and anyway, I had been told not to speak about things I had heard at home. I was actually a quiet little girl. That's why most of the workers really liked me. I was not in their way, and I would help if they let me. I watched them and loved to imitate their working or eating habits. The latter needed to be corrected sometimes by Oma when at our own dinner table.

To me, there was nothing as wonderful as being with Oma in the country, but I was not always with Oma—only when taking care of four children became too much for my mother. In 1941, my youngest brother was born. My mother had to get ration cards for food, stand in long lines for groceries, and conduct the household chores. She did have helpers, who were of Polish descent. There was a nanny named Lydia, a washwoman, a cleaning woman, and another household helper for cooking and ironing. None of them could assist my siblings with their schoolwork, nor could they buy food for us, because they would receive lesser quality. They could not pass on family traditions at Christmas, birthdays, or Easter. In the evening, all returned to their homes. Then Mother was alone to take care of whatever happened to us during the night. By now, my mother had to cope with the alarms that warned us of bombing raids, although Thorn saw less destruction than Stettin or Danzig. For my mother, it was a relief to have one fewer child to care for, and since I was well-liked by the relatives, it was easiest for her to send me. I never felt abandoned by her. I'd rather stay at Oma's, although since 1940, I was no longer the only child. Aunt Ursel had given birth to a little boy, Hermjörg.

Oma lived in the main house of the converted cloister. That was much more interesting than the apartment in Thorn. The old buildings surrounding the courtyard might once have hosted cells for the monks, but already years ago, they had been converted into stables downstairs and storage for grains and feed upstairs. Some of these buildings had cellars underneath them. We used them for growing mushrooms and keeping potatoes, firewood, coal, and other typical things one stores in a cellar.

My uncle planted sugar beets. Every part of this plant was used. The large leaves were put into long piles, resembling a grave for a giant, and covered with soil. They fermented and were used in winter to supplement the cattle feed. The beets were carted to a sugar factory, where they were washed, shredded, pressed, and processed to render sugar and beet syrup. Uncle Martin stored the dried leftover beet particles in one of the storage rooms above the horse and cow stables. The shreds still had enough nourishment to be added to the cattle feed.

After my cousins were born in 1940 and 1942, I discovered that someone had built a swing in the shredded-beet storage room. It was a long, airy, and well-lit place. Most of its windows faced the courtyard; only a few small upper ones opened toward the street. I loved to swing there for hours, singing all kinds of songs I had learned. Occasionally, Oma climbed up the steep staircase. She went to the adjacent room where the flour was stored. Here, too, were the rooms for some of the prisoners who chose to become civil workers.[56] They were not kept in prison cells; they slept in beds and had feather covers. Oma and the maids changed their sheets regularly. In fact, I never knew that they were prisoners.

Across from the horse stable was the wash kitchen, called so because it boasted two huge brick stoves. These stoves had no cooking surface. Instead, a large kettle could be suspended inside of each bowl-shaped opening in the center. Here, water was heated for the monthly laundry. The laundry was washed in wooden troughs, shaped almost like wide, crude rowboats. One was for the linens and the other for the work clothing. I remember several washwomen coming regularly each month to wash. They used detergent, but mainly soap and washboards. All of this was interesting for me, but I had the most fun in two rooms indirectly associated with the wash kitchen. Underneath that kitchen was a cellar that flooded sometimes. Then, under the supervision of Uncle Martin, my cousins and I sat in the wash troughs and used crudely made rudders to row around. My cousins had competitions to see who could cut the corner the fastest. Usually one of them landed in the cold water.

The other room was the attic of the main house. Here, lines were strung to hang the laundry when it rained. A second staircase shaped like a ladder with wide rungs led to another attic above it. There, Hildegard and I found dishes. They belonged in Oma's former household but now were stored here. The doll dishes came in a complete set with soup plates, dinner plates, soup terrines, vegetable bowls, and platters. After my mother had to leave our

---

56 See Chapter 5, where the difference between POWs and civil workers is explained.

belongings in Thorn in 1945 and we started anew in 1947 in Hamelin, we used these dishes. They supplemented the ones Mrs. Homburg let us use in exchange for my mother cooking the meals every day for her family, her relatives, and us. Often we were twelve people for the main meal at noon.

On sunny days, the laundry hung in the open place in front of the new attached house. That building was an eyesore. My grandfather had asked an architect to build a new house adjacent to the old one. The architect had no concern for the old building, which hugged the ground with its thick walls. It was well-balanced, spread out generously, had vaulted ceilings and windows that could be closed with heavy wooden shutters, and featured an inviting doorway in the middle of its front. Its walls were covered with light blue stucco, and later with a vine.

Onto this majestic old building the architect plastered a huge yellow brick building in the style typical for town buildings at the turn of the century. The new building had three floors. It could be reached from the old building through its second floor. One of the old house's rooms was converted to a semi-throughway, with steps leading up to the second floor of the new building. The stairs led directly to the master bedroom. A huge dressing room, a nursery, and a bathroom without a toilet were attached to it. Uncle Martin instructed a plumber to build a water closet in a corner of the old building, because Aunt Ursel had told him before they married, "Martin, I am not using one of the two outhouses in the courtyard. If I marry you and live in that old cloister, I want a toilet inside of the house." Well, I guess Uncle Martin loved her enough to have her wish fulfilled.

The nursery could be reached from the master bedroom and the hallway as well. The rooms had much higher ceilings than the ones in the old building. The main entrance for this new house was in the courtyard. Steep, long stairs led to the upper rooms. On the first floor, the architect constructed two large rooms that served as Grandfather's laboratory. Above it were the nursery, the bathroom, a bedroom, and a dressing-room. The second flight of steps led to two bedrooms meant for live-in maids. It started with a two-step ledge, from which a door led to the long roof over the grain storage and the wash kitchen. The roof extended over the adjacent potato-cooker room, the pig stable, the two outhouse-type toilets, and the carriage shed. We could walk all the way across it to an old pigeon loft that was located above the gateway. We children climbed through the pigeon loft onto rafters that supported the huge barn roof, where the hay and straw were kept.

We loved to play catch on the beams above the hay. We laid boards across them. On these, we had to balance to reach the wider beams. When I think back, I shudder at how dangerous these games were, twenty to thirty feet above the ground. When we played catch, we climbed two long ladders, ran across beams, and balanced on boards, all the time running.

In the winter, we loved another form of hazardous entertainment. We fastened our sleds together with ropes and hitched a horse to the front sled. We traveled through the village that way, with the last two sleds weaving back and forth after a curve and sometimes tumbling over, spilling us into the street. We did not need to fear cars. They were seldom seen during the war, with gasoline being rationed and only made available for emergencies, but there could always be a tractor or other horse-drawn vehicles on the road. We also could wind up in the ice-covered creek that runs through Klostermansfeld.

I entered first grade in Thorn, where I heard Polish and German. I'll talk about how I was registered for first grade in the next chapter. Anyway, I soon was back in Klostermansfeld. I had to go to school in the village. I understood math very well, was good at drawing and especially at learning poems by heart and reciting them with gusto, but my big problem was spelling. Now exposed to the Saxon dialect again, I made even more mistakes than before.

My classroom teacher, Miss Karsdorf, was concerned and talked to Oma about that quiet but a little backward child. Oma let me take tutoring lessons with that very teacher, who got paid with sausages, soups, and salted meats in the fall when we slaughtered pigs and calves. Miss Karsdorf tried to train me and I cooperated, but I often misunderstood her. Back in school, she urged me to participate. I just stared at her and kept silent. She often became irritated with this stubborn child and sent me with a push on my shoulders back to my seat. For the rest of the day, she would not speak to me.

Oma realized that I dreaded to go to Miss Karsdorf's tutoring sessions. She said, "You soon have vacation, and then you do not need to go to your teacher anymore." I just hugged her and thought, *Now fun times start again.*

When my mother came to visit and brought my sister and my younger brother along, I had to watch him and my younger cousins during the hour after lunch. This hour is like a siesta in Germany. Then even the grocery stores closed from noon to two p.m. It seemed like all grown-ups took a midday nap. You did not dare to make any noise. Somebody had to entertain the youngest children. The babies took their naps too, but the three older ones had to be kept quiet. I, with my talent for reading stories or telling fairy tales, seemed to be the elected one to babysit.

Sometimes Oma got up during her naptime, came to the pantry window, motioned to me as I was quietly playing with my friends, and handed me a basket. I had to take it to one of the special friends she supported. This only happened when the boys had gone with their parents for a visit.

After 1945, I had to take these trips more often. So many people were starving, even in the country. Oma paid for tailoring, shoes, and other necessities with food. It seemed we were back in the dark ages when people bartered work, clothing, and utensils for food—and in my ears rang Oma's plea, "But don't tell anybody, not Uncle Martin, Aunt Ursel, and especially not your friends."

Chapter 4

Thorn—War Years

When the Stammtisch met in midsummer of 1940, Germany had seen considerable expansion beyond its eastern borders as established by the Versailles treaty. The headmaster praised the cunning of Adolf Hitler when he announced, "It is such a pleasure to teach Germany's geography again. Germany not only received back its Saar Basin in the southwest, but it has also grown toward the east."

The pharmacist, rather exasperated, interrupted him with, "Yes. Yes, we know."

"Wait, wait, don't turn me off so fast. Have you observed how courageously Hitler went into Denmark and Norway? They welcomed him. Some of their best Aryans volunteered for the Waffen SS,"[57] the headmaster continued. "And that is not all; we have gone to the west as well. It was about time we taught the French a lesson. The British did not know what hit them when they heard of Belgium being overrun, and the French were just as surprised when they saw German panzers driving into Paris and German soldiers marching through the Arc de Triomphe."

The headmaster would have continued, but the minister stopped him. "Teach, you will have to play cards without me from now on."

All of them looked at him in surprise. Even the innkeeper paid attention

---

57 Between 1940 and 1945, other non-Germans were allowed to join the Waffen SS if they met the rigorous standards for SS volunteers. In 1940, the first volunteer division, the *Wiking* (Viking), was established for the Waffen SS from Denmark, Sweden, Finland, Estonia, the Netherlands, and Flanders.

to him and asked, "Pastor, is my beer not good enough for you anymore? Still want to try the Munich beer? You know I have imported beer from the former Czechoslovakia. There is Budweiser and Pilsner."[58]

"No, innkeeper, it's not your excellent brew. I might try Russian beer or vodka soon. I have been called to minister in the military," the pastor explained.

"Vodka in Russia? Who is talking about war with the Soviets?" asked the farmer.

The minister expounded, "Well, with France being an ally to Great Britain and Russia … what do you think will happen?"

The headmaster was not short of an answer. He declared, "Not another Great War! I assure you, we will overrun them just as fast as we did the Danes, Norwegians, and Dutch. It is not 1914 with a Kaiser[59] in control. Now we have our Führer. He saw the war firsthand, he knows how to wage wars." The man could not be halted in his praise of Adolf Hitler.

Meanwhile, the pharmacist, keeping his eye on the rambling headmaster, whispered to the farmer, "You know, Hitler did not keep his word to Chamberlain. The Führer is deceitful. I hardly trust anybody anymore. When Hitler wanted Lebensraum[60] in the east, the other European nations negotiated with him for the sake of keeping peace in Europe. Czechoslovakia was sacrificed for that peace. After they realized that they cannot trust Adolf, they were still unable to stop him when he attacked Poland in his Blitzkrieg last September."

The farmer nodded. "You heard Teach at that time. He was and still is so elated about Germany's military success. He wears his NSDAP button all the time …" He lowered his voice even more. "I wonder if he and the innkeeper are spies for the Gestapo?"

The pharmacist gave a quizzical look, thinking, *I should not discuss things like these with the farmer, either. Who knows if he isn't an informer too?* He turned back to the headmaster's account of the Nazis' military success.

---

58 Budweis (Budejovicky) and Pilsen (Pilzen) were Bohemian towns famous for their breweries. After Hitler annexed Czechoslovakia, the old German names for the towns were used again. Today, the Czech Republic is proud to export "Budweiser Budvar" and "Pilsner Lager".

59 *Kaiser* is the German word for "emperor." Emperor William II reigned during World War I.

60 *Lebensraum* means "living space," and was a major political campaign idea of Adolf Hitler.

"Denmark and Norway were powerless when the German army occupied in April," boasted the headmaster.

The mayor, whose son had been drafted shortly after the farmer's son, added, "They were still helpless when my son, with the 7th Panzer Division, drove via Belgium into France in May. That boy never thought he would see Paris. Now he is stationed there."

The pharmacist pointed out, "Your son was lucky to have fought under the Wüstenfuchs.[61] He is the best general we have. He spares his soldiers, but did you ever think about how many lost their lives in the battle against General Charles de Gaulle? Close to 360,000 French died, and we lost 35,000 German soldiers in our divisions."

To avoid further discussion with the headmaster reiterating the propaganda they all had heard during radio reports, the farmer reminded them, "What are we here for? Let's stop discussing the military and politics. I'll pay for the beer tonight, since it's the pastor's last game with us. Let's play our round of cards! Eh, Innkeeper, we need a round of beer! It's on me! Teach, you shuffle, and Mayor, you sit out this time."

But the headmaster snuffed, "It's not fun with you anymore, gentlemen. I'll have my drink at the bar. Thanks, Farmer, it's appreciated." He left the group and went to talk to the innkeeper.

Prior to this meeting of the Stammtisch, my family had moved to Thorn in the early summer of 1940. For the summer and fall, I was back in Klostermansfeld. Ernst continued elementary school, and Hildegard entered first grade. Normally, the school year started after Easter, but now, they shifted it to the summer. My sister learned to write in Latin script, and my brother had to change his handwriting from Sütterlin[62] letters to the new ones as well. The government decided to cast Sütterlin away because it was reminiscent of the Weimar Republic. Looking back, it seems strange to me that handwriting was converted but printing was not. The old gothic

---

61 The "Desert Fox," Erwin Johannes Eugen Rommel, was a brilliant tactician. To the German public, he symbolized Germany's military strength. After the invasion of France, Hitler sent him to help Mussolini out of Italy's predicament in North Africa. Rommel's unconventional tactics in battling the British earned him the name "Desert Fox."

62 *Sütterlin* script is named after its creator, Ludwig Sütterlin (1865–1917). This script standardized the formerly different chancery writing mainly used by government officials in the various German states. It was taught from 1915–1941 in German schools.

letters prevailed for propaganda pamphlets, posters, and especially books published under the Nazi regime. Censorship had reduced the stacks in public libraries, and pretty soon, everybody was sternly directed to put away certain magazines and books[63] they possessed. I did find books in the back row of the double-stacked shelves in the gentlemen's room in Klostermansfeld, but none of these were in Thorn. I just looked at the pictures in them. After all, I had not learned to read yet.

When I arrived in Thorn shortly before Christmas, my sister had the whooping cough. The community nurse, Anna, a deaconess, came and advised my mother, "Best you put all of your children together, then they will contract the whooping cough at the same time. Medication and treatment can be done in one room, and in a few weeks, the whole ordeal will be over with." My parents followed her directions and let us sleep in one bedroom. In those times, "sweating it out" seemed to be the cure for all sickness. The nurse and my mother wrapped us in towels and covered us with featherbeds. We laid there until the perspiration dripped down our foreheads. Then they uncovered us, washed us, and wiped us dry.

Actually, we were not so sick that we could not listen to Ernst read fairy tales to us. We also took turns telling stories to each other. I was surprised when Hildegard and Ernst laughingly said, "Hello, Fatty, tell us more about Uncle Martin and Oma!"

Were they, just for once, interested in what I had to say? I could hardly believe my good fortune and questioned them. "Do you mean it? You want to hear about Anton and Hans and the pigeons ...?"

My siblings burst out laughing. I wondered why, but I continued to tell them about farm life, every so often provoking an outburst of laughter from Hildegard and Ernst. My mother entered the room and listened. She grew very serious. "Ernst, Hildegard, shame on you! Both of you stop making fun of your sister!" Now it occurred to me that they did not care what I said. They only wanted to hear me talk, because I spoke with a rich Saxon accent.[64] *P* sounds often like *B*, most *Ts* sounds like *D*, and some *Gs* sounds like *J* or *K*. They heard *bijeon* instead of *pigeon*. *Tongue* sounded like *dung*, and *goose* like *juice*.

Needless to say, I became very quiet again. I listened carefully to my

---

63   In 1933, the SA and SS had already burned books by Jewish, Communist, or anti-Nazi authors. In 1938, the Nazis staged book burnings in many Jewish communities. After annexing Austria, they burned books in Salzburg.

64   It was the vernacular of Saxony Anhalt, which borders two states at its panhandle that extends into Saxony on the east and Thuringia on the west.

mother and imitated her. She pronounced words very clearly. After she had given birth to Ernst, one side of her face had been paralyzed for a short time. In order to speak again, she had to put pieces of amber in her mouth and practice pronunciation. Only a person with the energy and willpower of my mother would be able to regain full control of her facial muscles through that method.

I did not completely shed my accent. People who know German dialects still can detect a slight middle-German pronunciation when I speak.

My siblings were really not nasty to me. Ernst let me play with his farm buildings and all the wonderful animals in the barn. One day he asked, "Ilse-Rose, what do you think? Should we add a fence around the barn, so the cows have an enclosed paddock?"

I was eager and added, "And the sheep need a fence for their pen too."

My brother built it, as long as I would gather twigs from the trees that grew on the street leading to our apartment house. I went downstairs, crossed the Schlageterplatz,[65] and started to pick up branches, just the right size for a rustic enclosure. Upstairs again, I held the twigs so Ernst could nail them together. Now an appropriate fence surrounded the farm buildings. It looked very realistic.

When Ernst's friends came over, they played with their toy soldiers, guns, panzers, cannons, ditches, bunkers, headquarters, and Red Cross stations. They laid out battle plans over the whole everyday dining room. I was only allowed to play with them if they needed help moving soldiers into position. The boys probably thought, *What does a five-year-old know about strategic tactics?*

One day, I pulled a little sweater too hard over the head of my celluloid doll, named Hans. He lost his head. I cried, and Ernst saw me. Patting my shoulder, he said, "I fix Hans; only, you will not be able to turn his head anymore." I gave him the rump and the head, and he proceeded to our playroom, which was not too far from the toilet. You must know that in Germany, the bathroom is often separated from the toilet. My parents thought it rather practical to select the room closest to the toilet as the playroom.

It was during naptime in the early afternoon when my brother Ernst lit a candle and asked me to hold the rump of my doll. He trickled melting wax on the neck to fasten the head back onto the body. Now, celluloid is highly

---

65 Albert Leo Schlageter (1894–1923) was regarded as a martyr for the Nazi ideology. His name was used when renaming street addresses in annexed areas. Our address in Thorn was Schlageterplatz 7.

flammable. It did not take long until the head started to burn. *What to do next?* must have been running through his mind. *How to squelch the flames!? My hand is burning!!!* He dashed to the nearby toilet—dripping burning celluloid behind him—opened the door, and plunged the burning head together with his hand into the toilet bowl. I saw how the floor started to burn and screamed, "Our house is burning! Help! Our house is burning!" My mother came running from her bedroom, where she had been resting. She immediately helped Ernst. In the meantime, Nanny Lydia appeared out of nowhere and stamped on the spots where the burning celluloid drops started to ignite the paint of the wooden floor. She managed to extinguish them all. With a pail full of water, she wiped the burned places clean, although the floor was marked for good. Meanwhile, I just stood with the doll's rump in my hand and sobbed.

My mother turned to me. "Ilse-Rose, darling. Stop crying. We will bring Hans to a doll doctor. There, they will repair him. He will be like new." I was not to be consoled. She called Ernst into the room. "Look, Ilse-Rose, your brother is not crying. Look at his hand." I saw a blister almost as big as his fist on his wrist. He was in pain, but he also was in the Jungvolk. He was German, and German men do not cry. They can withstand pain like the American Indians did when they were tortured. My brother had read Karl May's books about the Appalachian Indian Winnetou and his white friend, Old Shatterhand.[66] Almost every child in Germany knew about the adventures of these two friends who lived on the prairie in America. We admired how brave and honorable they were. We knew their values and desired a friendship like theirs.

The leaders of the HJ and BDM[67] incorporated some of the values of these American heroes into their training of German children. Hitler approved of it. He also had been influenced by May's books. According to Albert Speer, when faced with difficult situations, Hitler would find courage through them.[68] Some of May's stories were revised during the Nazi

---

66   Karl May (1842–1912) wrote a series of books on these two characters. Adolf Hitler read them as a schoolboy in Vienna.

67   The "Hitler Youth," abbreviated HJ, was a paramilitary organization of the Nazi party founded in 1922. The HJ was for male youth ages 14–18. The younger boys' section, Deutsches Jungvolk, was for ages 10–14. The girls' section was called *Bund Deutscher Mädel* (BDM), "League of German Girls."

68   "Karl May," *Wikipedia*, last modified August 17, 2012, http://en.wikipedia.org/ wiki/Karl_May#cite_note-TNR-20. Albert Speer (1905–1981) worked closely with Hitler as minister of armaments and munitions.

era, since May spoke of nonwhite races quite favorably. A few of his books were edited to incorporate anti-Semitic passages. This was one of the many ways the regime used well-known and beloved literature to indoctrinate us children. Another means of eradicating the authorship of Jewish poems or songs that had become folk literature was to publish these anonymously.[69]

I remember one Christmas in Thorn when my father bought a tall, symmetrical, beautiful blue spruce. It smelled wonderful. He placed the tree in the formal dining room and closed the doors. Every night when he came home from his office, he disappeared behind these locked doors. He decorated the tree, and he built a railroad scene for Ernst on top of the fully extended dining-room table.

In one corner of the large room, he set up a doll's bedroom with white and pink furniture for Hildegard. In another corner, he placed a toy bedroom for me. The repaired Hans and a yellow teddy bear sat on the little beds. My furniture was painted in farmer style. It had decorative flowers against a blue background. Of course, we did not see any of this until December 24, the evening when Germans receive their gifts. We never had to unwrap presents. My mother or father unpacked the packages that the grandmothers and godparents sent. My parents assembled everything so it was ready to play with when we entered the room.

My mother gave all of our helpers the day off. She cooked a light meal, which we ate in the everyday dining room. Then my father disappeared again. We heard the ringing of a little silver bell. That was the sign for us to enter the formal dining room.

What a festive display! The Christmas tree stood in a corner. This year, it was decorated all in silver and white. Silver Christmas balls in various sizes and shapes hung from the branches, covered with silver tinsel and glistening white angel hair. The tree moved ever so gently because of the many candles on it, which burned and lit up the whole room with a warm glow. I stood transfixed, looking at this beautiful tree. My brother spied the landscape for his train set—but first, we had to recite some Christmas poems and sing a few songs.

Finally, my father switched on the train set. The whole scene lit up. Several trains ran at the same time; one crossed a bridge, another went

---

69   The song "Lore lei" by Heinrich Heine was sung often. It had become a folk song. It takes generations before folk literature will be forgotten by the people. Often these are used in other countries and kept alive there. Heine's "Lore lei" has become a standard poem and song for German studies in American schools.

through a tunnel, and one stopped at a station. Little people stood and waved, while others held suitcases. A mother held her child's hand and pushed a stroller. A HJ boy held up his right arm in the Hitler salute. The conductor wore a red hat. His arm could be lifted. In his hand, he held the signal for the train to start or stop. I just looked and looked. "Rosebud, this is electric. You may not touch any of it, or you might get a shock," my father explained to me.

Then I heard my sister shouting for joy, "Bärbel, my Käthe Cruse doll!"[70] She hugged the doll and then checked it out. "She has real hair. May I comb her?" she asked our mother.

"Yes. Look, there is a dressing table for your doll; it has a comb and brush for her."

Now Hildegard discovered the bedroom set. She immediately started to play with Bärbel, opened the little closet, and discovered dresses, coats, shoes, skirts, and blouses. Mother pointed to a little jacket and a sweater, saying, "These, Grandma made for your doll. We have to write a thank-you note to her."

I saw my presents. Hans had a new head, and he too had new clothing, but he was a Schildkrötpuppe.[71] They do not have real hair. These dolls are more practical for younger children. I liked my teddy bear. He had an artfully crocheted vest on, another of Grandma's creations. He had considerably long fur. I went to the bathroom, found a comb, and started to comb him. I combed his fur in different directions, even gave him a part on his head. Hildegard was able to braid Bärbel's hair, but Teddy's fur was too short to be braided.

We were allowed to play as long as we liked. The candles started to burn down, and Father replenished their holders with new ones. I must have fallen asleep. I woke up the next morning in my bed with my teddy bear at my side. At noon, we ate dinner as usual—only this time, we had a roasted goose that mother had stuffed with apples. The goose was Oma's

---

70   In 1905, Käthe Kruse dolls were made from material that did not break easily. Mrs. Kruse made these dolls first for her own seven children. After she exhibited them in Berlin, she received two big orders from the United States, which motivated her to establish her own doll company. To this day, her dolls are well sought after.

71   Since 1889, a German company called Rhenishe Rubber and Celluloid Works had found a way to improve celluloid so it could be used in toys. Soon the company was known as Schildkrötwerke. Their trademark is a turtle, for which the German word is *Schildkröte*.

Christmas gift for all of us. To keep the tradition of Father's family, my mother had cooked red cabbage with apples, a smidgen of ground cloves, salt, pepper, a little vinegar, and a trace of sugar. She had made Thüringer Klöße, which are dumplings made from raw potatoes. The dumplings are cooked in simmering water until they rise to the surface. Mother always roasted some bread cubes and put them in the middle of the dumplings. For dessert, we had her delicious caramel pudding.

In 1941, my mother had given birth to her fourth child—the son my father had wanted five years earlier when he had to settle for me instead. My younger brother had blue eyes and fair hair. Our nanny Lydia took care of him. She adored him. When she gave him a bath, she stroked the back of his head and remarked, "Handsome boy, has neck for a German officer's uniform." Did she say that to show loyalty to the German government? She had been Germanized,[72] as so many who worked for German natives were. She did not care for me. To her, I was a little awkward farm girl. She thought of me as an intruder into the tightly knit family, one who suddenly showed up, lived with the family for some months, and then left again for the farm.

The other servants had less to do with us children, although I was fascinated with the work one of them did: she ironed our clothing. She even let me try to iron a handkerchief. She and the cleaning woman brought bedsheets and table linens to a place where they had a big mangle.[73] A mangle was one of the things I missed when I came to America as an immigrant in 1964.

I did not like the cleaning lady. Somehow, I was always in her way, and she let me know it. I cared for the woman who came to do the laundry. She reminded me of the workwomen at Oma's. I liked her the most. She hardly ever was in our apartment. Once a month, the tenants of our building rented the wash kitchen in the cellar. When it was our turn to use the laundry room, I went downstairs to visit with her.

I was already several months in Thorn when, at the evening meal, my mother asked, "Who likes to take care of Reinhold tomorrow afternoon?"

---

72   The German word is *Eingedeutscht.* Eingedeutschte were of other native origins. They went through the process of belonging to Germany but did not have the same status as *Reichsdeutsche* (native Germans).

73   These mangles are run commercially throughout Germany. A mangle is a rotary iron. Its cylinder drum is so long that it can accommodate the length of a bedsheet or a tablecloth.

Hildegard right away said, "Let Lydia do it. She loves that baby."

I quietly ate, leaving the conversation to my older brother and sister.

Mother continued, "But tomorrow is Lydia's day off. You do not have to do much; just push his baby carriage back and forth in front of the church. I'll work here and can watch you from the balcony."

Ernst had an excuse. He needed to attend a meeting with the Jungvolk. He pointed out to us, "I must be at the HJ ward, and anyway, Mom, it looks ridiculous for a young man like me to push a stroller."

Hildegard chimed in, "And I am invited to play with Gertie at Sabine's house."

I nodded, "I'll do it." I took care of my little brother that afternoon. I did it so well that pretty soon, it was understood that I would always watch him. Reinhold rewarded me with his brotherly love and trust.

One Saturday, when Reinhold was not quite one year old, we children sat around the play table and my siblings had an idea. They had been a little jealous of all the attention their brother received from Grandma, from Father, from Nanny Lydia, and especially from Mother. They also knew how much he liked sugar. Ernst said to me, "Ilse-Rose, here is a teaspoon with salt. Give it to Reinhold. That should cure him wanting sugar all the time."

Hildegard added, "Let's watch his face. It will be hilarious."

I felt important that those two let me take part in one of their plans. We had no idea what so much salt could do to a little child. I took the spoon, and Reinhold, trustingly me completely, opened his mouth wide to receive the "sugar." His loud scream shocked us.

My mother came dashing into the room. "What happened? Why is he screaming? What does he have in his mouth?"

Instantly, we knew we had done something terribly wrong, but we did not want to explain anything. My siblings only told her, "Fatty has given him a spoonful of salt."

First, my mother took care of my little brother, making sure she retrieved as much salt as possible from his throat and mouth. He helped by spitting it out. Then she gave him a lot of milk and water to drink. By that time, milk was rationed. We had to do without it for several days after. Later on in the week, when my mother took the older ones to the theater and I had to stay home, I thought of it as a punishment for me. In reality, I still was too young to participate in some of the cultural events my mother selected for my older siblings. Still, this episode haunted me. One day, my mother told it to Reinhold when we all were reminiscing about our childhood. Years and years later, my younger brother included it in his speech on the occasion of our mother's eighty-fifth birthday. By then, I was fifty-five years old, and he still thought it had been my idea to give him salt.

Before I entered school, my mother had been asked—actually, ordered—to send her daughters to the German Kinderhort.[74] No child of Polish heritage was allowed to join, and definitely no children of Jewish descent. My wonderful play hours were forfeited in order for me to belong to the Kinderhort. Two energetic young women ran the Hort. They kept us disciplined. Siglinde told us, "You draw pictures now! Later, we'll put puzzles together, and then we'll play picture lotto or build with blocks."

I saw a book that interested me. It had a photo of a European finch on its cover. "Auntie, there is a book with bird pictures. May I look at it?"

"No. You just do everything according to our plan, just as everybody else does. Look how well your sister behaves and is exactly part of the group. Do you always have to have your own way?"

My eyes filled with tears. I did not mean to be difficult. I just wanted to see the picture book. At Oma's, I had access to many books, especially ones about horses, cows, chickens, and their diseases. I knew a lot about their anatomy already, and especially about the different types of domestic animals all over the world.

"Now, don't be a baby," the young woman scolded. "Stop sniffling. Listen, a Spartan girl would not sniffle, and we of the Aryan race are even tougher than the Greeks had been." To become as tough as a Spartan was the rule of the day. For years, I made it a great goal to reach. I would tell myself, *Swallow your tears; don't let anybody know you have feelings or any emotions. Be tough. Be able to withstand the coldest or hottest days. Be ready to defend the country and the Führer.*

I sat at the child-sized table and played with blocks. We had to build bridges. I noticed a red half-moon-shaped block inside of a blue rectangular one. Slowly, I withdrew the red one and dropped it into my apron pocket. I turned the blue one on its base, and *voilà!* I had a bridge. I started to draw wiggle lines resembling water underneath my blue bridge. Siglinde saw it and reprimanded me. "Oh my, what are you doing now? Who told you to take a crayon? Drawing time was earlier, not now. Build a bridge!"

---

74 A preschool and after-school program established by the Nazi government for the children of German nationals. The indoctrination of children started early, before our minds could be filled with religious or parental values.

I pointed to the block. "But I have a bridge, and this is the water. I'll draw fishes, and frogs, and salamanders, tadpoles, ducks, and geese …"

"Stop right this minute! You are disrupting the class. Give me the crayon." Both women stared at me in disgust. I had to fight tears again; I could not speak, could not utter an apology, I knew I would start crying if I opened my mouth. I gazed at my bridge. Suddenly, Erna grabbed my arms, pulled me off the chair, and transported me to the corner of the room. "That's where you belong when you are stubborn."

In the corner, I watched a little spider crawling up and down a thin strand. Would it build a net like the ones I had seen in Oma's garden? I focused so much on the spider that I forgot I was standing there as my punishment.

Finally, the Kinderhort ended. On our short way home, I skipped happily alongside my sister. We climbed the stairs to our apartment on the third floor. Here, Nanny Lydia took our jackets and aprons to hang them up for the next day. A little red half-moon-shaped block fell out of my pocket. Hildegard gave me a dismayed look. "Now what have you done? I did not think you stole the crayon, but you surely stole this block!"

A fight followed. My mother came to inquire about it. She listened to Hildegard's explanation, watching my reaction. Slowly she drew me to her chest and whispered into my ear while Hildegard continued to chatter about her sister's disgraceful behavior. "My little Rosebud, would you like to stay home tomorrow? Oma is coming."

A loud, happy squeal interrupted Hildegard's flow of words. She stopped her babbling, threw her head back, and left the room, the righteous judge.

The next day, I had to bring the block back to the Kinderhort, but I did not stay. My mother was with me and explained that I would leave soon for Middle Germany, where I would enter the same type of establishment. I was looking forward to Oma's visit. Now wonderful times would come again. Oma could make Nanny Lydia understand that I was a good child and was able to accomplish more than a typical five-year-old usually does. Oma knew how responsible her grandchild already was. She had sent me on errands nobody was to know about, and I kept it as a secret between us two.

Oma stayed a few weeks and then took me back to Klostermansfeld. Already on the train, she explained to me that I needed to go back to Thorn when I had to start school. To me, that was an eternity away. I'd rather think about the farm, my friends, the old dog Karo, the cows, calves, chickens, ducks, geese, and all the people who worked for Uncle Martin. Oma noticed that I was not interested in school. She told me about the two new black horses Uncle Martin had gotten. They were not the big Belgian horses; they were meant to draw lighter wagons, and best of all, they would be hitched in front of the new buggy, which was really an elegant carriage.

I entered first grade in 1942. My Aunt Ursel brought me back to Thorn. We took a long train ride and stayed one night in Cottbus to visit with Aunt Mertens, the mother of Aunt Ursel. That night, I experienced my first bomb scare. We heard the "forewarning" and left the apartment to go to the bomb shelter, which was located in the cellar. The main warning never came. After a half hour, the "all clear" sounded and we went upstairs again. The next day, we continued our train ride to Thorn.

Aunt Ursel took me to my first day of school. I left my Zuckertüte[75] at home. My mother had filled it with an apple, pears, hard candy, and marzipan from Lübeck. She also stuffed it with some playthings I liked and some utensils I needed for school: a coloring book with coloring pencils, some play dough, an extra slate stylus, and a little spare sponge. I carried a brand new leather satchel on my back. It contained the slate board on which I learned to write letters, do my math, and draw pictures. There was also a little sponge hanging from a hole in the frame of the slate board with which we could erase our work. We did not learn to use paper until we entered second or third grade. Using a slate board eliminated the lovely custom American mothers have of putting their children's artwork on the refrigerator door. Of course, my mother could not put it there even if we had paper pictures and magnets, since we had a wooden icebox in our pantry. At least once each week, a maid bought a huge ice block from the iceman, who delivered it to our kitchen. He used the back steps. I was only allowed to use this steep, tight stairwell when I wanted to visit Anneliese, who lived across the narrow courtyard between our L-shaped building, the hospital, and her house.

I am not sure why my mother could not take me to my first day of school. She was very occupied with my little brother. In addition, she had to stand in long lines to get food for the family. Just once, she had sent one of our maids to the market, and as a result, she had to point out, "These apples are shriveled up, and the plums are worm-eaten. At which stand did you buy them?"

---

75 This is an oversized, brightly colored cone made from cardboard. It is filled with candy and other goods. It should, supposedly, sweeten the start of the school year to come.

The maid replied, "I went where they had the shortest line, so I could be back soon."

Mother had to get food by herself. In the shops, she received better service than the maids. She had to pick up our ration cards in order to obtain food from the grocery store, but she also bought fresh produce from Mr. Schirkovski. He and his wife owned a big nursery and a hunting area, where my father was invited to hunt. During one of my stays in Thorn, I watched my father put a hare on a hook above the bathtub, so my mother could take its pelt off and prepare it for a roast. She had a superb talent for preparing game.

Any of the activities mentioned above would be reason enough to understand why my mother was unable to take me to my first day of school, but it is also possible that this was the day when she had to attend a meeting at which the mothers who had more than three children were honored. She received the bronze Mutterkreuz.[76] She used to tell us about this event. "All of us mothers were sitting in a big hall, waiting to be honored by the Gauleiter,"[77] she said. "When he entered, everybody got up and raised their right arm in the Hitler salute. I remained seated. My neighbor whispered, 'Get up or you wind up in prison.' I retorted, 'Who is being honored here? He or we?' But I did get up. I did not want to cause any trouble for my husband or my children."

The elementary school was a big building; my aunt and I got a little lost in it. Luckily, we found Hildegard, who directed us to the correct classroom and Miss Sanowski, a pretty, young woman who had to handle thirty-five to forty pupils. She asked us, "What is your name? Who is your father? Where do you live? Is this your permanent address?"

Right then and there, I became confused. Did I live with Oma or with Mom? But Aunt Ursel helped out. When Miss Sanowski asked, "Who is reichsdeutsch?" only five hands went up. The rest of the thirty-five pupils were either eingedeutscht or volksdeutsch.[78] That is one reason why, at recess, I only talked and played with two classmates who spoke German,

---

76 The Nazis handed out these medals in the form of a cross to honor mothers. When the woman had eight children, it was gold; for six children, it was silver, and for four, it was bronze.

77 *Gauleiter* was the title of the head of a Nazi administrative district.

78 *Volskdeutsch* referred to a person of German descent who applied for German citizenship because he or she was born in a foreign country that now was occupied by Germany. For the English translation of *eingedeutscht*, see footnote 72 in this chapter.

Anneliese and Ulla. I learned math very easily. I actually liked it, but orthography was terribly difficult for me. I liked to spell words according to the way they sounded to me. Of course, I had heard Oma and my friends in Klostermansfeld speak with a Saxon accent, where the *T* and *D* and the *B* and *P* often interchange, therefore called "hard B" or "hard D"; the *K* and *G* were mixed as well, and even vowels would sound different.

I loved to draw, but ran into trouble with communication again. One day, Miss Sanowski ordered in her slight Polish accent, "Now all of you draw some Hühnchen (little chickens)." I understood Hündchen (little dog). Lovingly, I drew a dog resembling Karo, the German shepherd at my Oma's place. "My, my, don't you even know that chickens have only two legs and not four?" The teacher shook her head.

Ulla and Anneliese, my classmates, giggled when the teacher rebuked me. I blushed, but the rejection of my friends did not last. At recess, the girls comforted me. "Even we have trouble understanding her sometimes," said Ulla, adding, "I hate school!" Her father was the janitor of the veterans' hospital adjacent to our apartment house. Anneliese's father worked for the railroad.

The family background of my friends was quite different from that of Hildegard's girlfriends. Sabine's father was a medical doctor, and her other friend's parents had a business in Holland. They lived in a luxurious apartment. I only visited there once. I remember that I seemed to be in everybody's way and did not take part in any games. The mother of Hildegard's friend came into the room and said anxiously, "I lost the stone out of my earring. It must be in this room." She started to look for it. I wanted to make a good impression so my sister would not be embarrassed because of me again, and I started to look as well. Finally, I mustered the courage to ask, "How big is this stone and what color is it?" I was informed that it was a half-carat, very clear, really expensive diamond. The lady showed me its counterpart, still hanging from her earlobe. I thought it was awfully small to make such a fuss about. My marbles were bigger than that. By now, all of us were searching for it in the thick oriental carpet. We never found it.

At home, I told my mother about this episode. "She was so upset about that tiny stone. She told us that it was very expensive. I do not believe it. The stone was not any bigger than my thumbnail, Mom."

But Hildegard gave details. "It was a diamond, Mom, a special cut of a half-carat diamond."

My mother told me, "Hildegard is right. These things are very valuable."

I was too young for Hildegard's friends, and anyway, I did not want to be with them. My sister always seemed to outshine me. I felt I never was good enough for her. I did not possess her polished manners with the guests who visited us or lived with us. I mispronounced and misspelled words, and especially names. In short, we seldom played with each other. She had her friends, and I had mine.

Ever since my mother had taken us to see the ballet *Sleeping Beauty*, my sister wanted to become a ballerina. My mother did not want to hear any of it. On the other hand, Hildegard wanted to join the BDM. The Nazi government financially supported the two youth groups, HJ and BDM and gave their members special privileges. For boys, the Jungvolk and, later, Hitler Jugend were compulsory. When Ernst entered high school, he had to join the Jungvolk.

The rules for the girls' groups were not as stringent until 1936, when belonging to the BDM became compulsory for girls as well. Each town or village was divided into small wards that could easily be reached on foot. In them, a BDM youth leader would meet with approximately fifteen girls twice a week. They designed the meetings so that they would appeal to children. They sang and played games. At the same time, the Nazi government systematically indoctrinated the children to first and foremost pay respect and give absolute loyalty to the Führer, to be proud of their Germanic-Aryan heritage, and to conform to the Nazi ideology, which included the Gleichschaltung[79]. It forced us into line with the Nazi standards and eliminated all opposition within the political, economic, and cultural institutions of the state. How did this work in reality?

Well, one day, when my sister was nine years old, she wanted to wear kneesocks like the BDM girls did, but my mother declared, "Honey, it's too cold today for bare knees. Here are your long stockings."

Hildegard looked at her defiantly. "You just wait until I am ten, then I join the BDM, and then you have nothing to say to me anymore." She left the room in triumph.

However, parents all over Germany could find ways to delay entry into

---

79 Gleichschaltung could be translated as "coordination" but really meant for the German youth "making all of them the same" or "bringing them into line" with the Nazi ideology.

the HJ, BDM, or special schools. When Hildegard was close to ten years old, my mother went to our pediatrician, who certified that Hildegard was not advancing at the normal rate for her age and therefore should be considered unfit to join the BDM at this stage of her development. I never thought my sister was weak, but the doctor found something to justify his statement.

Wolfgang Hamberger tells of a similar case in his book, *America*…. He describes how he, as a Jungvolk member, had been selected for the Reich School in Feldafing on Lake Starnberg. Although he wanted to enter this school, his parents were against it. First, his father took him to the office of the "Gauleiter" (district director). Hamberger writes:

> We weren't invited to sit down. While Dad said what he had come to say, the District Director … kept shuffling some papers, and his eye continually roved back to me as if he wanted to sum me up and find out what was behind my father's wanting me to stay home in Bensheim. After Dad had explained he didn't want to relinquish the responsibility for bringing me up, the district Director said … "It is no longer up to you to decide what school your son attends. It's for the party to decide now. With his athletic aptitude and other achievements, there is absolutely no reason to exempt him from attending the Reich School. … Even if I wanted to, I can't help you. As a last resort, a medical certificate might amend the situation.[80]

Hamberger's father remembered the district director's "last resort." He knew of a nose-and-ear specialist in his neighborhood who shared his political views, and from this doctor he obtained the certificate for his son. The boy was exempted from entering the school away from home.

My parents went with Hildegard to the BDM leader of our ward just before March 15,[81] the official last date when girls and boys who were

---

80 Hamberger, *America—my fascination*, 42–45. Here "Gauleiter" is translated "district director" which is not quite correct. "Gau" was a tribal district (@150 BC to 600 AD) The Nazi regime liked to use terms from "Germany's" ancient history. They called an administrative district "Gau" under the Nazis. Gauleiter was often the highest position in a district .

81 The induction into the Jungvolk, HJ, or BDM always took place on Hitler's birthday, April 20.

turning ten in the calendar year had to be registered with their respective Hitler Youth leader. They took the certificate from the doctor with them. My sister told me that the BDM leader, after scrutinizing her papers and listening to my parents, said, "All right, she does not have to enter this year." Then, looking at Hildegard, she remarked to my parents, "Well, your daughter really does not resemble the typical Aryan BDM girl anyway." Hildegard was slender, with beautiful big brown eyes and brown hair. She did have long braided hair—at least that was typical of BDM girls.

I never really got acquainted with Thorn. Hildegard had shown me which streets to take to walk to our school. She was in a higher grade. Her classes often started and ended at different times. Therefore, we very seldom went to or from school together. The women who worked for my mother did not live within walking distance and had to take the streetcar to come to work. Most of them spoke broken German, and they had no interest in showing me their homes.

Only once did the washwoman take me to one of the beautiful brick Gothic churches. I was amazed at its rich interior and mysterious dimness. It had a distinctive smell of dying flowers, burning candles, and incense. One more time, I entered a Catholic church in Thorn, but I only remember the casket in the foyer. One of my Polish-German classmates had died. She succumbed to an inflammation of her brain, I was told. Now she was laid out in a white lace dress with a lovely veil over her dark hair and a lily in her folded hands. To me, she looked so lovely, just like a beautiful angel. We passed slowly by her casket. I wanted to stay longer to look at her. It was not allowed.

The garrison church across from our apartment also was a brick building. Germans call these architectural structures Backsteingotik.[82] I remember having been in the garrison church only once, when a military minister baptized my younger brother. This church, which was used for Catholic and Protestant services for the soldiers, did not have the elaborate artwork and mysterious smell of the Catholic churches in Thorn. It was more ornate on the outside. Scenes of Christ's mission on earth were depicted on three of its outer walls. Iron fences protected the bigger-than-life sculptures from desecration by people or animals; only the ever-present pigeons had to be dealt with occasionally.

---

82 Gothic architecture built out of brick is typical in northern Germany, especially in West and East Prussia.

It was my brother and, after entering school, my friend Ulla who helped me to become better acquainted with the town. Ernst walked with me to the famous town hall.[83] In front of it was the old midtown square. There, maps of the eastern front were displayed. For a few pennies, we could buy small nails with different-colored heads. A man handed us a hammer. We went to a map on a wooden board and Ernst marked the "front" by hammering nails along a line indicated on the map. It showed how far the German army had advanced into Russia.[84]

This was one of the many fundraising events the Nazis held. A special task for the BDM girls was to collect money for various projects. They sold little flowers or other trinkets as fundraisers for vacation homes for mothers, children's homes, the Red Cross, the winter-help, and the wounded soldiers, among other causes and organizations. The BDM girls had designated streets on which they offered these trinkets to pedestrians. People proudly pinned the emblem on their clothing, thus showing their support for the different institutions.

The garrison church stood on a spacious square that became my playground, except when the soldiers of the garrison lined up for parades. In this case, the yard of the former high school bordering our apartment house sufficed for play. The building had been turned into a huge hospital for wounded veterans. Big sandboxes sat in the yard. They were meant for dowsing fires created by phosphor bombs. Fortunately, Thorn did not see many bomb attacks. My friends and I used these big sandboxes to build our own little world.

When asked by the town authorities, my parents agreed to let people stay in our apartment. These were families who wanted to settle in Thorn and were looking for a suitable place to live. My mother was also volunteered to have officers of the army and their families share our apartment. Since I often lived with my Oma, I only remember two men in uniform who stayed with us, except for my father. He had been drafted in late 1943.

In the fall, my Uncle Hans[85] was on a short leave and visited with us. We sat at the dining-room table. I had collected a few colorful leaves. They lay in

---

83　The old town hall dates back to 1274. It is one of the most enormous town halls in central Europe.

84　On June 22, 1941, the German military launched Operation Barbarossa, the invasion of the Soviet Union.

85　Apparently, the military did not consider his epilepsy too severe for him to be drafted into the army. At the end of the WWII, he was in a POW camp in France. He was released soon and went to St. Bernhard.

front of me. I tried to draw a scene with trees and their leaves. He took my pencil and said, "Look at a leaf of a tree. Look how the whole tree resembles the shape of its leaves." To make his point, he started to draw what looked like a scribble to me, but turned out to become a pine tree, then the oak and linden tree followed. I started to guess what he would depict next.

The other officer I remember was Major Alfred Conn. His family lived with us, although I do not recall any of them. We called him Uncle Conn. He seemed to prefer me to my siblings. When he was back at the eastern front, he sent me a package with a sweet cherry preserve. I was lying on the couch in the gentlemen's room with a slight cold when my mother brought it to me. She had a letter in her hand from him.

"Look what Uncle Conn sent you, Ilse-Rose! These are special cherries; we cannot buy them here. I opened the jar for you. Taste them."

They were delicious and cool, the best medicine I ever had. Mother proceeded to read the letter to me. I did not understand everything. Sometimes she stopped, as if to skip a line or two, but one sentence the major wrote I never forgot: "I am sending you a jar of my bloody tears I collected when I cried thinking about being unable to see you."

I looked at my mother and asked, "Did he really cry bloody tears?" I guess I would have tried hard to cry this type of tears, but my mother introduced me to analogies and symbolism at that time. I only tasted those cherries once. After a few days, when I asked for more, they were gone. My mother was very angry. She could not find out who ate them. She suspected our servants savored them. With ration cards, we only could get the necessities, never delicacies. The temptation must have been just too great.

My mother also had to get theater or concert tickets for the officers. The best seats were reserved for the upper ranks of the military personnel and their hosts. Therefore, when children's plays were performed, we were fortunate to sit in the front rows. Twice I saw plays at the theater when I spent Christmas in Thorn. I especially loved *Hänsel and Gretel* by Engelbert Humperdinck.[86] The ladder leading to heaven from which the angels came down to protect the two lost children was very impressive. Hänsel and Gretel were sleeping on the ground in the dark woods near a deep cavern.

---

86 Engelbert Humperdinck (1854–1921) wrote other operas, but this fairy-tale opera is his most famous one. He mostly composed children's and folk-tale operas. He was strongly influenced by Richard Wagner, and he in turn influenced Arnold Schönberg with his *Sprechgesang,* a vocal technique halfway between singing and speaking.

It is a children's opera with songs that are unforgettable. My sister and I sang the melodies and danced to them. Oh yes, when it came to music, Hildegard and I understood each other. We both loved to sing and dance. She danced with very graceful movements, and I enjoyed our rounds—even if once in a while, I stumbled over my own feet with those insole shoes. She developed a high soprano and I an alto. We could sing duets together, to the delight of the grown-ups.

Another thing Hildegard and I had in common was our perception of the hierarchy in our world. My sister asked me, "Who has the highest position in the world?"

I answered, "God."

"And who comes next?"

"That must be the Kaiser," I said. At Oma's, in Klostermansfeld, I had seen a big picture of one of the Prussian emperors hanging on the wall. In Oma's room was a picture of Queen Luise. Oma belonged to the Luisenbund.[87] It was clear to me that the Kaiser had to be next in line. In Thorn hung a photo of Adolf Hitler, so he held the third position in our pyramid of importance. Then came the kings, the dukes, the counts and the barons. We were still very much attuned to aristocracy, as we knew them from our fairy tales.

That year, I also saw *Thorner Katharinchen*, a play depicting the discovery of the recipe for the aromatic cookie. I never forgot the analogy between the scent of carnations and cloves, one of the major spices in the treat. The year before, I had seen *Sleeping Beauty* but was not too impressed, since the hedge of thorns was not realistic enough for me. Nevertheless, I loved the theater, and at home, I imitated all the characters in the musicals and plays. My mother helped us to dress up our dolls and my teddy bear in dwarf costumes to play *Snow White and the Seven Dwarves*. Hildegard always was the beautiful princess. I took all the other roles, even if it was the prince, the bad queen, or the stepmother. I just loved to act. I seemed to be destined to become an actress.

My father was wounded twice during the war. The first time, he was hurt by friendly fire. He had to train young recruits. One of them did not follow his directions; he shot my father through his wrist. My father

---

87   *Bund Königin Luise* was a monarchist nationalistic women's movement during the Weimar Republic. It was founded in 1923. Although the goals of this association were the same as Hitler promoted for Germany's women, it was abolished under the umbrella of the Gleichschaltung in 1934.

reflected, "I was lucky. The gun was not loaded with live ammunition." The second time, a Soviet bullet penetrated his upper left arm. "It is only a flesh wound, no damage to my bones," he used to say. He recuperated in Scandinavia. Sometimes he served in Denmark or Norway, but mostly he fought in Russia. We were relieved that he was not with the 6th Army when it collapsed after fighting for over a half year in Stalingrad.[88]

Soon, the civilians had to cope more and more with the effects of the ongoing war. Danzig, Stettin, and other East German cities were bombed. My mother, as with so many German women, had no help from her husband. She had her hands full when all of us four children were with her. My father was somewhere with the military. When she wrote letters to him, she never knew if they were opened and either forwarded to him or destroyed. Often she waited for weeks before she received an answer. By that time, she'd had to make decisions by herself. She had to deal with the rising difficulties for us all. Not only was it harder to get enough food for us, but also, living in Thorn became more dangerous.

For example, one day Ernst had to swim with his Jungvolk group and his leader in the treacherous Vistula. There were eleven boys with their leader when a whirlpool pulled several of them under. The leader realized the danger and dove in to rescue the boys caught in the downward swirl. Ernst managed to get out of it by himself. He swam to shore, watching the leader diving again and again—one of his young Pimpf[89] was missing. This boy was Ernst's best friend. He drowned that day. The death of his friend was hard on Ernst, although he did not show his grief.

Ernst was excellent in school. He soon was chosen to transfer to a special school called the Adolf Hitler School. My mother was not very excited about the suggestive political curriculum of this school. My father, on the other hand, was proud that his son was selected from among so many. He persuaded my mother to let Ernst go and pointed out two convincing arguments: firstly, they taught different subjects, and secondly, the school was in the heart of Germany. She liked the emphasis on languages, science, and sports, but more important for her was that this school was located in Middle Germany near our grandmothers. She thought, *In his vacations, Ernst can easily visit with my brother and mother in the country, away from*

---

88   The battle of Stalingrad was the turning point of WWII in Europe. It lasted from the middle of July 1942 until February 1943. In the end, the German 6th Army was destroyed. About 2 million casualties among Russian and German armies and civilians have been reported.

89   *Pimpf* is a term for the ten- to fourteen-year-old members of the Jungvolk.

bombing raids in the cities. It was good for Ernst to leave Thorn, his HJ group, the HJ leader, and the boys who constantly reminded him of losing his best friend in the Vistula.

Mother knew that in the heart of Germany, her children would be safer than in the east, so close to the Soviets and exposed to the hate of some Polish people. Most of the Poles never became true naturalized Germans, especially if they had a communistic background. They influenced their children, and nasty encounters occurred. We experienced this once while we walked in front of our house. Suddenly, some older boys passed us and threw sand in our eyes, screaming profanities at us. My mother concluded, *It is time to send my children away under some pretense.* For Hildegard, who was an excellent student, Mother again relied on her daughter's delicate body structure and health to get permission to send her away from Thorn. At the school office, she claimed that it was advisable to let her daughter finish the school year, but spend the vacation with Oma on the farm, where she would toughen up and have better food.

Grandma came to Thorn to help with my younger brother. Their love for each other was mutual. After some weeks, Grandma took Reinhold with her to St. Bernhard. He was too young to be in any Kinderhort, let alone school. In my case, my mother told the principal of our elementary school that I had to visit Oma, because in Klostermansfeld, I apparently learned well, at least better than in Thorn, because there I had a good tutor and NSDAP teacher, Soon I said good-bye to everybody again and went with Oma back to Middle Germany, to the farm, to the old dog Karo, the cows, calves, chickens, ducks, geese, and all the people who worked for Uncle Martin—and last but not least, my friends in Klostermansfeld.

Chapter 5

Friends

Many of the young male farmworkers were drafted into the military, after war was inevitable in 1940. Uncle Martin had to take in Polish prisoners of war, who had the status of civil workers. The Nazi government forced them into becoming civil workers. If they refused, they were sent to prison camps. Some of these workers were not familiar with farming. Uncle Martin had to instruct them how to care for domestic animals and how to plow, sow, plant, and harvest. I liked Anton the most. He was in charge of my favorite horse, Hans. This was an old farm horse used to pull a heavy wagon, but Anton let me ride him when going to work in the morning. Anton treated Hans well. In the evening, he drew water from the big iron pump into the long trough for Hans, who drank alongside of the other horses. We took Hans to the blacksmith, Mr. Fleming, across the street. Anton held the horse while the smith took off the old horseshoes. I watched and asked, "Does that hurt Hans?"

The blacksmith was a little gruff. "Does what hurt?" he grunted.

"I mean, pulling all those nails out of his hoof."

He loosened up and explained to me, "No, of course not. Does it hurt when your Oma cuts your fingernails?"

I had to laugh. "No!"

He continued cutting the hoof into the correct shape and said, "See, now I am cutting his nail. His hoof is really like his thumbnail or toenail." After he had formed the hoof, he shoed Hans with shining new horseshoes.

Every so often, the blacksmith came into the courtyard to take care of the cows' feet as well. That was especially necessary since my uncle's cows hardly ever left the stable and could not walk off the horn on their feet. Sometimes a few cows were put into the fenced-in square in the center of the courtyard. It was heaped full of used straw and other refuse from the stables. A shallow ditch surrounded it. It was no wider than a gutter to catch the liquid manure trickling from it. It ran down to the horse stable, where a big tank had been built into the pavement. It was covered with thick wooden planks. In March, the men loaded the manure heap onto wagons and carted it out in order to fertilize the fields. The tanks, two at the cow stable, one at the upper horse stable, and one at the pigsty, were also emptied for the same purpose. Every March, our courtyard stank.[90] Oma and I did not leave the bedroom window open during that time.

The chickens, ducks, and geese were kept in the courtyard. They scratched among the big quarter-stones that are used to pave the streets and yards in the Mansfeld district. These stones are so tough that even heavy panzers rolling over them did not leave track marks.[91]

Once in a while, Anton made a windmill out of straw for me, or he braided wreaths for Thanksgiving with wheat stalks. At Christmas, he showed me how to make stars from straw for the Christmas tree. It was easy to weave these stars. I still make them and decorate our Christmas tree with them. I had no idea that the Polish workers actually had fought against German soldiers and should be considered enemies. Here, they were not in prison camps. There was no barbed wire to keep them confined. They slept upstairs in some rooms above the horse stable. None of them thought of escaping. They would not have gotten far if they attempted to flee. The German police would have picked them up very soon. Anyway, where could they have gone? Their homeland, Poland, did not exist anymore; it was divided between Russia and Germany.

When the Polish prisoners opted to become civil workers, they forfeited

---

90   At that time, the whole farming country reeked. It was, and in some areas still is, customary to have dung heaps close to the house, even located near the kitchen windows.

91   These stones are made from *Mansfelder Schlacke* (slag). Paving and building stones made of copper slag and sulfuric acid are byproducts of mining copper. In the Mansfeld district, we find a type of shale that lends itself to be formed into tough stones to be used for paving the streets.

their legal protection under the ICRC.[92] It was contrary to the rules set up in the 1929 conventions in Geneva that prisoners of war could be turned into slave workers. Of course, the Nazis would not use the term *slave*. They had a way of covering up their most horrible actions by using "pretty" names for them. *Civil* sounds much better than *slave*, just as *crystal night*[93] seems less threatening than *pogrom*. Therefore, becoming a civil worker could be fatal for a POW. Some farmers in our area treated their workers very badly; they did keep them as slaves. Oma never allowed such acts. She instilled in us that God created all people. We should respect God's creation, and humans are part of it.

My uncle and aunt did not adhere to the regulations for civil workers. One of the rules stated that workers should not receive meat. On our farm, their food was much the same as ours. The soups had chunks of meat in them, and at Christmas, Oma roasted a turkey or goose for them as well. The civil workers had to observe a curfew and were not allowed to have friendships with Germans, especially relationships with German women. In spite of these rules, the Polish workers did treat me kindly, so that I regarded some as my friends. My mother observed, "Martin and Ursel always have one foot in prison themselves." If anybody reported my uncle and aunt, they could be incarcerated, or at least made to pay a hefty fine.

Uncle Martin did not treat his civil workers like detainees. They received the same respect as his German workers had, who helped on the farm before the war. I never thought of Anton or his fellow workers as bad people. Some of them were my friends. I did not even realize that they spoke with an accent, did not use correct grammar, used unfamiliar words, or, if they thought nobody was listening, spoke in a foreign language to each other.

In 1943, when I came back to Klostermansfeld during my school vacation, there were more foreign workers. Two Russian women lived in a room above the wash kitchen. One of them was pregnant. Oma helped.

92　The legal basis of the International Committee of the Red Cross's (ICRC) responsibility was the Geneva Conventions in 1929. The committee members visited POW camps, organized relief programs for civilian populations, and administered the exchange of messages regarding missing persons and prisoners.

93　On the night of November 9 into November 10, 1938, when the Nazis destroyed Jewish establishments and synagogues and brutalized Jewish people, they called the night *Kristallnacht*, meaning "crystal night." This referred to the many shattered display windows and the glass-splinter-filled streets. See also footnotes 46 and 47 in Chapter 3.

She gave the woman clothing and diapers for the baby. She also called for a midwife when the woman's time for delivery was near. The Russian women were quite different from the Polish workers, who had been here for such a long time that I considered them part of the farm. The *Flintenweiber* ("gun wenches," as the British soldiers called the Russian female soldiers) had no word of thanks for anybody. Oma took me upstairs to see the little baby. The room was in shambles with sheets, clothing, and foodstuffs everywhere. I had a hard time finding the baby. It lay in a crib, no doubt also supplied by Oma. Both women shouted something I did not understand. Oma tried to signal to them. She knew French, but not Russian or Ukrainian. These women just refused to see that Oma cared for them by bringing her grandchild to see the newborn. She turned to me and whispered, "You better leave." She did not need to repeat it. I hoped never to see those two again, or even consider forming a friendship with them as I had with others.

I was all too happy to run downstairs and across the courtyard into the cow stable. Here was Mr. Rosenhahn who took care of the cows like they were his own. He knew how to treat each individual animal. He let me feel the rough tongue of the little calf. "Ilse-Rose," he said, "dip your hand into this milk. It is still warm from milking the calf's mother. Now, let the calf smell it." Sure enough, the calf recognized the milk and started sucking on my hand. It felt funny. It tickled. Mr. Rosenhahn had shown me before where the calves liked to be stroked and scratched. I stayed with him until it was time to eat the evening meal.

It was a simple meal. In fact, Uncle Martin had said that Aunt Ursel should cook simpler meals for dinner, just peas or bean soups and a piece of bread with it. Dinner was always at noon; Uncle Martin came home from the field for it. In the evening, we had cold cuts, or cheese, or just a pancake. We were not allowed to drink with our meal at noon, but in the evening, Oma had tea or hot milk for us. The grown-ups sometimes drank beer from the nearby pub.

How do you form a friendship? You need to understand the environment, behavior, and differences of the one you want for a friend, especially if it is an animal. As a result of my misinterpretation of the courtyard dog's behavior, I was unable to build a trusting relationship with him. Karo was chained to the hut in the doorway. He was let loose at night to roam the enclosed courtyard. The dog was supposedly vicious. He barked loudly when a stranger entered the yard. He knew I belonged to the family and did not bark when I approached from the house. But when I entered the courtyard from the outside, he still growled until he recognized me.

Oma had introduced me to Karo by having me feed him. I was afraid he would tear me to pieces. One day, when I was alone—my uncle and aunt were visiting friends, and Oma was taking her midday nap—I gathered all of my courage, asked God to make the dog friendly toward me, and approached him.

First, I threw some extra morsels to him, staying far enough away from the dog, who was bound by the length of his chain. Then, carefully, one step at a time, speaking softly, I moved closer. He looked at me. I slowly extended my hand and touched his throat. *What knotted hair he has!* I thought to myself. "Sit!" I whispered. He laid down, his chain loose alongside of him. "You smell!" I exclaimed. He had lain in his feces; it was all around him. "Can't you go to the bathroom when you are off your chain? What a mess!" I scolded. Carefully, I tried to untangle the snarls in his matted, knotted coat. He allowed me to do it, closed his eyes, and pulled his ears back. I jumped up. I knew when a horse laid its ears back, it was warning you that it was ready to bite and kick. *Will he attack me now?* The dog only gazed at me and then went into his hut. Later in the day, I asked Oma, "Did Karo get so nasty to people because of the chain and the dirt?" Many years passed before I learned that dogs might express trust and pleasure when they lay their ears back.

Since I stayed with Oma so often, I gained two close friends when I was in Klostermansfeld. My best friend was Klärchen, a heavyset, rather quiet girl my age who had older sisters just like Anneliese in Thorn. Klärchen lived in a small house. It sat to the right, facing our front yard. Helga lived across the street opposite Klärchen. Helga was really my sister's girlfriend. She was a year older than I. Her mother lived in Berlin. Her grandmother and grandfather raised her. The latter mined copper in the Mansfeld mines. I do not think he worked in the Zirkel Schacht[94] with the Russian civil workers. We found out later, in 1945, that they were kept like slaves in horrible conditions.

When Helga's grandfather had to work the second shift, we were not allowed to make any noise so he could sleep during the day. Then, we played in the front yard of Oma's house. One of our favorite games was Catch the Ball. We played it in a competition. The new yellow brick building attached

---

94 A *Schacht* is a mine shaft or deep mine. *Zirkel* was the name of this particular deep mine.

to the old farmhouse—the "eyesore," as the grown-ups called it—was ideal for this game. Helga and I liked that it had tall, wide walls on which we could practice our catching skills. Sometimes Klärchen joined us, although she was not the athletic type.

We devised the game with nine levels of difficulty, which one had to master without the ball ever hitting the ground. It started with nine throws against the wall caught with both hands; eight throws and catches with the right hand only; seven throws and catches with the left; six throws under the right leg to the wall and caught; five throws under the left leg and caught with one hand only. The throws and catches became more difficult until the last throw, when you had to turn completely around before catching the ball. When you dropped the ball, you had to start all over again. We could play this game for hours. Aunt Ursel forbade me to play it during her midday rest, from one to three p.m. Our ball bounced against the wall of Aunt Ursel's bedroom. It was impossible for her to rest with the constant thuds against the wall in her ear. Oma said about sleep, "Sleep is holy. Never wake anybody up. Be absolutely quiet." I did not forget Oma's words. They haunted me later, when I crossed the Russian border illegally.[95] I spent an uncomfortable night at an overcrowded station just to avoid waking up anybody I knew nearby.

The hired hands in the household also had these hours of rest. Usually, they went home to take care of their own place and children until they came back for the afternoon. Mrs. Rabehl often brought her daughter, Christa, with her. When she did not have to watch Aunt Ursel's children, she joined us in our games. The men and women working in the fields took a shorter break of about one and a half hours. I remember when I was with them, the woman in charge called, "Lunchtime!" The workers all laid down their tools, got their bags or lunch pails, and looked for a shady place to eat. They sat in the grass and put an empty horse's feedbag down for me to sit on. We ate and then most of them leaned back to take a short nap. During their rest, I went to see the horses, or spoke to one of the workers who did not sleep. I talked about school, but never about what was going on in our house. Uncle Martin, Aunt Ursel, and Oma made that clear to me. They said, "Do not tell what we eat, what we drink, who is coming to visit, what we are discussing. If they ask you questions, say you don't know." That sounded rather stupid

---

95 After July 1945, the border went through the center of Germany, dividing it into the Soviet-controlled eastern sector and the western sectors occupied by British, American, and French forces.

to me, but these were my instructions, and I followed them out of fear of Uncle Martin.

When Hildegard visited, she claimed Helga for herself. Sometimes they let me join in their games. Helga did not care whose friend she was; she just loved to play with anybody from the farm. I, in turn, loved to go to her house, where I often stayed for dinner, eating the meager meal with the miner's family. I could have had much better food at Oma's, but maybe I was trying to avoid Uncle Martin's steel blue eyes looking straight through me. I wondered, *Is he seeing what I did in the wheat storage room?* or *Does he know I brought a basket of food to Oma's friend?* I was afraid of him. I sometimes did not know if what I did was destructive, forbidden, or dangerous. For instance, when I played with my friends in the stored wheat, we trampled it down.[96] Usually it was the boys in the neighborhood who suggested games like these. "Let's play tag on the grain," they would say. "It's harder to run there, but softer when you fall down."

Uncle Martin reached occasionally for the switch to hit me when I had done something precarious or damaging. I did not mean to be disobedient, but it was safer to stay out of his way. Decades later, after my uncle had died, my Aunt Ursel said to me, "I had pity on you when your Uncle Martin looked at you and you started to cry out of fear."

What the older boys and girls suggested sometimes was downright dangerous. We hauled boards up the ladders to reach the rafters under the barn roof. We connected the beams with the loose boards and played tag on them, high up above the hay. Often, the only escape from being tagged was to jump into the hay, scramble through it, climb up the ladder, swing onto the beam, and start all over again. Sometimes, bailed straw was stored with the hay. The huge cubicles were hard to jump into. It is amazing how little we were injured. It was especially hazardous when we played tag on these beams after winter, because then, only a thin layer of hay and straw remained. If we had ever fallen down the thirty feet, we could have been killed or badly hurt. Once, when we played above the low cover, I jumped down into the hay, but fell through the thin layer, landing on the bottom of the floor. I felt a dull pain in my lower back in spite of having bent my knees to lessen the impact. I never told anybody about it, fearing Uncle's stick. A few years later, however, the school doctor found an unexplainable abnormality on my spine.

---

96 My uncle grew seed grain, a very expensive commodity. The damage we caused cost my uncle thousands of Reichsmarks.

Helga's grandma, Mrs. Nebert, set the table in her kitchen. This room was small, oblong, and always dimly lit, since it had only one window high up against the ceiling. We sat very tightly together. Helga's grandfather sat in the corner; next to him was one of his daughters, and then his grandchild, Helga. They placed an extra plate for me at the corner of the table. Here at the end of it, they put a high chair for Helga's little cousin. Mrs. Nebert sat across from us. She had not much room either, since the stove in the corner took most of the space. Behind Mrs. Nebert stood a washbasin; above it hung a small mirror that Mr. Nebert used when he shaved. They left the kitchen door open to allow light to come in the kitchen and into the short, linear corridor, from where you entered straight into their narrow yard. Here, they kept their chickens, which scratched for food between the cobblestones. A high fence, made from thick wooden boards, separated the baker's yard from the miner's yard. The fence extended into a stone wall on one end. Here was their chicken coop. Helga's house was attached to another lower house. Its front door also faced the yard. Everybody in the two homes shared the outhouse. It stood above a dung heap, leaning against the boarded wall opposite the houses.

Mrs. Nebert's pudding soup was my favorite. One day I asked, as I had so often, "May I stay for dinner?"

Helga's grandma answered me. "You get better food at your house. You do not need to eat away the little we have." It never occurred to me that I was consuming the food meant for their family. I did not know that they were poor. They always had been very friendly to me and protective of me.

I remembered the time when I used their outhouse and the rooster pecked my behind. I screamed. Helga's grandma came dashing out of the house, grabbed the barnyard fowl, and threw him into the henhouse, closing the door tightly. "Whenever you have to use the outhouse, let me know," the old woman said. "I'll get rid of the rooster. He's a nasty critter." I trusted her almost as much as Oma.

I fought back my tears and went to Oma. Sniffling, I told her about the rejection I had just received. I was hurt; I did not want to go to Helga's house again. Later, Oma heard that one of the older daughters was "in a bad way." She was pregnant and had gone into labor too early. Oma stayed with her for hours. When I was sent to look for her, Helga was playing in the attic. Her grandma sent me up to stay there with her and told me not to come down until asked to do so. I found a wonderful doll kitchen up there. Helga informed me, "This is where I play with Hildegard. She likes these things a lot."

I agreed. "I like them too. Let's play with the kitchen," I suggested. "I promise to be careful."

Some hours later, Helga's grandmother called us into the living room to look at a tiny, healthy baby. "I am an aunt, you know," Helga said proudly.

That evening, I had my favorite soup at the miner's house again. Oma had talked to Mrs. Nebert and asked what they needed, and then she sent food across the street whenever possible. She often helped people in the village. In the evenings, she sold milk to our clients. She generously measured liters into the milk cans that people handed her. Sometimes she deliberately would ladle whole milk into their cans but ask to be paid the lesser price of the skim milk.

Now and again, when a poor woman died, Oma gave away one of her pretty nightgowns for the dead to be buried in. Oma's nightclothes had lace trimmings and were embroidered, so the deceased was dressed decently for burial. I ran errands for Oma. She was wise to send me, because it saved the person in need from embarrassment or looking like a beggar when an adult hands out food. Nobody rejected Oma's help that was given through a young child.

When Hildegard came to visit Oma, Helga played with her. I sat with Klärchen in the Victorian garden house that was covered with climbing clematises, shading its south side. We drew pictures. Paper had become scarce,[97] even in school. We had to be careful not to use up too many pages in our notebooks. The teachers handed out only a certain number of sheets per pupil. Therefore, Klärchen and I used unfinished cigarette-card albums. We penciled our pictures inside the designated squares where the cards that depicted historical scenes of Germany[98] were missing. War pictures dominated the albums' themes. I especially remember the ones from the Thirty Years War. Klärchen's father had given us the albums. He owned the tobacco shop in Klostermansfeld. He had many of these books for collecting

---

97   For instance, the postwar author Wolfdietrich Schnurre used the blank back of *Münchner Bilderbogen* (Munich picture sheets) to write down a whole novel. It was never published. It is kept in the *Deutsches Literaturarchiv* (literary archive) in Marbach, Germany.

98   The Dresden cigarette-card service supplied the pictures. Especially popular was the *Great War* album depicting WWI. Cited in Hamberger, *America—my fascination*, 9.

cigarette cards. His clients would get the pictures when purchasing tobacco products. When they grew tired of gathering these cigarette cards and gluing them into albums, they returned the unfinished books.

Klärchen was Catholic and would draw religious symbols. She had just entered Communion classes and was looking forward to dressing like a little bride on the day of her First Communion. We drew a dove with an olive branch, the symbol of peace, right among battle scenes. Klärchen drew the cross often, but her Jesus was never good enough for me. I was afraid to attempt a picture of Jesus. He was too celestial, too beautiful for me to do Him justice with my clumsy pencil. I knew Jesus through my nightly prayers. Here, He was so tiny that He could fit into my heart. I also knew Him through a church song: "Fairest Lord Jesus." In the song, He was described as being fairer than meadows, woodlands, flowers, sunshine, and stars. I would opt for stars, the sun, and the moon, arguing with Klärchen that these were symbols for Jesus. We scribbled angels among pictures of fighting warriors, knights, and mercenaries of the Thirty Years War.

The garden house was a retreat, but it also functioned as a throughway and entrance into the garden. It had a bench for us to sit at the oblong table. Here, Klärchen drew many symbols that I did not recognize. "Let's draw a white dove," she suggested.

"Fine, but why white? All of my uncle's doves are blue, gray, and brown," I questioned her.

"You are talking about pigeons," she explained. "I mean the dove, which is the Holy Spirit."

I thought, *What or whoever is this spirit?* and carefully copied Klärchen's dove. "It looks like a pigeon to me," I said.

She did not want to argue, so peacefully, she suggested, "Now it's your turn to say what we draw." I wanted to mention something I could do well. "A flower."

Klärchen wanted to be specific. "What type of flower?"

I looked around the garden. Behind us stood several lilac trees under which my grandfather's hunting dogs had been buried. The names of the dogs were carved on gravestones. Lilacs would be too hard to draw. The lattice wall on the opposite side was covered with dark blue clematises. "Clematis," I declared. When we were finished with our flowers, I had to confess hers had the better resemblance.

It was Klärchen's turn. "Now, let's draw a heart."

"Fine." I knew how to do that, but when I looked over at Klärchen's square, she had drawn an arrow through her heart and drops of blood were oozing from the wound. Now, I wanted to know specifics. "Why is this heart shot through the middle? Mine is just a plain red heart."

Klärchen sat up straight and looked at the ceiling of the garden house, as if she could look right through it into heaven. "It is Jesus's heart, pierced for our sins."

Although I had started to have enough of this religious stuff, I found it fascinating. It was so different from my church. On Sundays, I went to the children's service in the Protestant church, where my grandmother had reserved seats for the whole family. There was no fear that these would be worn out, as it was seldom that any of the adults went to church, except for Oma. Our church had an altar, but there was only a small cross without Christ on it. Two angels were portrayed there. The organ stood opposite the altar on a balustrade above the pews. When I was older, I sat up there, since I sang in the children's choir.

As a rule, most of the German schools separated boys from girls into parallel classes. The exceptions to this regulation were very small villages, like St. Bernhard, where they still had a one-room schoolhouse. Klostermansfeld had enough inhabitants to afford a large school building. There were so many children that we needed several parallel classes for the girls alone, with thirty to thirty-five pupils in each of them. Klärchen and I went to school together. We were in the same class. Oma might have arranged that the school did not place me in the parallel class. She had quite an influence in the village. Even the mayor would listen to her suggestions.

Klärchen was much better than I in orthography, but I outshone her in math and sports. Our classroom teacher was Miss Karsdorf. Now and then, Oma sent me to her with a little container filled with soup, or a basket with sausage, some milk, and even a piece of cake. Times started to get tough, even in the country. All of us had ration cards. Each year, the individual provisions on them diminished. Oma paid Miss Karsdorf for my tutoring sessions with food. Although I disliked her, my mother had told the headmaster in Thorn that I would get help with spelling from an NSDAP teacher. I still did not fancy her or the tutoring; it took away from my playtime with Klärchen or Helga.

Klärchen did not like physical games. I was often too active for her. I also played with other children in the village. Their favorite games were hide-and-go-seek or catch. Uncle Martin allowed them to play in the barn if I was there too. They would set rules: "No hiding between the horses, cows, or other animals." The stables and the grain storage rooms were off limits ever since we had trampled down the wheat. Home base was near the ladder, leading high up into the hayloft. I climbed silently up the ladder, careful not to let the seeker know where I was going. I climbed into the rafters under the roof, balancing myself while running on the wooden beams to the other side of the barn. I waited in the shadow of the rafters until the seeker climbed the ladder on the opposite end of the barn. I would watch him pass, and then I snuck up behind him, right above our "free base." I jumped into the hay just in front of it. "Free!" I screamed with delight when I had outsmarted the older boys. They sometimes did not like me to play with them because I was a girl and too young, but they had to let me be part of the game or else Uncle Martin would not allow them in the barn. I had no fear of heights. When my mother visited with my siblings, Ernst took part in the games, but Hildegard rarely did. She was too refined for farm games. She was actually smart, because when it came time to take our baths, the little scratches on our legs and arms we got while playing in the straw burned badly.

Saturday baths were an adventure. First, two of the male workers went upstairs into the attic to bring down a bathtub shaped like a big cradle. You could rock back and forth in it. "Make sure the water does not splash onto the floor," my mother warned us when we attempted to rock the tub. The men put it in the ironing kitchen. Here, a servant heated water on a coal stove. In summer, this room was hot like a sauna. My mother always opened the window when it was our turn to take a bath.

The tub was not big enough for all of us children. Hildegard and I took our bath together, and then it was Ernst's turn in the same water, which had been used before by my cousins, Hermjörg and Lutz. The whole house did not have a shower. I preferred Oma's sponge baths.

I celebrated some of my birthdays in Klostermansfeld. Two of them I remember especially. Once, Oma had planned a party for my friends and me. We sat around the table in the garden house. We ate the cake, which was decorated with a pretty number 6 carved from wood and painted. It had a candle. After I blew the candle out, Oma allowed us to use one of her daughter's cooking stoves that she had stored in the attic. It was not a pretend one. She poured some kind of fluid into a little canister attached to the stove. You could turn the knobs and a row of little flames heated the baking compartment, or you could cook on the stovetop. Oma gave us an egg to fry and some dough, reserved from the cake, to bake in the oven. We heated milk and drank it out of tiny cups.

From then on, I often begged Oma to let us cook. Sometimes Uncle Martin shot sparrows because we had too many of them. When I fed the chickens, they flew into the courtyard and ate the grain. They became a menace. Uncle Martin gave us the dead sparrows to cook. He showed us how to pull off their feathers with their skin attached in one stroke, so only the meat and bones were left. Oma showed us how to remove the innards, and then we were allowed to cook sparrow soup. I never attempted to roast one. They were just too small.

Another special birthday came in 1946. The war was over, and we had experienced a lot. A world had crumbled for my family and me. In St. Bernhard, children had called me a Nazi pig. Here in Klostermansfeld, my friends wanted to show me that they liked me after all. Helga and Klärchen, along with cousin Hermjörg, my brother Reinhold, Hildegard, and the young apprentice, Eberhard Fleisher, built a birthday wagon for me. It was a handcart that they had converted to be pulled by a goat. They put willow boughs across the wagon, decorated with flowers, with a seat under those boughs reserved for me. They carted me through the village. The goat behaved well. It refrained from eating the flowers that decorated the wagon. I was rather uncomfortable; the seat was too high, the boughs were too low. I had to stoop low, crouch down, and pretend to be happy doing so.

Soon I told them, "Let's go and have cake." Oma and my mother had set the table in the garden house. There, we were crowded, but we did not mind. Oma even had juice for us, which was a rarity by then. The farmers had to deliver their fruit to the Soviets. They could hardly keep any for themselves. To have cake and juice was a feast for my guests and me. Later, my mother played games with us. We played her preferred games, through which we could learn geography, get acquainted with artists and their works, and recall the names of animals, towns, rivers, and famous people. Mother avoided history, since she was not sure how much the teachers were told to distort this subject in our Soviet-controlled schools.

I do not remember any birthday party for me in Thorn, although at the breakfast table, my place had the traditional decorations every birthday-child received. Flowers surrounded my plate, and a burning candle stood in front of it. Nobody else was allowed to blow it out; only the birthday-child could extinguish the flame.

I recall the times when my mother played out scenes of fairy tales with us children. She included my friends Ulla Spatkovskie and Anneliese Blomann. Both were in my class. Anneliese, the railroad conductor's daughter, lived in a house in the back of our apartment building. She was the youngest of several daughters; the rest were already married. We played with dolls handed down to Anneliese. We had to be careful not to undress them or comb their hair. I had a hard time understanding this—after all, I liked to get to the bottom of things, and wanted to play real-life stories. Putting dolls to sleep, undressing them, washing them, combing them were all a part of life. Why were we not allowed to play like that? Once, I undressed one of them. I had to loosen the thread of the clothing that had been stitched onto the doll's body. My sister heard of what I had done and told me, "These dolls are very expensive show dolls. They portray people from other countries. They wear typical clothing called *costumes*. They are collector dolls to be placed on shelves and are not to play with."

I had my own ideas. "How good is a doll if you only look at it, if it is just a dust-catcher sitting on a shelf?"

At home, Hildegard had dolls that I could play with and imitate real life, but she did not like it when I used her toys. I did have Hans. I played with him, but I would have preferred a girl doll with long hair like Hildegard had. When Anneliese came to play at my place, we built a house under the big dining-room table. We hung blankets and tablecloths on either side of it, dividing this "house" into kitchen, bedroom, and whatever living quarters we needed. Sometimes Ernst and Hildegard joined in, but unfortunately, we usually ended up quarreling, and I gladly left with Anneliese.

One morning, Anneliese's older sister took her to school. Ulla picked me up and said, "Let's skip school." That was all right with me. She advised, "Put your school bag in this dark corner; nobody will notice it there. We'll be back home when school is over." The staircase in our apartment building was very dark. The first steps of the staircase were built around a corner. They had the shape of uneven triangles; one of them had the darkest corner, just big enough to hide my satchel. I asked Ulla, "What shall we do now?"

Ulla had it all planned. She said, "Let's get tadpoles at the Gristmill pond."

I shook my head. "Can't do. I don't have money for the tram, and it's too far to walk."

Ulla had thought about this. "We can use the money we were supposed to bring today as contribution for the Reich's Mothers' Homes."[99]

---

99 Called *Mütterheime*, a retreat for mothers to have a vacation.

Without any qualms, I agreed, "Okay. Let's run. We might catch the next tram to the pond." Off we went, happy to spend the sunny spring day in the country.

We found an old can and collected many little tadpoles. Some of them already had legs; others had only a body and tail. We even found a cluster of frog eggs. We loved to catch the slippery creatures and gather them in the rusty old can.

Suddenly a bicycle appeared on the horizon. A heavyset man strained to get up the hill. "There you are!" he yelled. "Ulla, Ilse-Rose." We were startled. Ulla's father ordered us to dump the tadpoles back into the pond. He lifted Ulla onto the bar in front of him and ordered me to climb onto the carrier behind him. Home we went. It was too late for school. Years later, my mother told me that she quite often had to ask Mr. Spatkovskie to find Ulla and me. Our teacher sometimes called my mother, wondering why those two girls were absent from school.

Ulla and I liked to roam through the hospital instead of going to school. I loved to play with Ulla. She was an only child. Her parents lived in the cellar quarters of the hospital. The pipes of the heating track ran under the ceiling of their kitchen, bedroom, and living room. We often played in the long hallway. Mr. Spatkovskie gave us play dough the wounded soldiers used for their rehabilitation therapy. We formed the neatest doll furniture, pots, pans, and dishes for our dolls. Hour after hour we spent in delightful play. The play dough had an army-green grayish color, but we managed to get some brick-red clay to "bake" layered cakes with little balls as cherries on top. There was no limit to our playful fantasies.

Ulla was smaller than I. She had a dark complexion, black hair, and black eyes, and she was quick as mercury when allowed to run loose. She always had new ideas for games. Anneliese was taller than both of us. She had very curly blond hair and blue eyes. Her behavior reflected the strict upbringing she experienced from her parents and her older sisters. One time, we lingered around in the hospital's big yard. At its end stood a high flagpole. Every morning, wounded soldiers raised the flag, and in the evening, they took it down again.

Ulla looked at the flag and said to me, "Ilse-Rose, I dare you to touch the flag when I let it down." That was not a great adventure for me. Ulla unfastened the rope and brought the flag down. It was made of strong material, stark red with a white circle and the black swastika in the middle of it. I touched it. Ulla looked at Anneliese and asked her, "Would you help me pull her up with the flag?" I thought it might be fun to be lifted up high above the ground.

"Just let me get a good grip on it," I said.

The two girls had to strain to pull up the flag with me hanging on it, higher and higher, and … suddenly, two soldiers came running out of the hospital, yelling, "What are you doing to our flag? Desecration! Shame!" My girlfriends let go of the rope and bolted as fast as they could out of the yard. Luckily, I was not too far off the ground. My weight and the flag came whirling down; one of the soldiers caught me before I could hit the cement slab. He was wounded. He had only one arm to break my fall. I tore myself loose and dashed after my friends with the soldiers running after me, but the moment I passed the gate, they stopped. Apparently the wounded were not allowed to leave the hospital grounds without permission. In the meantime, the ward appeared. He could have caused trouble for the two soldiers if they followed me outside the gate. For a few weeks, Ulla and I were afraid to be seen in the hospital. We stayed in the cellar and played there.

Ulla's father took care of the hospital. Whenever he had to carry out special errands for the doctors, or for military officers, he invited his daughter and me to come along. I recall that, during one Advent season, my mother went to the specialty store to buy authentic Thorner Katharinchen, a big, aromatic cookie. When she left the store with her precious purchase, she saw a huge wagon drawn by two large horses. On its flatbed stood overstuffed leather easy chairs, a sofa, and a giant oak desk. She could not believe it—took a second look—was this her daughter on top of the wagon? Snuggled in the easy chairs sat two little girls, one of them her daughter, looking like a queen in a parade through town.

The Nazi government employed artists, singers, comedians, and magicians—anybody who could lift the morale of the wounded soldiers. The shows took place in the auditorium of the former school. My mother, after conferring with Mr. Spatkovskie, allowed me to watch these. The first time we went, Ulla and I sat in the front row. We were fascinated by the magic, but the other performances were rather boring for Ulla and me. The jokes were over our heads. We were familiar with the songs, but were not allowed to sing along. We watched more of these events, but we never sat in the front row again. Ulla suggested, "Let's sit in the back, so we can sneak out when it gets boring." I readily agreed.

I visited with the wounded by myself when Ulla was not at home. One of them taught me how to play chess. I caught on readily, to the delight of the other patients in the room. They showed me certain moves, and once in a while, they let me win. I was too young to become an expert player, but it was fun for the soldiers. It was a change from their boring routines and their therapy. They laughed when the nurse asked me to leave the room because one of them had to get an injection. I experienced how some of the soldiers had traumas, which they refused to notice out of fear of being branded as cowards.

One time, a nurse came with a big bowl of steaming water. She went to one quiet soldier, whom I had watched carve a beautiful statue out of clay. "Okay, buddy, here comes your inhaler session," she said.

He lifted up his arms, crying, "Nurse, please, not again; no, no, not again!"

I anxiously turned toward him. *Why was he screaming at the nurse?* I wondered. I had seen his composure when they tore caked-on bandages off his chest, and he never flinched when getting an injection. He only needed to put his face over a bowl to let the nurse cover his head with a big army blanket. He was told to breathe in the aromatic steam. *What was so bad about that?* I thought. Now I realize that he probably suffered from shell shock or another trauma. Under the Nazi regime, psychological problems were not tolerated. They showed weakness, which an Aryan should not exemplify. We were taught to be tough like the Spartans.[100]

My friends were girls and boys from good hardworking families. Most of them had blue-collar jobs. I befriended former Polish soldiers in Klostermansfeld and German soldiers in Thorn. There was no difference between them for me. They were people who shared their skills with me. I liked them all, and yet, I lost contact with every one of them. Blame forty-three years of a divided Germany for this. After 1951, it became almost impossible for me to cross the border into the Russian zone. Keeping contact by letter soon became hopeless. We had to be increasingly careful about what and to whom we wrote, so as not to endanger the addressee or our own families. The Cold War reared its ugly head after 1951. It developed into a monster until 1989, when it died with the tearing down of the Berlin Wall.[101]

---

100 Spartans inhabited a Greek city-state. Their social system and constitution focused mainly on rigorous military training and education, with the goal of excellence in both programs. They were considered undefeatable by the other Greek states.

101 The Berlin Wall was erected in 1961 by the Soviet-controlled government of the Russian sector in Germany. It separated the three western sectors occupied by French, British, and American troops.

Chapter 6

"Paula, I have to make it short," Uncle Reinhold[102] said over the phone. My mother was surprised that he was able to get through to her. The phone lines had been down in many areas of Germany. "You have to get at least the children out of Thorn. The violin teacher, Mr. Sternmann leaves tomorrow for Cottbus. He can take the girls with him. I wait for them in Cottbus. I'll bring them to Klostermansfeld." *Click.* He hung up before my mother could answer or have any other suggestions. She was grateful that Uncle Reinhold had made arrangements with the violinist to bring us to Oma. Only my ten-year-old sister Hildegard and I still were with my mother in Thorn. Ernst was already in Thuringia, where he attended the Adolf Hitler School, and Grandma had taken little Reinhold with her when she went back to St. Bernhard.

My mother could not leave right away. After we had moved to Thorn, my parents offered their assistance to the town when new people wanted to move to this West Prussian city. We had enough room to accommodate families who looked for a place to live here. Currently, Mr. and Mrs. Reusel rented a room from us. Mother had to help them make arrangements for

---

102 My younger brother was named after Reinhold Seume, whom my parents met when they had to do their family tree that was required by the Nazi regime. His wife, Aunt Anna, was my third godmother along with Aunt Ursel and Aunt Klara.

another place to stay in Thorn. She also had to take care of father's office. In the back of her mind lurked the fear that she never would come back to Thorn after forsaking our apartment. What about our furniture, our dishes, the 800-carat silverware, Father's hunting guns, Ernst's coin collection, her daughters' favorite toys, the bedding, the curtains, and so much more?

She contacted the violinist and said, "Reinhold Seume told me you are willing to take my two girls with you to Cottbus. Can you take a few suitcases as well?"

He replied, "No problem, Mrs. Höfer. I only have one briefcase."

The next day, we stood with the violin teacher on the platform of the station. The train arrived. It was already overflowing with passengers. Mr. Sternmann managed to squeeze into one of the compartments somehow. The locomotive pulled out of the terminal … and we? We still stood with Mother in front of the empty tracks. There had been no chance to enter the train, let alone follow the violinist.

"That's it," Mother said. "Next time, we go together."

We went back to our apartment. Mother took care of all the pressing errands, and then she packed only one suitcase.

Two days later, we were at the station again. While Mother stood in line to exchange our tickets and obtain one for herself, I observed a banner with the slogan, "Räder müssen rollen für den Sieg" ("Wheels have to turn for victory"), and posters that warned against spying enemies. One showed two masons working on a wall, talking to each other. A man's shadow covered both men. Behind the back of the one worker was the warning, "Pst—Feind hört mit." ("Hush—enemy is eavesdropping.") Another poster showed two secretaries. One of them tells her associate, "Hans writes his division will go to …" with the same slogan in the right lower corner of the poster. The Nazis warned us about sly enemies who supposedly used terrible, despicable, cruel means to obtain secret information because they wanted to defeat Germany.

The Hitler government officials were instructed to discourage us from fleeing the encroaching Soviet Union army. Actually, the Nazi regime wanted totality—either Germans won the war or all Germans should perish. Most of the German people did not believe Goebbels' speeches anymore. They doubted the reports on the radio or in newspapers when the announcer or editor described an orderly retreat of the German military. We lost hope in those wonder weapons we had heard about. Scientists had allegedly developed and worked on them near the Baltic Sea. Would these be ready for combat soon enough to turn the war around for Germany?

My mother informed us, "We have to be on platform four for our train." We went down the steps to the underpass, underneath platform one and two, and up the stairs to platform three and four. Many people stood there, waiting for the train to arrive. My mother was anxious about how she could get close enough to the incoming train that she could reach the door before others would. After the disastrous experience of trying to enter the compartments two days before, my mother instructed us, "You have to stay close to me. Ilse-Rose, you hold on to the suitcase. Hildegard, you hold my hand. When I reach for the door handle, grab my skirt and don't let go."

Then we heard a pleasant female voice over the loudspeaker: "Attention, attention. The train to Cottbus will not leave from platform four. It will leave from platform eleven." The whole mass of people who were waiting became one huge wave of movement. We were pressed against the banister, not able to reach the steps. The people dashed like mad to get to platform eleven.

Mother sighed, "So be it." She waited until the crowd thinned out and then went with us to the Red Cross station. "Would you have some milk for my girls, please?" Mother pleaded.

The nurse inquired, "Do you have your ration cards with you?"

"Yes, here they are. This one for my daughter, Hildegard, and this one for Ilse-Rose." The woman snipped several squares off the card and gave us a small cup of milk. Mother saw the amount of milk stamps the nurse had cut off and gave her a puzzled look.

The woman shrugged her shoulders. "That is all the milk I have."

Hildegard and I shared the little cup, while my mother inquired about the train. "Do you have any idea if the train to Cottbus will be punctual?" The nurse told her that she was not the information booth. At that moment, we heard a sonorous voice behind us.

"Lady, don't even try to make this train. People have been at this station for two days already. Everybody tries to get to the center of Germany. The tracks around Berlin are bombed. No train goes there."

"But I bought tickets to Klostermansfeld via Cottbus and Halle an der Saale," my mother informed him.

The owner of the deep voice motioned her to the corner of the room. I clung to the suitcase, Hildegard to Mother's skirt. He whispered, "Take a different route. Go via Posen. That train leaves in an hour from now on platform four. In Posen, you take another train to Cottbus. That one is scheduled to arrive at the platform right across from where the Posen train stops. In Cottbus, ask for the train to Halle, with railroad cars designated for Göttingen."

My mother was not sure if she should trust this man. She saw that he did wear the typical conductor clothing. He had a little coal dust in his eyebrows; maybe he was the stoker or boiler man of a locomotive. "Thank you!" she said.

He continued to advise her. "And lady, go to the front of the platform. There are the cars reserved for the military; they will let you enter with those lovely young girls of yours." It was true children were loved, and often the soldiers made room for them. Mother paid for the milk, thinking, *I hardly have enough ration stamps for milk left for my girls … but at Oma's, there are cows, and where there are cows, there is milk.*

We had to go back to the ticket booth to exchange our boarding passes. The station hall was crowded. Long lines had formed in front of the little windows behind which the railroad clerks sold the tickets. Mother looked at the clock; the line moved ever so slowly. She had to get back to platform four in time to reach the front cars of the train to Posen. After forty-five minutes, she knew we would not make it. She left the line and went with us to platform four—but first, we had to pass the control booth again, where they punched a hole in your ticket. The railroad clerk, without looking at my mother, mentioned, matter-of-factly, "Your tickets are already punched."

"Yes, I know, but we were unable to get the train to Cottbus from platform eleven," she tried to explain, anxious about the further delay.

The people behind us pushed against us. We clung to Mother, pressed between the gate rail and suitcases. The clerk looked up and waved us through, yelling, "Good luck!"

Platform four looked deserted. We were able to walk to the front part of it. At that moment, the train rolled in. Would it ever stop? We saw the uniformed men in the front cars. The train slowed down and came to a screeching halt. The military cars stood beyond the platform, where it ended in grass. We stumbled off the concrete walk and through the vegetation. During this time, people streamed from all the other platforms toward our location. Apparently, everybody was hoping to enter this train, but the wagons were already filled with soldiers who were being ordered to the western front[103] and with many civilians who, just like us, were trying to leave Prussia.

My mother is not tall, and not having a platform to stand on, she hardly

---

103 Soldiers were pulled from the eastern front to fight on the western front because German intelligence hoped that Stalin would delay the Soviet offensive once the German assault in the west (Ardennes) had begun and wait for the outcome before launching his offense.

could reach the handle of the compartment door. Some people had caught up to us. They pushed Mother aside. Somebody pulled me into the car. Another person grabbed Hildegard, but where was Mother? The soldiers were standing in the passageway; the compartments were filled. They passed us over their heads to the middle of the wagon, where they put us into one compartment. We cried, "Mother, our mother!"

We heard her yelling outside, "Hildegard, Ilse-Rose, where are you? Where are my children?" Her voice was filled with panic.

"Hello, Mom, here they are," a soldier called, leaning out of the window. "Give me your suitcase." He lifted it into the compartment above everybody's head into the nets above the seats, and then he reached out again. The train had started to move already. "Fast, Mom, your hands," he shouted. My mother threw up her arms and the soldier lifted her right through the window into the car. Not until she was inside did the train roll faster. The conductor had watched the whole maneuver and made sure we were not separated. Was he the man with the deep voice we had met at the Red Cross station?

My mother was very grateful for the soldiers. She stood between two of them, not able to even turn around. I sat on the lap of one and Hildegard was crammed between two more. Seeing the anxious look on my mother's face, they handed us to the place where she stood, squeezed in between everyone else in the compartment. During the trip to Posen, we stayed in our positions, unable to move, let alone go anywhere else from there. Mother explained to the soldiers that we had to take another train in Posen. Two of them told her they also had to depart there and take the train to Cottbus. They would help her.

In Posen, they and we climbed out of the window. The ones left behind handed us the suitcase. We followed the two uniformed men, who had special privileges to get through the controls. When asked about us, they just said, "They are with us." We found the platform with the train and followed the soldiers into a compartment. We were on our way to Cottbus.

Again the train was overcrowded, but those soldiers even secured a place for my mother to sit. I leaned against her. "Where is Hildegard?" my mother called out.

My sister answered, "I am behind these big boxes. Somebody put them in front of the WC while I was using it." They had placed huge artists' cases in front of the dislodged toilet door, not noticing that my sister was in there. One of the soldiers leaned against the containers, reached over, and grabbed Hildegard's hands. He pulled her out and handed her again over the heads of all the people down the wagon to where we were. We took turns sitting on Mother's lap, and Hildegard even managed to sleep for a short time. In Cottbus, the track to Halle was still in working order. We were able to get on a train to Halle that had some wagons attached, designated for Göttingen.

You must know that the German railroad system always functioned well and still does. To eliminate frequent changing of trains for travelers or freight, long-distance trains take along wagons designated for different destinations. At major trade centers, these cars are disconnected and pulled over several tracks to be attached to another train. This process is repeated until the traveler or freight reaches the final stop. Halle was one of these trade centers, where our wagon would be hitched to a train going to Göttingen. On its way, this train would stop in Klostermansfeld.

By the time we departed Cottbus, the train was so overcrowded that people were standing on the wagon steps and hanging from the compartment doors on the outside. Fortunately, we had reached our car going to Göttingen early. Our luck lasted until we reached Halle. Here, everybody had to leave the train because a full alarm howled over the city. An air raid was in progress. All of us were directed to the station's waiting room or a bunker outside of the terminal. When we arrived at the bunker, it was closed. An elderly man with a band on his upper arm told us to go back to the station's waiting room since the bunker was full. We returned and sat on our suitcase, waiting for the bombing raid to subside. By now, people asked a consistent question all over Germany: "Will we get out of here alive?"

At the end of February 1945, Wolfgang Hamberger lived through the worst of all the bombing raids on Mainz. He tells about his experience and the advice some veteran soldiers gave him. They said, "Don't go in a shelter. There, you are trapped. There is no way out. You suffocate or burn to death." He stayed with the soldiers and survived.[104] We might have been lucky not to sit in a bunker. My mother had seated us close to the door. Somebody wanted to order us farther into the room. Mother only said, "No, we have to stay here until the 'all clear' sounds."[105] He did not argue. Bombs were

---

104 Hamberger, *America—my fascination*, 78.

105 The warning system for civilians was organized: First, we heard the forewarning. Usually we had some minutes to get our emergency knapsack or suitcase and gas mask together and go to a shelter. Next, we heard the full warning. Usually now the bombs were starting to fly. After the planes left, we heard the "all clear," and then we could leave the shelters.

falling, and he went back to the others. "Put your hands over your ears!" Mother said and covered her own.

Finally, the "all clear" sounded. The station had been bombed; tracks were torn apart. The sound system was broken. Where could we go? We had to find out if we could continue to Klostermansfeld. Which platform was still accessible? After a long time, a train entered the station. My mother asked for the destination of that train. "It goes to Göttingen," they said. We could not use the underpass to reach our train. We had to climb over twisted tracks. My mother pushed us into an already overcrowded wagon.

Klostermansfeld is not far from Halle. When we finally arrived at our destination, not one of our relatives was there to give us a lift to the farm. We had been expected two days earlier. "We have to walk to Oma's," Mother said. She headed to the luggage storage room and lifted the suitcase onto a low counter. "May we keep this suitcase here until tomorrow?" she asked. The clerk wanted to know if he should ship it ahead of us to another destination. "No, no," Mother assured him. "We stay here. I cannot carry the suitcase any further. Somebody will pick it up tomorrow." After the clerk handed her a claim stub for the suitcase, we walked the one kilometer to Uncle Martin's farm.

We arrived overly tired. Had we traveled one day or two? I do not remember. Normally, it took twenty-four hours to go from Thorn to Oma's. When we visited Oma before or when they came to see us, we often stayed overnight with Aunt Ursel's mother in Cottbus or at Aunt Bohne's apartment in Berlin, and then continued on our trip.

It was in the early evening when we entered the old familiar farmhouse. Oma had prepared my bed in her room and a bed for Hildegard in the adjacent transit room that led to the master bedroom. Mother could sleep in the guest room near the formal dining room, but first, we had to drink and eat something. There had been no nourishment for us since we drank the scanty cup of milk in Thorn.

Klostermansfeld had changed. Uncle Günther, Aunt Ursel's brother, had been killed during the battles in the Sahara desert. Aunt Ursel's third child had been born. Her sister, Aunt Bitta, had come to live with them. Bitta's husband, after being drafted and bringing his horse into the military expecting to be in the cavalry, had been placed in the bicycle infantry, fighting against the Soviets. In World War II, most of the transports for the army near the battle scenes were still done by horses.

The noon dinner table was periodically extended. From now on, many relatives, friends, and others who had lost their homes continued to come to Uncle Martin, seeking room and board.

Hildegard and I went to school in Klostermansfeld. We had to leave early to be back home by noon. We got up at six a.m. to be at school by seven. Between late fall of 1944 and 1945, the Allies had set up a regular schedule to bomb Berlin at noon. They often flew over our area. There was always the possibility of a damaged plane. In this case, the pilot unloaded the bombs, released the extra fuel tanks, and finally parachuted out of the plane. German civilians converted the fuel tanks into canoes. A disabled plane had landed on the high mining refuse mound near our farm. After the plane burned out, people tried to salvage whatever possible. We could use everything. Civilian merchandise had been scaled down to the absolute minimum, since Germany's factory production focused on the military. The women coveted the silk from the parachutes, if they could get a hold of them before the government confiscated them for the German military. I did see Helga's aunt wearing a silk blouse, but that was after the war.

The Stammtisch gathered as usual. The headmaster asked, "Where is the mayor? If he does not come, we won't have a round of three for Skat."

The farmer, who always came because of his love for Skat, mentioned how their number had dwindled during the still raging war. "First, Schumann left. He was Jewish."

The headmaster interrupted him. "No, not he, but his wife."

The farmer waved at him. "Yes, yes. They probably are not in southern France[106] anymore." He scratched his head and asked, "What do they call that little part of France? The new French state?"

"Vichy France,[107] since the armistice was signed on June 22, 1940," the headmaster was eager to inform him. "Hitler really shined that day," he continued. "He had the old railroad wagon pulled out of the museum and rolled onto the exact spot where the armistice had been signed in 1918. It ended World War I with a disgraceful defeat for us, as you very well know … but our Führer did not forget the humiliation of the Versailles

---

106 When Hitler overran the French with a Blitzkrieg, the French government in southern France had to deliver all of the Jewish inhabitants, especially the foreigners.

107 Vichy France was left from the division of France. Pétain headed this rump state in southern France after he accepted the status of a defeated nation. Italy occupied a small part in the southeast. The north and west were under German occupation.

treaties in 1919. He redeemed us. He showed them who is superior." The headmaster reveled when speaking of the victories of Germany a few years before.

The farmer interrupted him. "Now we are in World War II. We are at the end of it and will be humiliated again, I am sure. Look! Just look at how they have destroyed our cities, how even we in the country need to get into shelters because of all those air raids. American planes over us during the day, British at night!"

The headmaster resented the farmer's remarks. "Are you giving up?" he argued. "Did you not listen to Goebbels? He told us of a wonder weapon they are developing. They have tested the V I. It is a type of rocket. And now, they are testing the V II. They develop all kinds of secret weapons.[108] Soon, we can eliminate whole cities with just one rocket, or bomb, or rocket-bomb, or bomb-rocket."

The farmer, tired of the headmaster's enumeration, sighed, "I know. I heard about that tiny, courageous lady, Hanna Reitsch,[109] who already tested the V I. But I am more concerned about the Schumanns. Where are they?"

The headmaster had his own ideas about their former shopkeeper and stipulated, "As for Schumanns, they most likely went to the land of unlimited possibilities, to America, before the French could hand them over to the Gestapo." He stopped for a moment, thinking back to the friendly Stammtisch member, and then he continued. "If only Schumann did not marry this half-Jew." He paused, waiting for some opposition to his remark, but everybody in the room was quiet. He stood up and said, "And anyway, Jews belong to a much-too-old race. Old races have to go. They lose their strength, bodily and mentally. Hitler wants to cleanse Germany of all other races like Jews and gypsies. We want healthy Aryans and no physically and mentally defunct people. They have to be sterilized." He looked around the room and reiterated, "We want to keep our Aryan blood and soil free from unhealthy influences."

The farmer had heard enough. His blood started boiling. He faced the headmaster. "You are still a dreamer!" he chided. "You still believe this Aryan

---

108 The rockets were developed in Penemünde at the Baltic Sea.

109 Hanna Reitsch (1912–1979) was a famous German test pilot under the Nazi regime. She was the first female helicopter pilot. She was used for Nazi party propaganda. She flew many of Germany's latest designs. She became Hitler's favorite pilot and was awarded the Iron Cross First Class. In 1943, she piloted a rocket plane (Messerschmitt Me 163). In 1944, she flew trials of a jet aircraft.

stuff, don't you? You do not care if somebody like Lichtenberg[110] would have been killed if he lived under our Nazi regime. He was a hunchback as you very well know! I ask you, what is wrong with the Jews, the Sinti, and the Roma?[111] They belong to our culture, contributed to literature, music, sciences ..." At that moment, he saw the innkeeper reaching for the phone. "Hello, Innkeeper. Get us some beer, the local brew, please," the farmer called. The innkeeper gave him a contentious look. He put the receiver down and started to draft the beer as it is traditionally done in Germany. It takes seven minutes to draft a good glass of beer. It is never ice-cold, so it will not lose its flavor. In winter, some customers even like a hot metal stick plunged into the cool beer to warm it before consumption. The farmer's suspicions arose when the innkeeper looked for the phone. He had been successful in diverting him by calling for beer. Now, he had to deal with the headmaster. "Teach, you know how my tongue sometimes runs ahead of my brain."

"You can say that again!"

"Please don't tell the Gestapo about me. I mean, what I just said about Aryans, gypsies, and Jews. I just have a hard time with things like this. I know breeding. Give me a prize bull and a good milk cow and you get a good stock."

The headmaster nodded, "Yes. They already do this with excellent young German men and women who fit the standards for the Aryan race ..." He looked out of the window and saw the mayor crossing the street. He whispered, "Something is wrong with our mayor; he looks terrible." Both men watched as their Stammtischbruder[112] entered the inn and stopped at the bar, addressing the innkeeper. "Innkeeper, in two days, I want a funeral meal served in your special events room." He choked, but caught himself and continued. "My son fell in the battle at Normandy."[113] The headmaster

---

110 Georg Christoph Lichtenberg lived in the eighteenth century. He was a scientist and mathematician, but also wrote aphorisms and satires. He was one of the first professors at the Göttingen University. He was a hunchback.

111 The Roma roam through France. In August 2010, and again in 2011, the French government evicted several Roma camps and expelled hundreds of gypsies belonging to the Roma back to Romania.

112 *Bruder* means "brother." In some German regions, people refer to the members of a Stammtisch as their brothers.

113 Also known as D-Day (June.6, 1944). At the Battle of Normandy, the Allied forces broke the back of the Nazi army and hastened the end of Nazi Germany. News of fallen or missing soldiers was often slow to reach their relatives.

and the farmer got up, joining him. They wanted to console him. What do you say to a father who loses his son in a war that the military senselessly continues?

The farmer uttered, "Now your son too … our minister was killed in Stalingrad. We have not heard from the pharmacist since he had to leave for Yugoslavia."

The innkeeper poured schnapps for all of them and said, "I heard that the partisans are especially bad in Yugoslavia.[114] Maybe they ambushed him. Let's drown our grief with this."

The farmer chugged down his drink. *Who of us will be next?* he wondered.

Germans, especially in rural areas, had to make room for the many relocated people, refugees, and fugitives. Many city people had lost their apartments and houses. The destruction of civilian housing culminated in 1945, when the British decided to demoralize the German people by constantly bombarding cities, towns, and villages. Bombs had fallen on industrial cities before, in an attempt to halt the war efforts, but now culture centers like Dresden were destroyed.

My uncle had been ordered to take in evacuees. A young Berlin mother and her four children lived in the attached yellow brick building. They occupied the room high up above the master bedroom. Mrs. Kleefeld and her young children had been commanded to leave Berlin and stay in East Prussia. After living there for a short time, she had to flee from the Russian onslaught. The German government agencies shipped people wherever they estimated was less dangerous and where there was still some room for them. No wonder—the trains leading to the center of Germany were overflowing with evacuees and fugitives.

In spite of the bleak times, German traditions continued. Grown-ups did not want us children to go without some Christmas celebration. So a few days before Christmas Eve, Oma asked the owner of the grocery store to act as Santa. We were lined up against the wall of the hallway. Santa came to tell us all about our mistakes and our bad behavior, and he warned us to be good … or else! He had some sweets for us after we recited a poem and

---

114 On April 6, 1941, Adolf Hitler ordered German forces, backed by Axis allies, to invade Yugoslavia and Greece. Yugoslavia was defeated, but no efficient occupational forces could be employed because of Operation Barbarossa against Russia. Therefore, the partisans were able to commit their notorious cruelties without any restrictions.

sang some songs. I had learned the longest poem, which I recited with gusto. All were impressed, but it did not earn me anything extra.

This time, the tree was in the formal dining room upstairs. It stood in the middle of the long table. Around it were placed presents for everybody. Hildegard and I did not need much space for our presents; we only had one each. Grandma had managed to send a pair of knitted kneesocks for me and a sweater for Hildegard. My three younger cousins received the most. My mother just said, "The greatest present for me is that my daughters are alive and we have a good place to stay with Oma." Nevertheless, she said to Uncle Martin, "I have to go back to Thorn. I must try to get more things out of there. The girls need clothing. I hope Ernst and Reinhold are safe." The thought of her sons brought tears to her eyes. She swallowed hard and said softly, "They will need things too. We only could take one suitcase with us."

Oma tried to discourage her. "We can help you and supply what you need." Mother knew they would do that, but still, there were matters in Thorn that had to be taken care of. She needed to go back in January 1945.

On the radio, there was talk about the orderly withdrawal of the German army. "That is a lie!" Oma said bluntly. We'd already heard of soldiers who had deserted, fleeing the Russian onslaught. Between our stables and the walled-in garden of the neighbor stood two military medical cars. The medics fled on foot; their cars were out of gasoline. The doctor had permission to retrieve the medical supplies. After that, all of us rummaged through the vehicles.

January came and mother went back to Thorn. In Stettin, she had to leave the train and stay in a bunker. Bombs were falling in carpet fashion.[115] Running back to the station, she had to avoid the burning phosphor flowing through the streets. She never talked much about it. I do not know how she survived that bombing attack.

On February 27, 1945, Hamberger experienced the worst of all bombing raids Mainz had seen so far. He writes:

> What none of us could have known was that … an air fleet of more than four hundred *Lancaster* and *Halifax* bombers, flanked by one hundred and twenty *Mosquito*

---

115 Also known as carpet-bombing. A group of planes would fly in a "V" formation and release a bomb from each aircraft simultaneously. This was another attempt to demoralize civilians.

> daylight reconnaissance planes, was approaching the Continent, with Mainz in their sights. ... The order that was issued under the code name *Ramrod 1474* was to obliterate Mainz.[116]

We in Klostermansfeld experienced how a stray plane damaged by flack would dump its phosphor bombs. One of them fell on the farmer's stable up the street from us. "He is the only Communist farmer in our village," I heard people whisper about him. *Communist* was a word I would hear more often from then on. It was usually connected with horror.

When the bombs fell, my uncle stood on the roof above his grain storage room. He held onto an iron bar cemented into the wall. He told us that he had to hold on with all his might, or else the air pressure created by that bomb would have pushed him off the roof. He never came into the cellar when the alarm sounded. He would walk to his vantage point where he could watch all of his animals in their stables, ready to calm them if they became nervous.

During a British night air raid on Halle, he called me out of our bomb shelter. "Ilse-Rose, come upstairs! I want to show you the best fireworks you'll ever see." We stood in the front yard. The sky was lit up with "Christmas trees" slowly gliding downward. They were actually flares that the British planes dropped to mark targets for the following fighter-bombers. The "Christmas trees," as civilians called them, hovered, not moving against the firmament.

"What is that?" I asked my uncle.

He explained, "They are flares. Detonators create these flares, which are hanging on a parachute. You'll see them slowly float down to our fields."[117]

Nowadays, when we in America celebrate special days with fireworks, I always think back to the display I saw that night. None of our most spectacular fireworks can match those "Christmas trees." Can you imagine how it would be if one of those big, flowerlike fire-rocket displays did not vanish shortly after bursting, but hung in the sky for minutes? Now *that* would be a memorable firework!

---

116 Hamberger, *America—my fascination*, 76.

117 Hamberger also described this phenomenon in his book *America—my fascination*, 56.

Chapter 7
Toward the End of World War II

The headmaster, farmer, and mayor stood at the bar in their Stammtisch-pub. They spoke to the innkeeper about the "last stand" for Germany. "All of us are young enough to belong to the Volkssturm[118] Hitler activated last fall," the innkeeper remarked. Looking at his bulging beer belly, he added, "I am not in the best shape anymore. The practice sessions with our NSDAP leader are exhausting. I do not even know how to handle a bazooka."

"Me neither," the farmer said, falling into the innkeeper's account about the exercise drills. "You should have seen me when they explained that thing to me. I acted like an idiot. I know guns. I like to hunt hare and deer—not people."

The headmaster, as usual when the farmer spoke, was disturbed. "I fought in WWI. I know how to defend our Führer, our Germany. Farmer, you will learn how to handle the bazooka. Take an example from our boys! Last week, I watched the Hitler Jugend dig out trenches at the entrances to

---

118 The "Volkssturm" is a people's national militia. Hitler activated it in October 1944. All males between sixteen and sixty years old were drafted into it. Mostly Hitler Youth, invalids, the elderly, or men who previously were considered unfit for the military belonged to the units. Hitler relied on their number, strength, and fanaticism; to achieve the latter, the units were placed under direct command and training of the local Nazi party, but in actual combat, they were under the leadership of veteran soldiers.

our village. They do not give up. They will build barricades in the streets so the enemy cannot drive through—and we will too."

The farmer gave him a sheepish grin. "Yes, you will fight as long as you can get your milk, eggs, and other food from me." He put his hand on the mayor's shoulder and asked, "Mayor, you won't adhere to Goebbels' command to fight for every house in the village, will you?"

"What choice do I have?" was the answer. "They killed my son ... that British and American scum! I am burning with revenge." He turned aside and laboriously blew his nose, so they would not see his tears.

"Well-spoken," the headmaster shouted. "I like to fight alongside of you. You do not give up!" He added with a grim look at the farmer, "We need more people with his attitude. Heil Hitler!"[119] he saluted and left the inn. The mayor followed him, walking like a discouraged, dejected old man.

The farmer had just shown his hesitation about defending the village. He suspected the innkeeper to be an informer for the Gestapo. Now he was afraid the innkeeper might report him to the secret police. He knew he had to divert him again. He went over to the bar and said casually, "If I like to play cards tonight, I guess I have to ask the new Stammtisch members from Leipzig, Berlin, and Hamburg—have to ask if I may join them.[120] I saw some of them at our Volkssturm sessions. When do they meet?"

"You can do that. They will be here in a half hour at the corner table over there," the innkeeper informed him. The farmer ordered another beer, went to the reserved table, and waited for the new Stammtisch members, who were mostly his age. He kept his eyes on the innkeeper, wondering if he would reach for the phone to report him.

All the members of the new Stammtisch were marked by the two wars and political unrests Germany had seen since 1914. The one from Leipzig had an amputated leg. The Hamburger's left hand had been crushed during a bombing raid. The Berliner coughed a lot since his lungs were scarred by the mustard gas he had been exposed to during WWI. In 1919, he had lost an eye in the uprising of the Communists in Berlin.

When the three new members arrived, they welcomed the farmer. "Glad to see one of you villagers is accepting us," the amputee remarked.

The farmer told him, "We like all of you. You must understand that

---

119 *Heil Hitler* means "Hale Hitler." It was the customary greeting for people under the Nazi regime, often enforced by the local police or Gestapo.

120 He was referring to the evacuees from these cities. Although they were mainly women and children, some invalids and older men were among the evacuated.

we need to be on our guard. One never knows who is to be trusted in these confusing times."

"Do you mean 'Hush—enemy is eavesdropping?'" the one-eyed man chuckled. "Listen!" he continued, "although they have not called me for shooting practice, I am in the Volkssturm with all of you. I helped dig the trench where our Leipziger can lie with his stump. He shoots well."

The farmer pulled out his deck of cards. "Let's play cards. I heard you are very good at Skat too." For the next hour, they forgot about Germany's blight. They simply enjoyed a satisfying card game and each other's company.

In January 1945, my sister and I stayed with Oma. My mother had been with us for Christmas, but now she had gone to get more of our belongings from Thorn. She hoped she could make arrangements to even have our furniture shipped to Klostermansfeld. It was a hopeless dream.

On the radio, we heard about the "orderly retreat" in which the German troops were engaged. Everybody wondered how close the Soviets were to West Prussia. Was Mother safe? We did not dare to ask. Oma knew how to ease our worries. She allowed us to play in the upper attic and snoop around in the stored treasures from her past.

"How many interesting pieces of china Oma has!" my sister marveled. "Look here at this vase!" She held up a light green vase that was formed in the shape of a slender hand holding a cornucopia. There was even a pearl ring on the hand. It was a perfect example of the Art Nouveau movement (also called *Jugendstil* or "Secession") around the turn of the century. A doll service for twelve that was painted with little roses intrigued us. We found pretty decorated glass and porcelain lampshades that belonged on oil lamps. They were brought downstairs to be used again, since the electricity was cut off often.

In the middle of January, we still had not heard from our mother. Refugees passing through Klostermansfeld told us that the Soviet troops had taken Danzig, a harbor city not far from Thorn. We were used to not knowing where our father was. He fought at the eastern front, as so many of our friends' fathers and brothers did; but what about mother? Was she still alive?

Many women shared the same anxiety about their loved ones. What would the future bring? That was the big question for all Germans, even us children. We wondered why young brides and wives looked at coffee grounds or tea leaves, or held their wedding ring fastened to a string over a cup to find out if their fiancée or spouse was still alive. Our mother had told us, "Don't believe in these things. It is stupid to think that coffee or tea can predict the future, and if a ring will circle to the right or left over a cup and then bang against its rim. That depends on the shakiness of the holder's hand."

Oma frowned upon superstition as well. "Black cats, the number 13, and all of that stuff is nonsense," she said. "Our address is Thondorfer Street 13, but nobody can call us unlucky."

Now the German soldiers came closer and closer. Some deserters had passed by our farm already. Usually they were hungry and in bad shape, nursing a wound or two. They brought bad news with them. Oma quietly gave away clothing and food. She did this secretly, of course, or she would have been imprisoned for helping deserters and the soldiers would have been shot. She had to be especially careful since new families lived in the old farmhouse. They might have been tempted to disclose information to the police, hoping to receive a favor in return.

Mrs. Kleefeld, with her four children, still occupied the two rooms upstairs in the add-on yellow brick building. Now my uncle was ordered to take in a mother with her seven children. They had fled from the Soviets who had entered their homeland of Silesia. My aunt asked her servants to clean out one of my grandfather's laboratory rooms. It was big enough for a little cookstove, a table, some chairs, and several bunk beds, although the smallest children had to share a mattress. That became almost normal. Soon, Hildegard and I also slept in a bed together when we shared Mother's room.

Oma had given up her bedroom so it could be converted into a delivery room for Aunt Bitta. She would give birth to her first child any day now. She preferred home to a hospital. Anyway, by now, it was impossible to get a bed, let alone a room there. The hospitals had been bombed, despite of being marked with huge Red Cross symbols[121] on their roofs. There was also a severe lack of medical doctors. They had been called away to take care of the many wounded soldiers and the worn-out, displaced, or fleeing civilians.

Most of the fugitives were in bad shape. They fled on foot, a few with horse and wagon. Sometimes a mother would only have a baby carriage for her child and their belongings. They would collapse on their trek into

---

121 The Nazi regime started to mark factories for military production with a Red Cross, hoping they would not be destroyed. This method worked for a short time until British intelligence got wind of it, with the result that now, most buildings marked with a Red Cross were bombed.

central Germany. They did not have enough food. They carried diseases.[122] The winter of 1945 was especially hard. Many had frostbite. The elderly and the babies had the least chance of survival. Thousands died on the way. The haunting question was, "What to do with the dead?" None of the fugitives could adhere to the normal burial rituals. There were hardly any caskets, and if you could get one, it was too cumbersome to pull it along with your meager belongings on your hand wagon. Digging a grave was impossible because the ground was frozen too deeply. There was no time to wait for it to thaw. They had to hurry along to get away from the battle zone. Sometimes, they just had to leave the dead person in a ditch alongside of the street. One alternative was to put the frozen body in an empty sack and haul it along, hoping for an opportunity to bury it.

One day, I saw the street in front of Uncle Martin's house congested with long lines of refugees coming from the east to get ahead of the advancing Soviets. They brought stories with them of atrocities committed by the victorious Soviet soldiers. "They are especially dangerous when they are drunk. Most of the time, they are drunk," the refugees told us. If Uncle Reinhold had not warned my mother in the fall of 1944, we would have been among these unfortunate refugees. Thanks to his foresight and my mother's swift reaction, we were spared their misery.

At the end of January, my exhausted mother returned. She had left Thorn on the last locomotive, abandoning the town before the Soviets entered. Because of her former connections in Thorn, she was able to bring the big painted hope chest that we inherited. It was loaded into the coal bin of the locomotive. Through bombing raids, emergency repairs of destroyed railroad tracks, and many detours, she managed to get the trunk to Klostermansfeld. It contained featherbeds, Father's hunting guns, some clothing for our family—especially a civilian suit for Father—Hildegard's favorite doll, my teddy, some silverware, and some dishes.

Hildegard and I shared Mother's bedroom. It was located behind the formal dining room at the other end of the house. Aunt Ursel had moved us as far away as possible from Oma's room, so we girls would not witness Aunt Bitta giving birth. The former guest room was too small for another bed frame or mattress. Therefore, Hildegard would lie with her head close

---

122 The American Medical Department was prepared to deal with diseases of displaced civilians in Germany and other European countries. The most common ones were tuberculosis, typhoid fever, scarlet fever, dysentery, diphtheria, and typhus, spread by lice and fleas.

to my feet, and I would lie the opposite way, with my head against her feet. This way, we both fit best in the narrow bed.

Aunt Ursel often walked through our room, since it led to a temporary pantry where she stored the preserved fruit and vegetables. Glass lids placed on red rubber rings and clamped down with metal brackets sealed the jars, which were filled with the produce from our gardens and fields. By now, shortage of food had become normal for Germans, even in the country. It was not wise to store our winter provisions in the readily accessible pantry near the big farm kitchen where many people worked. They brought their children with them in the afternoon hours. They could easily enter the pantry and help themselves. Therefore, the walk-in closet in our bedroom was converted into a pantry, and the formal dining room was locked.

Aunt Ursel showed us where she kept the key. "Do not tell anybody," she warned us, "and always lock the doors behind you." The bathroom at the master bedroom was also used to store food. The sausages, hams, and bacon hung above the huge copper bathtub. The salted pork lay in its brine in wooden tubs nearby. There, the smoked and air-dried meats could not be stolen. My aunt stocked more food than usual. She anticipated that her servants, many relatives, and friends would come and seek refuge in the always hospitable farmhouse in the coming year.

Uncle Martin did not know if he could harvest any crops in 1945. His fields could become battlegrounds or be bombed. "So many mouths to feed," he said. "Such uncertainty where our food will come from. Better put what we have in a safe place, Ursel." She agreed with him and showed him the bundle of keys she had for the bedrooms and makeshift pantries.

After my mother arrived, her first question was about her sons. Had anybody heard from them? Was there a message from the town where Ernst, our oldest brother, went to the Adolf Hitler School? Did he get drafted like so many others his age? Had he been killed already or imprisoned? Reinhold, our younger brother, had been with Grandma, living in a tiny village in Thuringia. Was he alive? Bombs had fallen on a city near them. Were they affected? Where was Father? Was he in a prison camp? Was he missing in action? Was he killed—or might he have deserted too? Every night, Mother hugged us and prayed with us. I ended my evening prayer with, "And, dear God, please let Germany win the war."

With a sigh, Mother stroked my forehead and added, "Dear Lord, let Dad come home safely. Protect my sons, please. Bring us together again, please."

Until April 1945, we still started our school day by honoring the flag of the Third Reich with the traditional Hitler salute. Sometimes Miss Karsdorf would ask us to hold up our right arm for a long time. "Our brave soldiers at the front are suffering a lot. You can stand holding up your arm for them for that short time!" She scrutinized every one of us little girls to see if our arm was extended high enough while singing one of the many songs meant to make us proud of our Fatherland, our heritage, and our Führer. Our right arm got so tired, but we were not allowed to support it with our left hand. She proudly told us of the Spartans and how much we, her pupils, could become tough like them. Her slogan was, "Work hard, and fight for the Third Reich." She actually made us feel responsible for the fate of Germany.

New pupils entered our class. One was from the Balkan states. Miss Karsdorf made her stand in front of us and pointed to her brown arms. "This is a hardworking girl. She has arms like steel. Look, she is tanned from long hours harvesting in the sun, wind, and rain." We were supposed to admire her. She stood there and looked rather embarrassed.

At recess, I turned to Klärchen. "Maybe all the stuff Miss Karsdorf says about her brown, muscular arms is not the truth."

Klärchen informed me that her father had met the Balkan family. Their father had told him how they came to Klostermansfeld. Klärchen said, "She might not have harvested, but rather has been toughened and tanned from the long trek she and her family had to endure before they reached central Germany."

I drew my conclusion and agreed. "Just the same thing that the Silesian family had to go through before they came to us. You know, their little girl is very sick. Oma tried to reach a doctor for her."

The Silesian family still lived in the downstairs room of the add-on building. Their blight had not ended when they received shelter and food. Their little four-year-old girl succumbed to tuberculosis. Her mother told Oma that it was too late for a doctor. She had already died. Oma helped her wrap the little body in a white lace dress that was made from Oma's pretty nightgown. I was allowed to look at her. With her black hair draped in locks over her chest and a wreath of flowers on her head, she looked like a little angel. I found her very pretty, just as beautiful as my classmate in Thorn had looked when we buried her in the old Polish tradition, but the little dead four-year-old did not lie in a church. She lay on a blanket on the floor of Grandpa's former laboratory, the only room not yet converted into shelter for evacuees or fugitives.

Before her burial, I begged Oma, "May I see her again? She is so beautiful."

Oma nodded, took the key from the wall, and walked with me to the laboratory. "Wait behind me until I get that door unlocked," she said to me. She opened the door and looked into the twilit room. She stepped back and abruptly closed the door. I looked at her questioningly. "Ilse-Rose, my child," Oma sighed. "I don't want you to look at her again." There was tenderness mixed with firmness in her voice. *Do I see tears in Oma's eyes?* I thought to myself. *I will not plead with her anymore.*

That afternoon, I overheard a conversation between Uncle Martin and Oma. "You have to contact the priest today," she said.

"Dear me, woman! I have more to do than run after a priest," he told her.

"The little girl has to be buried today," Oma insisted.

"Why? She has only been dead for a day and a half. Her mother wanted to wait until she could get some relatives here for the funeral." My uncle grew impatient.

Oma disclosed, "Martin, the rats have eaten away at her." That settled it. Uncle Martin went to make funeral arrangements for the Silesian family. Now I knew why Oma did not want me to see the little dead girl again. It must have been a horrible sight, after the rats had gnawed on her face and body.

In April, my brother arrived. For over a week, he had walked with his best friend, Hermann, through the Thuringia Mountains to Klostermansfeld. Hermann was not allowed to go to his family, because they lived in a battle zone where the Germans were still fighting the British.

Another plane had crashed on top of the high spoils from the copper mines and was pilfered by the villagers. The pilot's parachute had been caught on the steeple of the Catholic church. It took the men of the village longer than necessary to get him down. He was wounded and half dead, they said. I heard, too, that they delayed his rescue because they had a lengthy debate. Some of the men wanted to shoot him. They argued, "After all, he dropped bombs on our houses."

Two huge craters in Uncle Martin's fields bore witness to the terrible, destructive power these explosives had. They created such strong air pressure that the tiled roofs of the houses on several streets flew off the buildings, and all the windows were shattered. Chunks of red roof tiles and glass splinters lay everywhere. Now our school was cancelled. The air pressure of the bombs' impacts had blown out the windows of the building. Our old farmhouse was about half a mile away. Nevertheless, we did not see any damage to it. These old cloister walls had held up during many wars that raged over Germany in the last six hundred years. They held up again, against modern, technologically advanced military forces. My grandparents, anticipating air attacks in WWI, had installed thick oaken shutters to protect the windowpanes.

I was not allowed to roam around anymore. I had to stay close to home and tell about my every move. Still, during the midday rest, Oma continued to give me some errands to run. She seemed oblivious to the danger I might be in at that time. I trusted her and took the food to its destination. Often, these little errands would coincide with other jobs I had to do for Uncle Martin or Aunt Ursel. I had to bring foodstuffs to the shopkeepers, from whom they got hidden-away merchandise—Friedensware.[123] I had to do it when their stores were closed to the public during the midday rest. By 1944–45, the food ration was calculated to a minimum for individual survival, and civilian consumer goods were of inferior quality. Everything was reduced to the mere basics—Kriegsware.[124] Bartering became the way of payment, as is typical when the black market flourishes. For food, one even could get good quality merchandise that had been hidden away like a good-smelling bar of soap. Yes, even soap was considered a luxury. Certain soap was made from animal bones. It was rather brittle and had a peculiar smell to it. We used it for the laundry. A few years after the war, I heard some people claim that the bones did not come from animals, but rather from the people who were killed in the concentration camps.

The British had decided to undermine the morale of the German civilians by bombing every major city during the night, while their allies, the Americans, had to fly the more dangerous missions during the day. American and British pilots had been ordered to strafe civilians on the assumption that this was also an effective way of demoralizing the Germans.

Wolfgang Hamberger lived near Darmstadt, a city in an industrial area close to the Rhine River. As a fourteen-year-old boy, he experienced how the trains were strafed, and also encountered strafing aimed at him:

> Shortly after the train left Nauheim station ... we heard
> the whine of fighter bomber engines and the rattle of the
> guns they had on board. I jumped off with the soldiers,

---

123 *Friedensware* was good, solid material left from Germany's peacetime.
124 *Kriegsware* consisted of shoddy material, made as cheaply as possible.

rolled down the railroad embankment and lay there … but luckily for us … part of the railroad track ran through woods. … No one was hit.

"Beginners," said a soldier next to me, adding with a swagger, "If we had their planes, they'd never touch a hair of our heads. We'd come out of the war as the winners."[125]

Before Hamberger had the experience with strafing planes on his train trip, he tells how, in his area, *"lightning* fighter bomber[s]" shot at civilians. He explains that he "understood why the stretch of railroad to Darmstadt … had to be bombed, why trains were being strafed," but he questions the "justification in terms of warfare" by asking, " …why should individual civilians be treated like sitting ducks?"[126]

The possibility of being strafed was remote for us until the beginning of April 1945. By then, our school was closed. We stayed around our own house or the house of friends who lived nearby. Nevertheless, we discussed strafing with four of our most trusted relatives and friends: Klaus, Ernst, Hermann, and Horst.

My cousin Klaus came to visit Uncle Martin and later went to Aunt Magda and Uncle Richard,since they had more room left in their farm house. Klaus' mother, Aunt Hilde, thought that her son was safer in Middle Germany either at Oma's or her sisters Magda's place, called Kaltenborn. The only bomb that was ever dropped on Heidelberg[127] fell in Aunt Hilde's garden. She feared that more bombs would fall on their town. From a few miles away, they witnessed the numerous bombardments Mannheim and Ludwigshafen had to endure. They watched the squadrons of planes flying over them, and then saw the sky above these two neighboring cities turning fire red.

Horst Bollman, who lived close to the farm, was Uncle Martin's HJ farm helper.[128] He and Klaus, along with my brother Ernst and his friend Hermann, told us how to avoid the machine-gun fire from American planes. But they had conflicting opinions about what action to take. "Stay close to

---

125 Hamberger *America— my fascination.* 76

126 Hamberger *America—-my fascination* 68-69 and 88

127 The western Allies agreed to keep certain places intact, since they wanted to station their headquarters there. Heidelberg was one of them.

128 The Hitler Jugend boys, too young to fight in the war, had to help at home. In rural areas, they mostly did farmwork.

the house walls! Duck under windowsills! Run into house entrances! Run right at the plane; they fly so fast, they'll shoot right over you! Stay under trees! Lie down flat on the ground, because they think you are already dead! Whatever you do, don't stay close together!"

In April 1945, the farmer, innkeeper, headmaster, mayor, and the evacuees from Hamburg, Leipzig, and Berlin met at the village square before they had to leave for the trenches near the village. They were called with their Volkssturm unit to defend Germany. The headmaster reiterated Josef Goebbels' speech: "Every house in Germany is a castle. Each one of us has to defend it until the last drop of our blood is spent. Goebbels asked us if we wanted cannons rather than butter. All of us yelled, 'Cannons!' And he asked us, too, if we wanted the total war, and we shouted, '*Yes!*' I would rather perish than give the enemy the satisfaction of destroying our Aryan blood and soil."

The farmer wondered about the logic of the headmaster's last remark. *Doesn't he give the enemy satisfaction if he, belonging to the Aryan race, perishes?*

In the background, everybody could hear the gunfire of a nearby battle. The innkeeper said, "We are in the middle of it. In the north, the British are fighting, in the west, it's the Americans, and in the east, the Russians. We will have to battle the Americans. The rumble and explosions sound like American weapons. How will they treat us when they defeat us?"

"Nobody will defeat us!" the headmaster exploded. "If we talk like this, we will defeat ourselves. We will deserve to be defeated. Don't forget, we are of the best Aryan stock." The full alarm sounded. "Now they try to demoralize us," he thundered. "Like you could do that?"[129]

"I have to look after my animals," the farmer declared. "One of my horses always shies when it hears the sirens." He grabbed his cap and left. Suddenly, they heard a whistle and shortly after, a loud bang. A bomb had fallen onto the farmer's stable. The barn started to burn. The fire alarm whined at the same time as the "all clear" sounded. Instead of marching to their assigned trench, the men went to help the firefighters as they rescued the animals and extinguished the flames. Only the headmaster and the

---

129 The remark of the headmaster was correct. The bombing raids, strafing, and bombing squadrons flying over us did not demoralize us. They had the opposite effect. Instead of stealing from or murdering each other, Germans held together and helped each other, making room wherever they could and sharing the little they had.

innkeeper went to the trenches, mumbling to each other, "All of them are deserters. They ought to be shot."

In April, when the fighting closed in on us, we did not know who would enter our village first. Would it be the Russians or the Americans? We prayed it would be the Americans. If it were the Russians, all women had to be hidden. We had heard horrible stories about how they treated civilians. My mother feared even for us girls. Fugitives told us that the Soviets took all jewelry from the women before they raped them. If a woman could not get her wedding ring off her finger fast enough, they would cut her finger off. They would rip earrings out of earlobes, and tear golden chains from around necks. They said, "Russian soldiers flaunt six, eight watches on one arm." All of us children had nightmares. We prayed that our father would come home safely. Where was he? He had fought on the eastern front against those terrible Russians.

Two days before the enemy entered Klostermansfeld, we watched clouds of airplanes block out the sun. That was another method of trying to undermine the morale of the German people. Our mayor had to tell us to defend the village, but many women pulled white bedsheets out of the drawers, ready to hang them out of the windows as a sign that we would *not* fight. Oma asked, "How can we defend against these clouds of airplanes?"

When my sister spotted the first soldiers entering our village, she ran into the kitchen. "Aunt Ursel, the Americans are coming!" she yelled. My aunt did not believe it; she went to look around the corner, and sure enough, it was American uniforms she saw. What a relief! She told Hildegard to stay inside. At that time, my uncle disappeared. Was he with the Volkssturm? Was he hiding somewhere where the Polish and Russian civil workers would not find him? What would happen to him—and us—when the Americans liberated these prisoners of war turned civil workers?

We heard a knock at the heavy oak door. My mother answered it. She was the only one who knew some English. She had brushed up on some phrases that might be helpful in communicating with the enemy. I listened for any sound from the hallway. I heard the door open, some words—not unfriendly—and then … quiet. What was going on out there? Oma, Aunt Ursel, Aunt Bitta, Hildegard, the young children, and I huddled together in the everyday dining room. We heard footsteps through the hallway, into the courtyard, and soon back again. Then we listened to the way the door was closed. My mother came to us. "It is okay," she said. "The young American soldier spoke German. He spoke with a Bavarian accent. He said to stay inside until the 'all clear' alarm sounds," she continued. "They still have to check many streets in Klostermansfeld. There is a curfew for today, and probably for weeks to come. We may feed the animals and milk the cows."

Oma said, "I am glad we have Horst, Ernst, and Hermann here to help. You know, the Polish and Russian civil workers will be set free by the Americans. They do not need to work for us anymore."

At that moment, the three teenagers entered the dining room. My mother turned to them and said, "Mr. Rosenhahn will help you with feeding and milking the cows. Then the horses have to be fed and led to the trough to drink; the cows need their turn after them. Pump fresh water for them." The boys were eager to help. Aunt Ursel and my mother admonished them to be friendly to the Polish workers and let them roam freely throughout the premises. "We have to be prepared for the worst," my aunt said, holding her youngest son in her arms.

The walled-in courtyard—cover during so many wars—again supplied shelter for animals and humans. We could observe the curfew and still take care of the livestock, since we did not need to cross any streets to feed them.

In the next chaotic days, this courtyard was our refuge from other Polish and Russian civil workers who had been freed. Horst Bollmann saw the Russian civil workers from the Zirkel mine plundering houses, beating people, and killing them. Our three Ukrainian women, the last of the civil workers we had to take in, ran outside to greet the Americans. They were ordered to stay out of the way. I never saw them again.

How would our Polish civil workers behave after the Americans liberated them? We saw them gather heavy clubs. *Good that Uncle Martin is not here*, we thought. My mother commanded us to stay in the house—better yet, to go into the cellar. Three of the Polish workers suddenly ran through our hallway and positioned themselves in front of the heavy oak door. The other civil workers barricaded the big gate of the courtyard. Two of them stood at the small entrance for people. When the former Russian civil workers came to loot, our Polish civil workers defended us. They spoke with the freed Russians, yelled at them, and confronted them with their clubs. It did not come to a fight. None of these Russians entered our house this time.

The next day, suddenly, my uncle was back. The civil workers demanded to go into the pantry and plunder it. Oma, grateful that they had defended us, let them enter. Actually, she had no choice, but our Polish workers were civilized, probably because we had treated them with civility. They took bread, some meats, milk, and cheese, all things they had gotten before anyway. Only now, they could gorge themselves on it. I was not there to observe this. I was at Klärchen's house. We were sitting in their kitchen when two of Uncle Martin's civil workers entered without even knocking on the door or ringing the doorbell. They looked different to me.

There were so many questions left unanswered for me at that time. Why did the Polish civil worker, Robert, and his buddy come to Klärchen's father and demand cigarettes? Why didn't they work for Uncle Martin anymore? Why did I hear about farmers being killed by civil workers? What right did they have to behave in such a manner? Who were those Russian miners? Where did they come from? Why did I have to stay close to home all the time? Why was there a curfew? How come Miss Karsdorf did not wear her NSDAP button anymore? She suddenly spoke in a friendly manner about the good Americans. Had they not been our dreaded enemies before? Didn't she tell us that the Americans were bad people? These enemy soldiers looked just like ours; only their uniforms were different. I did not understand the change in the behavior of so many people. Fear had stricken me. At night, I mistook the shrieking meows of several cats for the crying of a baby who might be tortured by the enemy. My mind, fueled by stories I heard, was filled with cruel tales about the occupation forces.

In the following days, we had to give up all of our guns, including the wonderful double-bore hunting guns my mother had rescued in the hope chest.[130] Their stocks had beautiful silver engravings. They were thrown in huge piles and burned. We had to hide the Nazi flag. Aunt Bitta said, "Best to cut it up and make a skirt from it for one of the girls."

Somebody said, "But the war is not over yet. What will happen if we do not have the flag anymore, when Hitler comes with his wonder weapon and defeats the enemy?"

Oma shook her head. *There are still dreamers among us,* she thought.

After the Americans had established some order, especially by demanding that the liberated civil workers leave and go back to their homeland, I experienced some wonderful things for the first time. The Americans gave some chocolate to my mother for us children. I was surprised she took it from the enemy. She explained to us that she was their official

---

130 My mother must have thought that father could use them when the war was over. After WWI, certain civilians were allowed to keep their guns. Maybe at the time of her flight, Mother even thought that Germans could still win the war.

translator, and the chocolate was like a payment for services rendered. That was the first time I ate chocolate. They offered her chewing gum, too. My mother did not want us to have it. She explained, "It is not ladylike to have gum in a slightly open mouth, and it is bad for your teeth." She only allowed us to chew the ones laced with the wonder drug Penicillin. It was amazing how fast our sore throats were healed by moving this gum around in our mouths. The Americans also gave us oranges. These were another treat I did not remember ever having eaten before.

Something else was a first for me—African American soldiers. One day, when the panzers rolled through our street again, I saw many of them sitting on the tanks or walking alongside. I was wary of these dark-skinned soldiers. I only saw them once, when they marched on the main street in front of Uncle's house. They did not stay with the military dispatch in our village. Many years later, I learned that in WWII, the African American and white soldiers were separated from each other. That was the reason they did not stay with the white ones who occupied the pub near our farm.

We watched the American soldiers behave in such a relaxed manner. They would put their feet on the desk while speaking with a German. They would sit on the broad windowsills, smoke coveted cigarettes, and listen to music I had never heard before. Its rhythm was enthralling to us. The Germans picked the cigarette butts up in the streets where they had been flicked away. They opened the butts, gathered the little tobacco left in them, and carefully put it into a cigarette paper to form their own cigarette. When they could not find any cigarette paper, the edges of newspapers would do for a few puffs.

Chapter 8

Trek to St. Bernhard

In the last days of the German soldiers' defense of Berlin, Hitler's orders verged on insanity. He commanded that all sewers in and around Berlin be flooded, thinking that this would stop the Russians. He did not consider the many refugees and wounded who died because of the sewage problems in the makeshift infirmaries and hospitals. He stayed in his bunker, where he met daily with generals and ordered armies to defend Berlin that did not exist anymore or had already retreated to the west to surrender to the American forces. He demanded that the middle part of Germany, still undefeated, be scorched and all factories and bridges be wrecked. In short, he ordered that Germany's entire infrastructure be destroyed.

His minister of armament, Albert Speer, did not heed this command, thinking ahead about how Germany could survive and rebuild after the war. Hitler named Kriegsmarine Admiral Karl Dönitz[131] as his successor. This was probably the only sensible act Hitler decreed before he died. Dönitz, like Speer, did not want more killings and destruction by burning or flooding the country. After Hitler committed suicide on April 30, German officers, as representatives of Dönitz, met with Eisenhower near Reims to end the war on May 7. A day later, the surrender was signed in Berlin with the Russians. Thus, on May 8, 1945, the war was officially over.

The Allies decided not to make the same mistakes of 1918 when the

---

131 Karl Dönitz was the head commander of the German navy. He was very well-respected, not only by the German people, but also by American and British navy personnel.

Versailles treaty was devised. This time, Germany did not have to pay reparations. Instead, the country was to be divided into four sectors, to be occupied by American, British, French, and Russian authorities. Germany's capital, Berlin, eventually surrounded by the Soviet-controlled sector, was also split into four districts. Originally, the four Allies envisioned governing Germany from their central seat in Berlin.[132]

Even before the war ended, the Big Three—Great Britain, the United States, and Russia—met in Yalta and, shortly after, in Potsdam. (France was not present, since it had been defeated by the German armies and was counted among the "liberated" countries.) They agreed on several procedures:

- Russia was finally to join the United Nations.[133]
- Germany was to be divided into four zones, occupied by Britain in the northwest, the USA in the south, the USSR in the east, and France in the southwest.
- Nazi war criminals were to be put on trial.[134]
- Poland should get a Polish Provisional Government of National Unity. Poland should soon have free and unrestricted elections.
- The Allies should help the liberated peoples of Europe to set up democratic and self-governing countries. They promised to help those new countries in maintaining law and order, carrying out emergency relief measures, setting up governments, and holding elections. This was called the Declaration of Liberated Europe.

---

132 It proved to be an illusion, because already in 1946, the western Allies realized they did not have much in common with their eastern ally, the Soviet Union. Churchill coined the term "Iron Curtain" at Westminster College in Fulton, Missouri, on March 5, 1946.

133 The term "United Nations" was first used by President F. D. Roosevelt in 1942. As an organization, it came into existence in 1945, after fifty states established its charter.

134 The war trial (it was the first of its kind) took place in Nuremberg between 1945 and 1947. To start with, five field marshals, twenty-six military leaders, fifty-six high-ranking SS and police officers, and fourteen officials from the SS organization were tried. Eleven men were sentenced to death by hanging, twenty-four were indicted, and seven received prison sentences from ten years to life. The trials continued in other locations until 1947. Many were arrested and tried, especially in the American sector. Since then, the IMT (International Military Tribunal) exists.

◆ A commission would be set up for reparations.

In the United States of America, in France, and in Great Britain, people celebrated V-E (Victory in Europe) Day on May 9, 1945. In the rest of the European countries, the millions of soldiers, freed civil workers, refugees, and other displaced people felt relief, but did not revel in the victory over the Hitler regime. They wanted to go home and rebuild their ruined places. Only the uprooted persons who originally came from eastern Germany hesitated to move back. They had heard about the Soviets' cruel revenge on the civilians.[135] They knew that they would not find their factories, businesses, or farms intact. The Russians dismantled anything of value in their sector of Germany and shipped it to the Soviet Union.

In the beginning, when enemy forces were entering Germany, the Stammtisch members had been under American control, but on July 1, 1945, the borders between the individual sectors were adjusted and firmly established.[136] The farmer went to the pub before the curfew came into effect at ten p.m. He wanted to talk to the innkeeper and set up a new time and day to meet again for their card games. He was surprised to see the innkeeper's wife crying hysterically. Her daughter tried to console her, but the young woman could hardly handle her own emotions.

The farmer spotted Leipziger and turned to him. "What is going on?" he asked, pointing to the two women. "Why all this screaming?"

Leipziger cleared his throat and whispered, "She found her husband when she wanted to go to the attic. The innkeeper had hung himself on the stairs."

"You don't say! But why? He did not lose his hotel in a bombing raid. He has a good family. We, his customers, are loyal ..."

Leipziger broke in, "Where have you been all this time? Ah, I remember ... you got clobbered by the Russian civil workers, right?"

"Hmm ... I did, and they thought I would not make it after they cracked my skull open. Almost bled to death, but the mayor found me and made

---

135 It is estimated that over 100,000 women were raped, and some did not survive.

136 The American forces had advanced into Germany close to 200 kilometers into the predetermined areas for the Russian sector. They had to give up Thuringia, Saxon Anhalt, and Saxony. They received a part of Berlin in return. Berlin had seen street fights between the German and Russian forces and had been occupied by the Soviet army.

sure I got medical help. But tell me, do you have any idea why the innkeeper would commit suicide?"

"You suspected it. Yes, he was an informer for the Gestapo. He tried to hide it from the Americans, but they found out about it. For once, somebody told on *him*."

The farmer could not understand why that should be the reason for killing oneself. He uttered, "But suicide? He was not in the Gestapo. He just informed, as many others did, like the headmaster …"

Leipziger interrupted him again. "Oh, the headmaster! He disappeared. The rumor has it that he bribed Berliner, who has medical training, to remove his tattoo …"

"What!?" the farmer interjected. "I knew he believed in the Aryan dream, but SS?[137] He never wore a uniform. I thought he was connected with the Gestapo. But SS! Wow!"

"Actually, he never was in the SS. When he was called to the Volkssturm, he just thought it a good idea to get the tattoo so his blood type could be readily identified if he got wounded and needed a transfusion while unconscious."

The heavily breathing and coughing Berliner had entered, accompanied by a doctor. He had heard part of their conversation and continued Leipziger's report. "And now, the innkeeper was afraid the Americans would arrest him, as they do with many SS members. He feared to be put through trials, and maybe he would be tortured to death."

The farmer sighed. "What will happen next in our little village? Can you, Leipziger, go back? And what about you, Berliner and Hamburger? Where will you live, with your homes in ashes?"

Berliner answered, "We'll stay here. We have permission until Berlin is divided into sectors, and Hamburg and Leipzig are under Allied control. Oh, you might not know, they straightened out the borders. We will be under Soviet rule. We supposedly get a new government. They want to help us to have free elections for democratic leaders."

"Or Communists, socialists, a mixture of the two," Leipziger enlightened them.

The doctor had seen the body of the innkeeper and wrote the death

---

137 SS stands for *Schutzstaffel*, meaning "protective squad." Originally, they were the bodyguards of Nazi leaders. They swore unconditional loyalty to Hitler and the Nazi party. Later, the Waffen SS (a special military outfit) was installed. The members of the SS had their blood type (A, B, AB, or O) tattooed near their left armpit. This tattoo was used by the Americans to find SS members.

certificate. He gave a sedative to the wife. By now, she sat sunken into herself, sobbing quietly. Her daughter stood behind the bar and served the people, thinking, *Somebody has to run the business.*

The farmer shook his head. "So many changes, so much sadness, and still, life goes on. There is a reason why I did not succumb to my injuries. ... The pastor died in Stalingrad, our pharmacist was ambushed by Yugoslavian partisans, our innkeeper was thoroughly disappointed about the outcome of the war and could not face the trials, Teach is somewhere in hiding with a new name, and our mayor, as do all of us, has to go through the Entnazifizierungs[138] process. Only for him, it will be more rigorous."

Wolfgang Hamberger refers to this process the Allies initiated in his book, *America—my fascination*:

> Those soldiers were arrogant, they acted as if all Germans ... were Nazi criminals, and most of them probably believed that was the case. The first measures by the "occupation power" ... seemed harsh and unrelenting. That was particularly true of the curfews, the often arbitrary checks, and especially the requisitioning of private dwellings accompanied by the command to vacate the premises within the shortest time possible. ... The Americans never stopped talking about wanting to bring liberty and democracy to us, but in fact they played the boss. "Reeducation" ... was their overarching theme. They actually knew next to nothing about Germany.[139]

Hamberger describes how his mother tried to explain to him what the American Allies hoped to do, after he asked her, "Why is it necessary for everybody to be reeducated, me too?" She said:

> "You don't need any reeducation from anybody, but you're not anywhere near finished with your education! What the Americans mean by 'reeducation' is a political agenda. They want to drive Hitler out of the heads of every last German. Maybe it would be better to say 'reevaluation' instead of 'reeducation,' for what the Americans are after

---

138 A process in which the Allied forces, assuming that every German was a Nazi, tried to eradicate the Nazi ideology out of all Germans. First, the Americans had Germans fill out lengthy questionnaires. Soon, they turned to reeducation.

139 Hamberger, *America—my fascination*, 118.

is to ensure that their, that means our, old spiritual and cultural values prevail. ... They have liberated us, but they still have to prove whether they can also teach us good conduct, morals, and culture. But many in our country are in urgent need of it."[140]

Reeducation took place with more or less rigor in every one of the four sectors of Germany. Hamberger writes especially about his experiences in the American-occupied zone. He lived between Darmstadt and Heidelberg, the very area my cousin Klaus went back to shortly after the war had officially ended. Eventually, all of the first influx of shelter-seekers left for various Allied occupied zones. Another who reluctantly had to leave my uncle's house in fall 1945 was Ernst's friend Hermann. His family lived near Hamelin in the British sector. Aunt Bitta moved to Freiburg in the French sector. We would eventually leave for St. Bernhard. This village was first under American control, but soon was turned over to the Soviet forces.

In Klostermansfeld, the Americans had chosen the hotel right across from our courtyard gate as their base, from which they carried out some of the procedures the Big Three had agreed upon. In the beginning, my mother was the only one in the village they asked to help with translations. She used an old English-German dictionary from her father to intercede on behalf of many individuals and their requests. She helped to clear persons of being imprisoned because of a mistaken identity. She solved their problems with curfews when they needed to take a trip to the hospital, or find their relatives, or locate a place to stay. There were so many displaced people all over Germany, the Americans had their hands full sorting out where these people should be sent. They decided to order all of the displaced back to where they originally came from, be they prisoners of war, civil workers, soldiers, evacuees, fugitives, or refugees.

At the end of May, my father and his army comrade, Martin Bosert, arrived in Klostermansfeld. They had escaped from a makeshift American prison camp. They had surrendered to the American forces because Martin had been badly wounded. He had been shot in his back. He also had a bullet stuck in his leg and a few shrapnel wounds. They hoped to get food at the camp and medical help for him. After a week of resting, although not comfortably, Martin felt well enough to sit on the bar of the bicycle my father had taken. They waited until an army truck would leave the prison,

---

140 Ibid., 118–119.

so they could coast alongside of it through the prison gate, unnoticed by the guards. Martin could not have escaped from the Russian invasion if my father had not helped him. My father never liked to talk about it, and in 1991, when I met Martin again, he—just like my father—did not want to tell anything about these devastating times. He was originally from Berlin, where he had dreamed of becoming an opera singer. He was unable to go back to Berlin and live with his parents. They had died under the rubble of their home, which had been destroyed during one of the many bombing raids on Berlin.

Aunt Bitta's husband came at approximately the same time. He, too, had a nasty wound on his leg and had to use crutches. His leg needed to be amputated later. Eventually, this wound caused his early death.

One of Aunt Ursel's friends suddenly dropped in. She had just given birth to a tiny baby. She stayed with us, too. By now, the old farmhouse was overflowing with people. Somehow Oma, in her resourcefulness, found a place for everybody to sleep.

The first group that had to go back home were the Polish civil workers. Some of them followed the command reluctantly. They had liked working for Uncle Martin, but they had no choice. With the civil workers gone, Uncle Martin welcomed anybody who could replace them. My brother and his friend Hermann had helped alongside the civil workers before the Americans entered Klostermansfeld. My father, along with Martin Bosert, offered their aid as soon as they arrived in May. Horst had liked his duties as the former HJ worker so much that he volunteered to stay on the farm. Some of the farmworkers who had fought at the various fronts returned and gladly performed all the tasks Uncle Martin asked them to do once again. They knew they could rely on Mr. Oemler not only to pay them on time, but also to supply them with food when their ration cards were depleted at the end of the month.

My father, with the helpers arriving, and knowing that he too would be asked where he belonged, thought of leaving before he needed to fill out forms. He feared repercussions, since he had not officially been released from the American prison camp. He talked to Uncle Martin. "We will leave for my farm in St. Bernhard," he said.

Uncle Martin agreed, although he would have liked to keep my father and Martin Bosert as farmworkers. But he knew that when they left, there would be six people fewer (his two nieces, his nephew, his sister) to feed and house. He pointed out to my father, "According to the rules of relocating—or should I say, ordering people back to where they came from—St. Bernhard is the place they will send you to anyway. After all, you inherited this farm. That overrules going back to Thorn, where you only temporarily occupied an apartment as long as your insurance company wanted you to stay in West Prussia."

We made preparations to leave. We hoped to find Grandma and my four-year-old brother, Reinhold. Nobody had heard from them. Uncle Martin understood very well why my mother was anxious to move out. He secured two small horses and a covered wagon that had been left in the courtyard by retreating German soldiers.

My mother asked the Americans for permission to trek to St. Bernhard with her children and two workers[141] who would help her with the horses and wagon. She called attention to regulations about displaced people in all four occupied zones. She told them, "We fled from Thorn, which now is Polish, I think, but Thorn was only a business post for my husband. We originally come from St. Bernhard, where my husband owns a farm. My mother-in-law and my youngest son are hopefully still there. I need to find out how they are getting along. Also, I am sure my husband will first search for us at his farm." Thorn was out of the question for her. The Poles would rule there soon. She made clear to the American officials that we originated from Thuringia, where father's farm was rented to a Mr. Rassmann The Americans did not like to lose their translator, but they accepted that she wanted to be with her youngest son and wait there if her husband ever came back from the front. My mother was afraid to let them know that my father was one of her two workers. Therefore, she made up names for my father and his friend Martin. She was able to get the necessary travel papers from the American officers. These documents allowed her to travel through the Thuringia Mountains to St. Bernhard with her children and two horse handlers.

Before we could depart, we children had to be vaccinated. The American medical teams wanted to make sure that all people heading home would not spread diseases throughout Germany. They set up an immunization program for all children and young adults throughout their occupied territories. They stuck the needles into our arms, chests, and behinds to prevent dysentery, typhoid fever, diphtheria, scarlet fever, and typhus. We were also tested for tuberculosis. To avoid the spreading of typhus carried

---

141 My mother could not disclose that one of those "workers" was my father. He would have been put into a POW camp again.

by fleas and lice, the Americans dusted us and everything else with DDT.[142] Our entire bodies became sore. We were vaccinated against all of these diseases in a short time. The different serums wreaked havoc in our bodies. Regardless of how we felt, we had to start on our trek to St. Bernhard.

When we left, Hermann stayed in Klostermansfeld. He loved to do farmwork. He decided to study agriculture. He would have liked to remain with Uncle Martin, but he was ordered to join his family after the harvest season. He went north to meet his parents and five siblings in the British zone.

We went south. We voluntarily left, not as fugitives, but as displaced people. It was heartbreaking for the fugitives from the east to follow the relocation rules. They did not want to be forced to go back to where the Soviets occupied their hometowns and fields. They had fled from the Russians before, because of the cruelties committed by the Soviet soldiers. In her book *Fliegen—mein Leben*,[143] Hanna Reitsch tells what happened to her family, who originally came from Silesia. Her father, a medical doctor, had been called numerous times into the surrounding villages that had been overrun by the Soviets and then won back again by German forces. He witnessed the horrible acts the Russians had committed on the villagers. In the last days of the war, he and his family had been evacuated to Salzburg, Austria. They were safe there, but then he heard that he and his family would be forced to go back to Soviet-controlled Silesia. He had been deeply disappointed in his belief in a superior Germany and could not cope with the defeat of the Nazi ideology. Now, the worries about exposing his family to the Russians added to his despair. He committed suicide with his wife and five of his family members.[144] Many Germans killed themselves for the same reasons. They were disappointed, and having been NSDAP members, they feared a harsh treatment by the Allies. Worst of all, they had lost all hope in Germany's recovery.

Not so my father! We loaded the painted hope chest under the canvas of the covered wagon. It was the trunk in which my mother had tried to save my father's hunting guns, only to have them taken away by the Americans. Did she really think, when she left Thorn, that we would be allowed to keep guns? Maybe she still believed in a German victory against all odds. Now,

---

142 Dichlorodiphenyltrichloroethane is a very harmful synthetic pesticide.

143 Hanna Reitsch, *Fliegen—mein Leben* Stuttgart: Deutsche Verlags-Anstalt. Passage from "Stuttgarter Hausbücherei" no date. Translated by Ilse-Rose Warg, PhD.

144 Hanna Reitsch, *Fliegen—mein Leben*, 305–306.

the old chest had room for some pots and pans, linens, clothing, and food from Uncle Martin and Oma. We sat on the featherbeds between the hay and grain for the horses when we did not have to push the wagon up the high mountains of the Thuringian Woods. I must say, we did not often have the luxury of sitting in the wagon.

We left Klostermansfeld in early June. Uncle Martin hitched two strong horses in front of the smaller ones to pull the wagon up the steep hill toward Bensdorf. Then he had to take his team back, and we schlepped along the many kilometers, trusting in the strength of our little horses. We always made sure we stayed in the American-occupied part of Germany. My father knew the mountains well; he avoided towns and large villages. He led us through deep woods and over less-traveled streets.

Martin Bosert started to sing. I joined him. It was a poem by Johann Wolfgang von Goethe set to an old German folk melody, as was customarily done to popular poems in the nineteenth century.

Ich ging im Walde so für mich hin, um nichts zu suchen, das war mein Sinn.	I strolled through the woods all alone, not to seek anything on my mind.
Im Schatten sah' ich ein Blümlein steh'n, wie Sterne leuchtend, die Äuglein schön.	In the shade I saw a small flower, Its beautiful eyes shining like stars.
Ich wollt' es brechen, da sagt' es fein: "Soll ich zum Welken gebrochen sein?"	I wanted to pick it, but it lisped: "Should I be torn away to die?"
Ich grub's mit allen den Würzlein aus, zum Garten trug ich's am hübschen Haus. Und pflanzt' es wieder am stillen Ort; Nun zweigt es immer und blüht so fort.	I lifted it up with all its roots, Carried it to the garden behind the house, And planted it again at a quiet place. Here it grows and blooms continuously.

I had my head almost buried in the crib fastened to the back of the wagon. With both hands on the trough, I marched and pushed with all my strength, still singing. My parents, Ernst, and Martin braced themselves against the spokes of the four wheels. Hand over hand, we forced the heavy vehicle forward, helping the little horses overcome the steep mountain road.

"Hush, quiet!" my father hissed between his teeth. I stopped singing immediately. We reached the plateau. A motion with his hand indicated that we had to disappear. Hastily, my mother, Hildegard, and I climbed into the wagon. We squeezed ourselves behind the big old painted hope chest. Ernst covered us with a blanket and skillfully rested a sack of fodder across the chest and a suitcase behind us, thus hiding us. This was our secret shelter whenever danger lurked. There were so many people, homeless and hungry, who just would have loved to have our food, our wagon, and our horses. Some of these homeless people had been criminals, kept in Nazi prison camps. They were arbitrarily freed with all the other inmates, who were politically or racially unwanted people under the Nazis. We had just passed one of the notorious concentration camps, Buchenwald.[145]

Now we saw, through a little hole in a board of the wagon, a group of men with shaved heads. They looked longingly at the wagon and the horses. What would they do to us? Were we safe? My father had gone to the horses, holding them by their halter, partially hidden by the horses' heads and chests. Martin limped behind him. Ernst sat at the "helm," holding the reins. We held our breath. At any minute, they could pounce on us, throw us from the wagon, and drive away with our last belongings. How could we defend ourselves? At that moment, an American patrol controlling the country road stopped us. Did we sigh with relief? Not really! Although we were sure that the liberated prisoners would not bother us as long as the Americans were there with their guns, anxious thoughts crossed our minds. *What will the American GIs do? Will they let us continue to travel? Are our papers good enough?*

My father showed the soldiers our travel permission documents. The officer looked at him questioningly, probably wondering where the females of the group were. He counted Ernst, Martin, and my father. There were three people missing, but they allowed him to continue on the journey. My father spurred the horses on to a faster gait. Looking back, he noticed an army jeep following us. What did that mean? Would they stop us again? Would they spoil our plans to find out about Grandma and Reinhold?

Actually, the soldiers' presence kept the people near Buchenwald at bay.

---

145 Buchenwald is the name of a concentration camp located near Weimar in Thuringia.

"You know," Mother whispered, "that these men with shaved heads are freed prisoners. They are thieves and murderers." Was she really unaware that politically unwanted people, gypsies and Jews, had been imprisoned here? Later, we realized that the Americans had protected us, but at the time, Father feared being asked about the women of the traveling party. There was always the possibility that the soldiers would take their unwritten right of the victors by raping the women. The American soldiers never asked about us. They rode in their jeep, smoking cigarettes and chewing gum.

It started to get hot underneath the blanket and the fodder. Hildegard experienced leg cramps. My arms grew numb. Mother held us tightly. She was ready to protect and defend us with all the strength in her small body. She had nothing to fear. As soon as the last former prisoner of Buchenwald was out of sight, the jeep left us. Now it was time for us to get out of our stuffy hiding place. I rubbed my arms. Hildegard stretched her legs. Gladly, we continued our walk behind the wagon and helped push it up the next hill.

Nightfall was near. Where would we stay tonight? Every evening, it was the same uncertainty. We had to observe the curfew. We could not simply stay at a clearing in the forest near one of the many springs in the Thuringian Woods. Father would leave the wagon on the side of the road, partially hidden by trees and bushes. He would walk to the next village, inn, or farmhouse, trying to find out if we could stay in an enclosed courtyard or a barn, where the horses might get some rest and his family could sleep. We slept under all kinds of conditions—on living room floors, in haylofts, or three of us in one bed. One of the men would always stay with the horses and the wagon to make sure nothing was taken.

Once we reached a little village where my father knew people from way back when his father had held the first chair of the Thüringer Landbund.[146] Here we found out from one of Father's acquaintances that Grandma and Reinhold were alive, and St. Bernhard did not witness much fighting. My mother sighed deeply and wiped away a few tears. She finally would be united with her youngest son again.

Father asked an old farmer if our horses could drink from the water pump and we could rest up in their barn.

"No, not tonight!" the old man replied. "The Americans are planning a party here. When they get drunk, nobody knows what they'll do. They might see the horses."

---

146 The Thuringia Farmers' Party during the Weimar Republic.

The old farmer wanted to continue, but his wife interrupted him. "There is room in the living room. You can sleep on the carpet," she said.

"Thank you. We have blankets and pillows. We will be fine," my mother said.

"The men sleep in the stable with the horses; we hide the wagon in the barn."

The farmer sighed. "You are always too trusting, Minna," he said to his wife. "But it's okay. Just as long as you know I cannot protect you and might get into trouble myself."

Ernst did not know if he was counted as a man too. He was thirteen years old and had done many a man's work already. Mother sensed his dilemma. "Ernst, you'll sleep with us in the living room. You sleep at the entrance. You are our protector if some drunken soldier should enter." The farmer's wife showed us the room where we could wash. She asked us to use the chamber pot during the night, since the way to the outhouse led across the street and therefore could not be used during curfew hours. Soon we were settled on the floor and fell asleep. Early the next morning, before we left, the farmer's wife brought some hot milk and black bread for us to eat.

It was a beautiful summer evening when we arrived in another village. My father remembered that his former classmate owned an inn there. Sure enough, he found it and was permitted to put the wagon behind the barn and the horses in a stable nearby. We went upstairs to a large room that served as a ballroom, theater, or auditorium depending on what function it was needed for at any given time. Martin drew back the curtains of the stage. He found a few props. He started to sing a *Rigoletto* aria.[147] He had a beautiful baritone. My mother joined in, laughing, and soon we played along, although we did not know the opera. We were led by the text Martin sang and acted out, offering different endings to the "play." Everybody laughed and had a great time until my father asked us to find a place to sleep in this huge ballroom. Somewhere among the stage props, I found a sofa covered with dusty red velvet. I curled up on it and fell fast asleep.

"Ilse-Rose!"

"Fatty!"

"Rosebud!"

I opened my eyes. The sun shone right into my face.

"Ilse-Rose!"

---

147 *Rigoletto* is an opera in three acts by Giuseppe Verdi (1813–1901) of Italy.

"Fatty!"

"Rosebud! Where are you?"

I heard my family calling. I answered, "I am here."

"Why didn't you tell us where you wanted to rest?" my father asked anxiously.

"I thought this was a good place to sleep when you told us to find a place to lay down."

My mother felt a disciplinary action by Father coming. "Let her be, Herbert," she intervened. "I never was alarmed about her. She is a resourceful child. She always knows how to make the best of every situation." I not only listened to her words expressing her confidence in me, but I remembered them for the rest of my eventful life. I would always try to find something good in even the most dreadful situations.

After a few more days of travel, we arrived in Father's village. It was my first visit to this remote place. It was the tiniest settlement I ever saw. Only three streets seemed to go up the hill and two other ones crossed them, with one at the top of the hill and the other at the bottom, where my father's farmhouse stood.

We could only enjoy the wholeness of an undivided family for a few weeks under American protection. On July 1, 1945, the borders of the four occupied sectors were designated, with the result that St. Bernhard fell under Soviet control. The Americans had to leave our district, and the Russians moved in. Since St. Bernhard was—and still is—so small, we seldom saw Russians. German policemen soon oversaw our region, though they had to enforce the new Communist laws. We lived only about ten miles away from the American sector, but it might as well have been a thousand. From then on, we were confined to the Soviet-controlled zone.

Chapter 9

Hardships in St. Bernhard

My grandma lived with my younger brother in St. Bernhard. They occupied a small two-bedroom apartment on the second floor of the farmhouse, which had two stories and an attic. Three buildings enclosed the courtyard. An iron fence at the street finished the quadrangle of the yard. The barn stood across from the main house and extended toward the street into the horse stable. The traditional dung heap lay at the gate across from a water pump, not too far from the kitchen.

When we arrived, my parents took over one bedroom. Grandma shared hers with us four children. All of us used the living room. Its couch served as sleeping quarters for Martin Bosert. The bathroom, typically without a commode, was converted into a kitchen. A coal and wood stove stood alongside the water heater. A board across the tub served as a counter. A small table occupied the limited space under the window, from which we could observe activities in the courtyard. Here we ate our breakfast before walking to the one-room school.

Our father had rented the farm to Mr. Rassmann. Their contract legally should have run for nine more years. Therefore, Father could not farm, but he had the privilege of taking care of the three forest lots belonging to the estate. Mr. Rassmann's big family occupied the lower rooms of the house. Hildegard soon befriended his daughters. She always could associate with people easily. It really did not matter to me; we had little time for playing.

Grandma believed in the old saying, "Early to bed and early to rise makes a man healthy, wealthy, and wise." She used many of these proverbs.

One was, "A girl may not rest as long as it takes for a chicken to pick a kernel off the ground." Therefore, she taught Hildegard and me how to knit and how to crochet, so we would not sit idle during a rest period. In the summer of 1945, she woke us up early so we could go with her into the woods to look for strawberries. Later, we picked raspberries, then blackberries, and at last the sloes, which were best after the first frost. In St. Bernhard, frost could come as early as September. After a rainy day, we looked for a variety of mushrooms in our woods. Grandma cleaned and sliced them, and then she hung them on strings close to the stove in the kitchen so they could dry. We gathered a good supply of them for the coming winter months. Grandma had the right to grow some vegetables in the farm garden. Her plot was not big. It was too small to grow cabbage or potatoes, but she had grown tomatoes in little containers in spring. She planted them outside in June. During the whole summer, I never saw a single ripe tomato there. Just before the frost came, she brought all the green tomatoes into the house. We had to carefully wrap them in newspaper and store them in single layers in the small hallway located in front of her apartment. We checked the tomatoes intermittently to see if they had ripened and then we used them. A few did spoil.

Grandma baked bread for all of us when we were able to get flour. She formed round loafs with her hands and put each onto a wooden slab. We helped her to bring these to the community oven. The oven, made from brick and fieldstones, stood by itself in the middle of the village. A strong wood fire heated the inner chamber. After the flames died down and the embers were covered with ashes, the villagers pushed their loaves of bread onto the hot ashes. In a few hours, the bread was baked. The fresh-baked bread always tasted very good, but we were not allowed to eat as much as we liked. The bread had to last for many days. My mother marked it, dividing it into daily rations. When we told Grandma that we were hungry, she answered with one of her sayings, "Praise be to what toughens you up!" Sometimes a neighbor gave us one of her slices of bread. She had a few cows. She scooped the heavy cream from the milk and mixed it with our strawberries to make a delicious spread for an open-faced sandwich.

My father had sold the small horses and purchased bigger, stronger ones. We called them Lise and Hans. Hildegard had a knack for making Lise listen to her, although the mare was high-strung and nervously twitched her ears. "She is prettier than Hans; she is my horse," Hildegard declared proudly. "Don't even think of getting close to her. Something might happen." What might happen, I didn't know.

In July and again in late August, we made hay for the horses. Father was allowed to cut the high grass and herbs in a meadow that was a long walk away from our place. Grandma, Mother, my older brother, my sister, and I raked the hay. Father used a scythe. He showed Martin Bosert and Ernst how to sharpen it and how to swing it so the grass would lay just right. We followed him and raked the grass into shallow rows. It needed to be turned often. Again, Grandma woke us up early and went with us to perform this task, so the evening and morning dew could not settle on the drying grass, causing the hay to spoil.

My grandfather, a forest keeper by profession, had taught his sons how to care for the forest. My father noticed that the beech trees needed to be thinned out. Now he decided to work as a lumberjack. With the help of Martin Bosert, he cut the trees down. Although Hildegard was only eleven years old and I had hardly reached nine, we had to help get the trunks out of the deep woods and onto the pathways, where they could be loaded into a wagon. We sold them in the nearby towns. Everybody needed wood, whether it was for firewood for the coming winter or for repairing the war-damaged houses. My sister and I had to lead the horses through the often-narrow spaces between the standing trees. The felled tree trunks were fastened with chains to the horses. They dragged them out of the dense underbrush. We girls had to find a way for the animals to pull the long logs toward the road. Often, the trunks would get hung up on bushes or smaller trees, and sometimes the horses, especially Hans, would have a mind of their own when it came to which way to drag them out. It took all the strength we two could muster to direct the big horses.

Ernst, Martin, and my father loaded the logs into a wagon and brought them into town. Firewood was very much sought after. Winter would be coming soon. Many people, like us, had no oil heat; either there was no oil available, or they simply did not have the luxury of central heating.[148] There was no coal furnace. Coal was sent to Russia or France, and there was seldom any coal left for household consumption by the Germans, although each family was allotted a small amount of lignite (brown) coal for their little stoves in their kitchens. We had heard that people would burn their

---

148 The first time I experienced central heating was in Mülheim on the Ruhr in the early 1950s. In villages, it was common to heat every room separately as needed. Usually the bedrooms did not have any stoves.

furniture to keep warm throughout the winter. My father either sold the wood or bartered with it.[149]

Coming home from a long day of work, the horses had to be fed and taken care of. One day, when I was asked to feed them, I entered Lise's stall from the wrong side, mixing up right and left as I did so often. The horse started to bolt. Luckily, Martin was standing near the stalls, but even he had a hard time calming the horse down. I pressed myself against the wooden plank that separated Hans from Lise. Hans started to get nervous as well. He turned his head toward me, showing big yellow teeth. I held my breath.

I heard Martin. "Ho, ho Lise, ho, ho!" To me, he whispered, "Slip out when I come from the other side of Lise." He had brought a shovel with oats, but the horse continued to stomp its hooves. Any minute now, she could start kicking. The neighbor, a blacksmith, heard the commotion. He came running. With a secure grip, he caught one of Lise's hooves. "Now, now, Lise, old girl," he said in his deep, calming voice. She responded to him. Martin started to pour the oats for Lise. "Out, out" he hissed to me. I stumbled out of the stall.

"Stupidity of stupidity! Don't you even know how to approach a horse? Can't you think? Can't you understand that the poor animal does not know what is going on behind her back? You scared her half to death. She could have trampled you!" My older brother was yelling at me, and of course, Hildegard had to chime in.

"You scared my horse. You ruined her. She'll never overcome this. She'll never be the same again."

Martin thanked the blacksmith for his help. The blacksmith waved it off with his hand and said, "Don't mention it. I saw what was going on. I naturally would help, as long as our Father in Heaven gives me the strength to do so," he muttered as he crossed the street and resumed splitting wood in front of his house. Everybody in the village knew that he was a God-fearing man. It was a blessing that he was always there when we needed help. Soon enough, we would have to rely on him again.

Deeply shaken, I slipped into the house. Grandma noticed me. "Finished

---

149 The black market flourished in all four zones. It stopped rather suddenly in 1948 in the three western sectors. In the Russian sector, it never stopped completely, but bartering had to be done secretly. When caught, the barterers were sentenced to prison and severely punished.

feeding the horses already?" she asked and then ordered me, "Go downstairs and help peel the potatoes."

Mrs. Rassmann handed me a dull knife so I would not cut myself, and I started peeling. "How slow you do this!" she remarked. "Look how many potatoes Lenchen peeled already, and you haven't even finished one!"

Grandma wanted me to be as accomplished as others in the village. She really did not mean to embarrass me in front of the Rassmann children, who were my schoolmates. She just wanted to spur me on. I was not competitive when it came to showing that I would be better than others. I could be very ardent when playing games, but even there, I cheated a little once in a while, so that the younger players would not lose all the time.

What was the use in peeling potatoes, if I could not satisfy anybody? I thought. I put the knife down, thinking all the potatoes we needed this day were peeled.

I went upstairs to play with my little brother. I would lie on the daybed in the living room. I bent my knees and let Reinhold ride on my lower legs. He was sitting just above my ankles. I would toss him up and down lightly. He laughed and relished every moment. He loved his sister, who always had time for him and could tell such interesting stories, read fairy tales, and even made going to bed fun. He just wanted to be tossed higher and higher. He threw his head back in delight … and then it happened. As he threw his head back, I hoisted him up again. Reinhold squealed with glee, flying up, when our hands slipped apart. He was thrown backward, and his head came down hard on the stone windowsill.

A scream, and then dead silence.

"Mom, Mom!" I wailed loudly. "Mom, I killed Reinhold, oh I killed him. I killed him, oh, oh."

Grandma was first on the scene. She opened the window and shouted for the blacksmith across the street. "Fast, come fast, the child … the child, he fell, his head, he is bleeding." Reinhold opened his eyes and started crying. My mother had heard the commotion while hitching the horses to the wagon on which my father wanted to load the last cut of logs. She left the team and ran up the stairs. She lifted my brother up and carried him to the blacksmith's place. The blacksmith calmly put a butterfly bandage on Reinhold's head after he shaved off a little of the light blond hair.

My mother could hardly hold back her tears. "Thank you, thank you so much. I would not know what to do without you. There isn't a nurse within five miles of here, and no doctor for at least ten miles. We could not pay them anyway."

He interrupted her. "It's all right, Mrs. Höfer." He looked at her again and felt compelled to speak to her. "May I say something? Just among us, I really do not like to interfere in other people's business. ... but I have seen how brave you are, how you face the people here. How you keep your children clean and neat and teach them good manners. You are so slender, so tender-boned, so small. Your hands are not made for this farmwork, hitching horses, and milking cows. You do not belong here. I mean, my wife and I will always help you and your family. There are a few others who will help you, too." He stopped a moment, making sure nobody was around to hear him. He continued, "But the Russians will now take over this part of Germany. Who knows how they will treat us? Soviets, Communists! Sooner or later, we all have to become Communists working in communes, doing even the toughest chores together."

Observing my mother as she reached for my brother, he sighed. "And the harsh winter in our mountains is approaching. I say go back to your family, to your home. This village is not the place for such a refined, sophisticated lady like you." The blacksmith seldom spoke as many words as he did this time.

My mother looked into his good-natured eyes. "As long as God gives me people like you, I can stand it anywhere," she said, and she took my brother from the blacksmith's lap, carrying him tenderly upstairs to Grandma's apartment.

At our meager dinner of potatoes with sour milk and a few strawberries that Grandma and Hildegard had picked, my father frowned. "Whose turn was it to feed the horses? When I went to give them water tonight, Hans looked like he did not get anything to eat. There was not a morsel in his hayrack. He had even pulled up some straw from his bedding to munch on. You know we need the horses in good condition to survive. We made hay last week. You could have given him a forkful. Can't I expect at least so much from you? Well, whose turn was it? Mother, Ernst, or Martin?"

I said, "I tried to feed them."

Father wanted to know, "Who has asked her to help?"

My mother answered, "Herbert, I told her to help me. Tenant Rassmann said we could have as many potatoes as we could peel in an hour. I went to work as fast as I could. Hildegard and Grandma had just come back from the woods, picking strawberries that Hildegard cleaned. I know Ilse-Rose is resourceful, so I asked her to help with the horses."

"Yes, and she was so dumb as to approach Lise from the wrong side, and the blacksmith had to come, and ..." Hildegard was ready to tell of all the events that happened on this day. I could not eat anymore. I tried to swallow hard. I did not dare cry. I just waited silently for my punishment, knowing Dad had not even seen Reinhold. He was in bed before Dad arrived. My father just nodded. He understood that his little Rosebud, his third child, was overtaxed. There would not be any disciplinary action.

That evening, he took the whole family to the barn. He wore riding boots, had a small whip in his hand, and was leading Lise into the barn. She wore a beautiful saddle. To this day I have no idea where he was able to get this luxurious riding gear. My father mounted the horse, rode two circles, asked Tenant Rassmann to open the barn gates, and rode off into the setting sun. The horse followed every slight command. Lise was a classic riding horse, definitely not a farm animal. I never forgot this picture: my father high on the beautiful mare, rider and horse in perfect harmony, encircled by the glow of the sunset, which intensified Lise's red-brown coat and reflected on Dad's shining boots.

In September 1945, all schools in the Russian zone opened again, although often only in cellars or other dilapidated buildings. My older brother could not attend a nearby high school. Usually, high-school students living in a village take the train or public bus in the morning, attend their classes, and come home the same day. Since St. Bernhard did not have a bus or train station, he needed to live in a town. My parents searched among their former acquaintances in Thuringia and found a woman who was willing to offer room and board for Ernst in return for his monthly ration card. Father supplied money for his stay, and Mother sent food packages so the lady could cook meals for him. My brother never saw what my mother sent. When the mailman came to deliver Mother's packages, Ernst was in school. The woman took the parcels and did not give anything to Ernst. She used the food for herself and for the black market. Ernst had to survive on what she allotted to him from his ration card.

Hildegard and I were still in elementary school. We went up the hill across the farm, through the old orchard and the churchyard to the house that hosted one room for grades one through eight. I liked this school more than Miss Karsdorf in Klostermansfeld, because the teacher left me alone most of the time. I seemed to learn everything without her tutoring, except now, we had to learn Russian.[150] I did not understand why we had to speak

---

150 Depending on which sector German pupils lived in, they had to learn the language of the occupying forces (French, English, or Russian).

the language of soldiers against whom my father had fought not quite a year ago. I just refused to learn it.

On October 19, when Hildegard and I walked home from school, we could tell that something was going on. The village seemed desolate, and still there was a sense of hustling and bustling behind the closed windows and doors.

"Look, Fatty,[151] there, see the cars?" My always alert sister pointed to two jeeps. They were parked in front of the farmhouse. We had not seen a car for weeks. We scampered up the stairs. We did not notice the spiteful grin on Mrs. Rassmann's face and the curious looks her children sent our way.

Our living room was a mess. Every drawer had been opened; their contents were strewn all over the room. Three policemen searched the beds, lifted mattresses. We looked at our mother, who stood against the warm tile stove. She motioned us to come to her side. She whispered, "Quiet, don't say anything." Hildegard gave her an agreeing glance out of her big brown eyes. I nodded silently. Reinhold, four years old, leaned against mother, sucking his thumb. My father stood at the desk, his hands in handcuffs.

"Aha, here it is. Here is a swastika, ja, Mr. Höfer, you gave this jewelry to your wife, ja?!"

My mother tried to explain politely, "Officer, this is the typical mother's cross every woman would receive after bearing four children. See, this one is bronze for my four children. Others received silver or even gold ones if they had six or eight children."

"Well, why do you still have it? There are no honors in swastikas, don't you know that?" My mother did not know why she still had it. She had lost most of her jewelry with all of the other belongings in Thorn. Why did she keep his one? She never wore it. It just so happened that when she packed the trunk in Thorn, it slid in amongst the dishes or silverware. She did not remember. Maybe she kept it because she was grateful to have given birth to four healthy, intelligent children. The policeman bent the cross and threw it into the fire.

"What do we have here? A letter addressed to Sergeant H. Höfer! Tsk, tsk, tsk! Let's see what's in it!" He showed it to his companion and began to read aloud what my mother had written to Father when he was fighting at the eastern front. It was one of her love letters to him, filled

---

151 By now, I was anything but heavy, but this was the name my siblings gave me when I was a toddler and it stuck, no matter how skinny I had become.

with tenderness and encouraging words for her husband. She told him that she expected a fourth child. My father had never received this letter. It had been sent back to my mother. Now, the envelope revealed that he had been a minor officer in Hitler's army and that he had fought at the eastern front. German police arrested my father because he had been in battles against the Soviet Union and our grandfather had been the leader of the conservative Thuringia Farmers' Party, formerly Thüringer Landbund, which was against Communism.

The policeman pushed my father down the stairs. My father turned once and looked at Hildegard. She interpreted his glance as, "Don't worry, I'll be back." They shoved him into the jeep and then sped away. My mother sank into a chair, tears streaming down her cheeks.

Grandma came into the room and tried to console her. "At least Martin is safe. He came from the stable when the police arrived. I pointed him toward your bedroom, and when all of the policemen were searching the living room, he climbed out of the window to hide in the woods behind the pasture."

"I hope the tenants downstairs did not see him and squeal on him or denounce him as well," my mother sighed.

"No, I am sure they were much too excited about what was going on up here to do anything else. They would rather watch what would happen to Herbert."

My mother collected herself and put on a courageous front. She would not let the family downstairs triumph over her misery. She prepared the evening meal as best as she could with the meager provisions we had. She made sure we washed our hands and sat at the table. "It is important to keep good manners. There are things nobody can take away from you. Always learn. Always behave well. Knowledge and civilized behavior are things nobody can take away from you."

"May I have another potato, please?" I asked.

Grandma let me know, "No, we have to keep some for tomorrow."

Late at night, Martin sneaked into the stable. My mother pretended to check on the horses. She gave the potatoes to him. They talked about different times and spots in the woods where she or Grandma could leave food and warmer clothing for Martin. We did not know if the police or the Russians were looking for him, too. He had to hide. We could not trust anybody in the village. He could not ask someone for food. It was too tempting for people to tell the police where he was in order to receive a favor in return from them.

The next morning, Tenant Rassmann asked my mother what she did in the stable the night before.

"Remember when my daughter spooked Lise? Ever since, the horse seems to get restless, and sometimes she gets loose. I had to check on her last night. You know my husband could not do it." Later, when she told Grandma how Tenant Rassmann spied on us, she concluded, "Thank God Rosebud spooked the horse!"

In a matter of fourteen days, Martin was able to cross the border into the American zone. On his way, he stopped at Oma's place to tell her about my father's imprisonment and in what a precarious situation her daughter Paula and her grandchildren were.

My father had to follow the police when they arrested him. He had turned his head to send a glance of good-bye before he was shoved into a jeep. On the outskirts of the small village a truck was parked, and he was told to climb in. The driver and the guards were Soviet soldiers. The Russians had sent the German police to arrest Father so they, knowing the German language, would find evidence in our living quarters for imprisonment. Now the Russians took over. When the truck stopped, my father was led into a makeshift prison cell.

With the first light of morning, he looked out of the barred window and recognized the town. Here he had gone to high school. He knew the apartment building across from the prison. He studied the windows, the last fall flowers in boxes on the windowsills. Pretty soon, here and there, women opened their windows, shook out the dust cloth or hung out one of their featherbeds to air in the cool morning breeze. Another lady appeared right across from his window. That woman looked familiar. She put away her flowerpots and cleaned the windowsill. Suddenly she stopped, looked straight at him, clasped her hand in front of her mouth, and disappeared. Now he remembered her. It was Marian Schönfeld his former classmate. The woman leaned out of the window, glanced up and down the street and at his building, and then stepped back further into the room and motioned to him. He just nodded.

My mother still wondered what criminal act or political affiliation sent our father to prison. The question haunted her. Was it because he had fought against the Soviets? Was it because his father had been a leader of an anti-Communist party of the Weimar Republic? Soon, she received an answer.

Mr. Rassmann had misinformed the Russians and German police

about my father. He denounced my father in hopes of receiving our farm as reward for his deceptive report. He must have deliberated, *My contract with Mr. Höfer will run out in 1954. I have five children. They are good workers, and with their help, I can make a go of this farm.* He further rationalized, *Mr. Höfer has hardly farmed here before; he only rented the place out.* Mr. Rassmann thought that now, with my father arrested and hopefully sent to Siberia, it was his chance to grab the farm. He showed his true colors.[152] They had been brown with the National Socialists when he rented the farm from Father. Now they turned red like the Communist Socialists. For him, it was time to switch to the new regime and get the most out of it.

After the rumor about my father's arrest as a "war criminal and Nazi" spread through the village, our stay in St. Bernhard became unbearable. Now we experienced a time of greater hunger, and even worse, a bitter disappointment in people. Tenant Rasmann's unfriendliness increased. The schoolchildren in the village started to call Hildegard and me "Nazi pigs." Once in a while, they threw stones at us on our way home from school. There was only one good turn in our unfortunate circumstances: the wound on Reinhold's head healed well. The blacksmith had done a good job with his butterfly bandage.

My mother had to bring food to the prison, which was twelve miles away. She arrived there in the afternoon. She had to give the sandwiches to the police. They searched them and told her they would give them to Father.

"Can't I speak with him, or at least see him?" she asked.

"No!"

She left, uncertain if he would receive the last of our smoked sausage stuck in between two pieces of brown bread.

About three days after they had taken my father away, Russian soldiers came up to our rooms. They demanded to know where my father was.

"He is in Hildburghausen in prison," Mother answered.

"No he's not, and you know it. He escaped. Where is he hiding?" My mother turned pale. She did not know where he was. Our emotions ran high. On the one hand, we were relieved he escaped, but on the other hand, where was he now? Why didn't he come to tell us?

As much as they tried to prompt my mother, she had no idea where

---

152 The color brown is associated with the early Nazi movement, since the SA had brown uniforms. Red stands for Communism. The background of most flags representing Communist nations is red.

Father might be. One soldier pointed a pistol at her chest. She held her breath and looked at us. She shook her head. Finally, she stammered, "I did not know he broke out. He never told us. He did not come here." What else could she say? She did not want to be killed in front of her children. My little brother started to cry. Maybe the Russian soldiers had children of their own. They saw us two girls staring at them and Reinhold whimpering. They must have realized that this woman really had no idea where her husband was. They probably thought that their escaped prisoner was too smart to go home after breaking out, knowing that the police would search the area where his family was first. He most likely was hiding somewhere far away by now. They knew they better leave and not waste more time on us.

After they left, my mother and Grandma sobbed. Then Mother straightened herself up, thinking to herself, *I may not give in. My children need me. I will be there for them.*

It was true. My father was only in prison for three days. He had scraped at the door hinges with a spoon until they gave way. He waited for the right moment and snuck out. He lived under an assumed name for one year, hiding and constantly changing his whereabouts.

In the meantime, the Russians confiscated our farm,[153] although it was not large enough to fall under the land reform. Large estates over 100 hectares were taken from their owners. The fields and animals were distributed among farmworkers, small farmers, and refugees who wanted to own land and were willing to farm. The original owners had to leave their homestead and the district. In the Soviet-controlled zone, smaller farms were often taken for political reasons. Usually some envious or disgruntled person denounced the owner by claiming that he was a war criminal, or belonged to the Nazi party, or worked against the Communist ideology.

For a short time, Mr. Rassmann had control over the farm, but soon it became a *kolkhoz* (collective farm) or VEB.[154] That meant he had to give it up. He received the order to work with the rest of the farmworkers and do all farm activities collectively, as the blacksmith had predicted, in a commune. Most of what they produced had to be delivered to a collection

---

153 This Land Reform started in late 1945. Under the same rule for dividing large farms, the Soviets would claim the right to confiscate whole factories, dismantle them, and ship them to Russia. The Land Reform was only partially heeded in the French sector and hardly at all in the British and American sectors.

154 VEB stands for *Volkseigener Betrieb*, literally translated, "folk-owned business." It had become nationally owned property, to be worked by the people, for the folk.

station from which it supposedly went to towns, but actually was channeled to Russia or privileged Communists. Our family had to leave the district; only Grandma was allowed to stay.

After Oma had heard about our situation from Martin Bosert, she took one of the overcrowded trains to Themar, a town about five kilometers away from St. Bernhard, and then walked the long path through the woods to us. She carried food for us. She certainly was not used to walking with a heavy load. My mother never forgot how Oma came to our rescue. She arrived in the beginning of November. She did not stay long. She suggested to my mother, "Paula, I'll leave soon and take Ilse-Rose with me to Klostermansfeld. Of course, all of you are welcome to come, too."

"I know, Mother. That keeps me going."

"Only, you cannot come with me right away. There is no room in our house."

"Why? You always managed to find a place for us."

Oma sighed, "Not only Herbert's farm was confiscated." Before she could continue to explain why we could not join Oma now, my mother suddenly realized that most of our relatives had large estates. She screamed, "Magda, Lisbeth, Richard, Wilhelm, Tante Klärchen?"

"Yes," Oma said, "all of them lost their farms and will have to leave them soon. First your sister Magda and her daughter claimed they could live with us. Then Lisbeth, with her three little children, and Aunt Klärchen declared our address as the place where they will stay. We still have Aunt Bitta's family living with us. There is Mrs. Kleefeld from Berlin, and we had to take in a new family from the Baltic states. They have two children."

Mother slowly sat down and put her hands in front of her face. She moaned, "Mother, we have orders to leave here in a few days. Where can I go? Should I try Hilde in Heidelberg? Her place is overcrowded as well, and they do not have food."

"Paula, I will find a place for you and Hildegard."

"Mother, you say Hildegard and me, but I will not be separated from Reinhold again. He already speaks in the St. Bernhard dialect. I need to take him with me, too. Grandma hardly has enough food for herself. Winter is coming. We had the first snow already."

"Paula, there will be a place for you, I promise. I only do not know …" Suddenly, her face lit up. She exclaimed, "Wait! I have it. Great-Grandmother! She has two bedrooms! Yes, that will work. You can stay with her in Edersleben until Mrs. Kleefeld moves out." As always, Oma would find the best solution for our terrible predicament.

Oma left and took me along. I had pretty much outgrown my clothing, but in those times, nobody cared. What counted was having something warm to wear, no matter if it fit.

My mother had to sell the last logs Father and Martin had cut, the horses, and the wagon, and she had to let the police know that she was leaving for Edersleben. These errands had to be done in the town where we were registered. In the morning, she and Ernst drove the horses and wagon to the town. Ernst had to take the train from there to his high school. He had to stay with the lady who had promised my parents to give him room and board. My mother did not know how to get back to us after she completed the errands. She had to face the long twelve-mile walk. Nobody dared to offer her a ride. The police had treated her rather harshly. They had taken away the horses. I do not know how much money she got for the wagon and logs.

Somehow, the people who purchased these things gave her a bottle of rum as well. She could use the rum more than the money. She would keep it to barter for food or clothing. It snowed when she walked back to St. Bernhard. Utterly discouraged and exhausted, she cowered down against a snow bank, closed her eyes, and envisioned how it would be if she drank the rum, fell asleep, and froze to death. All the pain, all the harassment, all the anxiousness about her children would be over. Startled, she thought, *My children! No … my children need me. I must be there for them.* She stood up and dragged herself to St. Bernhard.[155]

Soon she left with Reinhold and Hildegard for Edersleben. There, she stayed with our great-grandmother, who still polished her floors to a mirror's shine. One day, Hildegard slipped and sailed along the balustrade, almost all the way down the staircase. My mother had to ask the old lady not to polish the floors, especially since she insisted that everybody entering her apartment had to take his or her shoes off and walk around the place with socks on.

It was not easy for Great-Grandmother to live with young ones again. She had been a stern mother with her own children. My mother needed to explain to her that Reinhold was only four years old and had been away from her for a long time. He had just bonded to my mother again after

---

155 Years later, my mother told us about this moment in her life when she was ready to commit suicide.

living with Grandma in St. Bernhard. My mother promised he would lose his dialect and learn to speak High German.

Great-Grandmother had good connections in Edersleben. Soon they would celebrate Christmas. She was able to get the necessary ingredients for her famous delicious Christmas cookies. Hildegard watched her baking process. When the cookies were prepared that had a sweet, white lid, Hildegard asked her, "Why do you take two spoons to drop the dough on the baking sheet?"

"This way, all cookies get the same size and shape, Hildegard," Great-Grandmother told her. She filled several sheets with them, and then, instead of putting them into her oven, she stored them on the top shelves of her pantry. That prompted a new inquiry by Hildegard. "Why don't you bake them?" Patiently, Great-Grandmother replied, "They have to dry overnight. Tomorrow I'll bake them, and while baking, they will form their lid."[156] Everything was ready for Christmas. And then came the best surprise of all.

Shortly before Christmas Eve, my father appeared. He could only visit for a short time. He never dared to linger in one place. He had to stay ahead of the Russian and German spies. He had sent word to Aunt Ida in St. Bernhard that she should urge her husband, Hans, to leave right away whenever he would arrive. When Hans finally was released from the French prison camp and came to St. Bernhard, he either did not heed my father's warning or never received it. In a matter of two hours, the police arrested Uncle Hans. He was never seen by any of us again. We heard they had taken him to Buchenwald, the notorious concentration camp, which the Russians now used for their purposes to punish war criminals, SS members, other Nazis, political opponents, and many denounced people.

My older brother had his Christmas vacation and came to Edersleben, too. Only I, as happened so often, was away from my family. I stayed with my dear Oma and all the other relatives in Klostermansfeld. I did not know that my father was alive and in Edersleben, and neither did they.

---

156 I have the recipe, but my cookies never form that lid. I guess you need the moist winter air in Germany for the cookies to become *Deckelplätzchen* (lid cookies).

Chapter 10

Confiscation, Displacement,
Relocation, Hunger

Back in Klostermansfeld, I noticed that our school had changed. Miss Karsdorf was gone. We had a new, much younger teacher. When I had been in St. Bernhard, the Russian language had already become a requirement to teach in all schools. I reluctantly learned some of the vocabulary and the funny letters of the Russian alphabet. Soon, the street signs at the town and village entrances were written in Russian and German letters.

When I dressed for school, I did not have long stockings for the cold weather. I just wore a pair of old boots, a skirt a little too short, a jacket over a blouse, and kneesocks Grandma had knitted for me. While my knees were freezing, I thought, *Spartans were tough and so am I.*

One morning when my girlfriend Klärchen did not accompany me to school, I heard laughter behind me. "Look! The Oemler! She is wearing kneesocks in this weather."

Another voice: "Oemler does not need long stockings. Her fat keeps her warm. She gets all the food she wants."

I thought, *Okay, I have been here so often, that they think my last name is Oemler and not Höfer. Should I show them?*

Some of my friends were influenced by their parents. Most of them had been Communists before Hitler became a dictator. They never belonged to the Nazi party and wanted to show that they were in charge now. My mother had called Helga's grandparents "noble communists."[157] What she meant by this expression, I was not sure. But anyway, "noble" had a good ring to it. Not all of my schoolmates were my former friends from school. They were children of displaced people who were still looking for their lost relatives. They hoped to find them soon.

Uncle Große was asked to be the rector of our school again. He had been the headmaster before the Nazi regime. He disagreed with the National Socialists and never joined the Nazi party; therefore, they had ousted him. Now, in his seventies, the Russians reinstated him. He became my tutor, since I still did not spell correctly. He combined his dictation with anecdotes about Martin Luther, and usually stopped at the most interesting places. "What happened then?" I would ask.

"You will find out when you come back on Tuesday," he would answer with a friendly smile. By keeping me guessing about the conclusions, he made sure I did not skip my spelling lessons.

I brought vegetables, meat, and sometimes a piece of cake for him and his wife. Usually, when I arrived with my treasures, he and his wife would eat some of it before he started the tutor session. In his garden, he kept beehives. I admired him when he went to check on his bees without any protection except for the pipe he smoked. He reached into the hive with his bare hand, pulled out one of the frames, and gently tapped the bees off the honeycomb. If the frame was filled enough, he cut off a piece of the comb for Oma.

One of the first things I had to face in Klostermansfeld was another round of vaccinations. Did the Russians think the American injections from last summer were not good enough? Now I received a second dose of serums. Not long after, my head began to itch something fierce. Mrs. Ackerman, who washed our hair once a month, notified Aunt Ursel that I had lice. Oma ran a fine-tooth comb dipped into oil through my hair. She squashed the nits between her thumbnails. It did not help. Finally, we were able to get Kuprex.[158] After they had applied it to my head and hair—I had long braids—they wrapped my hair in a huge towel. Hours later, it was washed. The stench of this cure lasted for days, no matter how often we

---

157 In my mother's eyes, they were communists out of conviction. They envisioned sharing all the riches of the earth with each other. They definitely were not Bolshevists, or members of the Communist party.

158 A substance used to wash the hair without rinsing right away. It had to stay on the head for hours.

washed my hair. I stayed home from school during that procedure, which had to be repeated after a week. It worked.

"Rosebud," Oma said, "do not get close to anybody's head; you might get lice again. So your hair won't fly all over the place and touch others, I'll fasten your braids around your head." I must have followed her advice to a T. I never had lice again.

Later in November, Uncle Martin sent me to the butcher. "Ilse-Rose, tell Mr. Probst we need him next week to slaughter two pigs and a calf. Tell him he can keep most of the calf as payment for his service."

"Don't go into the store if you see people in there," my Aunt Ursel added. "Ring the bell at the gate to their courtyard. Somebody will open it. Tell them you come from Martin Oemler and need to talk to Mr. Probst personally." I walked to the butcher shop a short mile away. There were people in the store, so I went to the courtyard door. Where was the bell I was supposed to ring? I could not see it in the normal place for doorbells. There was no button, only an old string hung from the upper part of the doorframe. I tried knocking … nobody came. I watched as people left the shop. There was a moment when all the clients had left. I entered the store. The saleslady was nowhere to be seen. I stood there and waited. A new customer entered, and the clerk came back. She addressed the lady, "May I help you?"

The shopper said politely, pointing to me, "This child was here before me."

I stammered, "Oh, I can wait; I only have a message to deliver."

"Well, tell it to me," the salesperson tried to encourage me. I shook my head. Losing patience with me, she served the lady and then more customers entered the store to buy the sausages or ham that hung against the tiled wall. The saleslady snipped their meat stamps from their ration cards. I went home.

Aunt Ursel asked me right away, "When is the butcher coming? What did he say?"

"There were people in the shop and I could not find a doorbell button on the courtyard door. I knocked, but nobody came. I waited until the shop was empty, but …"

"Well, did you speak to Mr. Probst?" she interrupted me. I shook my head. "You did not give the message to the clerk, did you?" Aunt Ursel was definitely displeased. "Stinky Rose," she said mockingly, "there is no bell button. They have a string you need to pull. It is connected to a little bell in their house. You have to learn to understand that we cannot rely on electricity in these times. An electric button would not work, but a bell on a string works without electricity. So go back and deliver the message." I went back, pulled on the old string, and a dog started to bark loudly.

"Quiet! Bad dog!" I heard. Then the door was opened a crack.

"I need to talk to Mr. Probst personally; Mr. Oemler sent me." Uncle Martin's name was magic. The door opened wide, the dog was calmed, and I was led into the house via a backdoor. I faithfully delivered my message, wondering why the grown-ups made all that fuss. I could have talked to him in the store. I was not aware of the stringent rules the Soviet government had instated. Most of the meat had to be sent to the common market. Uncle Martin did not get much pay for it, but worse than that, he would not have enough left for his workers and his family.

A week later, Mr. Probst came early in the morning. They had prepared a roaring fire underneath both kettles in the wash kitchen. The first squealing pig was brought out by its hind legs and tail. The new farm apprentice held the sow between his legs and by its ears. The butcher plunged an instrument against its forehead and pressed a button; a short bang, and the pig was numbed. The butcher opened up the main artery in its neck with a big, sharp knife. He called to me, "Bring the pail!" Aunt Ursel had given me a big bowl. I had to hold it under the spurting stream of blood and stir with a big wooden spoon, so the blood would not curdle. When the red flow subsided, I carried the bowl into the wash kitchen, put it on the table, and stood in line with the rest of the children. The butcher jokingly said, "I have to measure your mouths so I know how big I have to make your very own sausage." He used a funnel and dipped it into the cooling blood. We had to open our mouth wide so he could literally mark a blood red circle around our mouths. Later in the day, we did get our own sausage. It was even marked with our names. These round sausages were stuffed with a mixture made from the blood, tiny bits of bacon, and the brain of the pig. They had been boiled in the kettle, where other sausages were swimming in the hot broth. It was a delicacy not many Germans could enjoy in 1945.

I also helped scour the bristles off the pig's skin after it had been doused with boiling water and was thrown into the big washtub. The water was poured through a fine sieve to catch the bristles. I had to deliver these to the brush maker in our village, who was glad to receive them, but I was not to tell that we slaughtered two pigs. The old man might have wondered what type of pigs Uncle Martin raised since one pig could render so many fine bristles, but he never asked.

The second slaughter had to be done secretly after the farmworkers and household helpers had left for the day. My uncle did not want to raise suspicion. We had to work through the night and put some of the meat away in the pantry upstairs, which really used to be a bathroom but never was used for that purpose. A good part of the pork was turned into ham, bacon, and sausage. Lesser cuts were laid in brine. The salt would preserve the meat during the cool winter months.

The butcher took most of the boiled sausages home to smoke them in his smokehouse. Intermittently, Aunt Ursel sent me to his shop to get some of them. Again, no one was to know that we had butchered two pigs. By not storing all of the smoked goods in our pantry, the helpers in the house could not suspect we had a secret slaughter feast. We could not trust anybody. It was even worse than when we lived under the Nazis. Then, we at least were not suspected of being against the Hitler regime. Now, with the political affiliation of my grandfather Höfer and my father's escape from prison, we knew that we were spied on. The informers of the Soviets used the same methods as the Gestapo. Now it was the Stasis[159] who targeted children for information that could be used against the grown-ups.

The Russians, governing all farm production, ordered each farmer to deliver a certain amount of eggs, chickens, geese, ducks, milk, goats, pigs, calves, sheep, and rabbits. Not only did livestock have to be handed over, but also milk, grain, and other farm products. My uncle grew carrots, cabbage, and onions in the same field. The soil in his fields was very fertile. He brought vegetables all the way to Leipzig for the common market. He was paid very little for these. He was expected to share his produce and animals with everyone. If the delivery of the assigned foodstuffs fell short, the farmer had to pay with other commodities or land in prison.

We soon needed all the food we could secretly put aside. When I arrived in early November 1945, I met Aunt Bitta and her family again. Aunt Ursel's mother had come from Cottbus, and Aunt Bohne had to leave Berlin-Charlottenburg. She would have starved to death if she stayed there. She was the mother-in-law of Aunt Hilde. Aunt Bohne could not join her daughter-in-law in Heidelberg because at that time in West Germany, food was just as hard to come by as in Berlin. Aunt Hilde's house was overflowing with people too, for whom she and Uncle Willi had to supply room. The two

---

159 *Stasi* is an abbreviation the East Germans used for *Ministerium für Staatssicherheit*, which means "Ministry of State Security."

elderly ladies had joined Aunt Ursel's friend and her baby. In early January 1946, my mother arrived with Hildegard and Reinhold.

Every one of us needed a place to sleep. My three cousins—Hermjörg, Lutz, and Jochen—slept in the small nursery off the master bedroom. For Eberhard Fleisher, the new apprentice, Oma and Aunt Ursel had prepared the room where the Russian women as civil workers had formerly stayed. The mother from Silesia with her six children had orders to move out. Her room was given to a family of four from the Baltic area. The Soviet Union soon started the largest exodus in history. The family from the Baltics was one out of the millions of families who were forced from their homes because the Soviet Union had acquired parts of former German, Hungarian, Polish, and Austrian areas. The Russians wanted to make sure that no Germans remained in these newly added lands under Soviet control.

The Stammtisch met at their pub again and talked about the new flood of people who were sent from the now Bolshevist-occupied areas. The farmer opened their conversation. "Margret, the innkeeper's daughter, runs this place rather well, don't you think?"

The former mayor, now released from interrogation, agreed. "She knows how to draw a good glass of beer. She and her mother recuperated rather fast. I guess in these times, you are forced not to mourn for too long." He knew it too well. He did not have enough time to grieve when his son was killed during the battle in Normandy.

They had met with Leipziger and Berliner. Hamburger had already left for his hometown, which was now occupied by the British forces. As soon as the relocation of displaced people had started under the control of the Allied forces, he had applied to go back to Hamburg. He wanted to find a place where his family could live, in hopes that they could join him soon. Leipziger and Berliner were not so keen on going back to their cities. Just like Hamburg, these areas were still in rubble, but that was not the main reason why they hesitated to relocate. Their cities were now under Russian control. Berliner wanted to find out which one of the sectors[160] would be assigned to him to reside in. His question was, "Will we have to live in an area controlled by the French, the Americans, the British, or the Russians?" Therefore he waited, especially since not all of his family had come with him to the village. He was still searching for his wife and youngest son.

---

160 Berlin was divided among the four Allies. The Russian sector was the biggest part of Berlin.

Berliner wondered what jobs would be available for him and his Stammtisch members, although Leipziger had been offered a position as a teacher at the elementary school. Of course, it was clear to him that the farmer continued to work his fields. He asked the mayor, "What are you doing now, since you lost your job as mayor?"

"I am helping the Red Cross relocate people, but more importantly, I help families to find each other again. You know how crowded our trains were when the people fled from the east. Many children were separated from their mothers and siblings. The Red Cross and other missions have taken care of these children, but their families are anxious to find them." He sighed and continued, "They asked me to help since I know how to keep records of people, how to file and …"

Berliner hit himself on his forehead and yelled, interrupting the mayor. "My, oh my, Mayor—I hope you do not mind that I still call you that—it is your voice I hear every night after the news on the radio, enumerating the many people who are looking for their relatives, and later on, describing the children who need to find their parents!"

The mayor nodded and said, "To make it simple for all of you, call me Mayor. I do not know what you would call my occupation right now, anyway."

"Radio announcer!" Berliner suggested.

"Family-reuniting-clerk of the Red Cross." Leipziger would come up with a lengthy title like that. After all, he had been a librarian before.

"Red Cross Helper," the farmer chuckled. He grinned since Red Cross Helpers usually were female nurses.

The mayor told them that the Red Cross was getting good responses to its search efforts. People who were looking for their relatives would call the radio station, and many of the missing ones answered within hours. He remarked, "The first attempts to locate lost relatives were just little notes pinned on makeshift bulletin boards at train or police stations."

"Yes, I have seen them," the farmer cut in, and added, "They would read: 'Anja Meyer is here; inquire at the school.' Or they gave an address or phone number where they could be reached."

The former mayor nodded. "But that left it up to chance if their relative would ever read the note, and young children could not read them. Yes, when it comes to lost children, we have an especially hard time. Ask a toddler his or her name, where he used to live, his or her age. It is impossible to get accurate information … and then, there are the soldiers who came home to find bombed houses. Their families have been evacuated, or were injured or died in a bombing raid."

"Yes, these are awful times for displaced people," the farmer agreed. Wanting to play cards instead of discussing all the problems they faced, he suggested, "Well, we will not solve all of these problems tonight. Let's have a good round of Skat. Berliner, it's your turn to deal." He shuffled the cards, and Berliner dealt the mayor a very good hand.

They were playing with concentration, looking into their cards, when a fist appeared on the table, knocking the traditional "Good evening."[161] All of them looked up. The mayor and the farmer stared at the somewhat familiar face. They recognized it, only it had changed so much. Finally, the farmer remembered it. He pushed back his chair, jumped up, and exclaimed, "Man, Pharmacist, I don't believe it. It's you!!"

The pharmacist nodded and answered in a hoarse voice, "It's me."

"But we heard you were ambushed by the partisans."

"There is truth to that. My whole company was, but I was not with them. I had dysentery. They let me lie in a horse stable, not able to take care of me, thinking I might die. But I packed myself into the horse manure filled with ammonia. It created the heat I needed. When I felt better, I could not find my company again. Found out that all of them had been killed. So I tried to avoid the partisans and the German military. I spoke little, gave myself another name, and worked with a doctor in a remote village in the former Polish area."

"Polish area?" the farmer wondered. "You were in Yugoslavia, right? Why go north?"

The pharmacist continued, "I know a little Polish, and before the war ended, many Germans still lived up there who did not want to flee and leave their businesses, factories, or farms when the Russians came. There were German troops. I tried to report to the German military, but just like in Yugoslavia, when I was on my way, hellish fighting started again, and I, without a gun—what could I do? Before I knew it, the Russians had control of that area again. It went back and forth several times between the opposing armies. The doctor had his hands full with so many injured people, and not all of them were hurting because of the fighting, but because

---

161 In Germany, when you arrive a little late and join your familiar group of students or Stammtisch members, you knock on the table to say "good evening" instead of shaking everybody's hand.

of the Russians, who took their revenge on the German civilians, especially on the women. I do not like to talk about this."

"We understand," the farmer said.

Leipziger was curious; he wanted to know how the pharmacist came back to his village. He asked, "But how were you able to come back here?"

"When the war was over and the borders between the Allies in Germany were established, the Russians forced all Germans to leave the now reestablished Poland under Soviet control. The Russians pushed the doctor and me, along with all the other ethnic Germans, to the station. They crammed us into an open wagon. Mind you, it had no roof. Animals are transported better than we were." The pharmacist sighed, "And we were even the lucky ones. We did not need to walk away. It was cold; we stood so close to each other that no one could sit down. We could not even help the sick, who would faint and lean on others with buckled knees. They brought us to Berlin first. When we exited the train, many a person's body collapsed … dead." All of them were quiet. What can one say when faced with this type of war aftermath?

The pharmacist continued after a short pause, "In Berlin, we were ordered into tents or barracks until they gave us the command in which part of Germany to relocate. We were shipped to various Allied occupied zones. The ones from Poland either stayed in the Russian sector or went to the British sector."

The farmer knew about it. He had to give rooms to people who had been thrown from their homes in the former Polish/German area. He noted, "I heard that the Soviets ousted over 3.5 million people who had any German affiliation. Ethnic cleansing, I call it."

"I can tell you many stories about it," the pharmacist replied. "Farmer, you said 3.5 million had to be absorbed from the Baltic and Polish areas, but what about the people from Czechoslovakian, former Austrian, and Hungarian areas?"

"I know about these," the mayor interrupted. "They were sent to the French and American sectors. I heard there were about 3 million as well. We at the Red Cross Search Station have the grim job of telling surviving relatives that their loved ones might have been among the estimated 2,111,000 people who died during these Soviet-ordered transports."[162]

---

162 Many people did not survive the transport in open train wagons, in trucks, or on foot.

"I don't know where these displaced people will find room," Leipziger wondered.

"Well, look here. My farmhouse is overflowing with people, and Berliner had to give up one of his two rooms to another family of four, whereas he himself has two children."

"And he is waiting to find his wife and his youngest son again," the mayor added.

Berliner sighed, "I am afraid they died on their way from East Prussia to here."

The mayor tried to comfort him. "You will find them. Just give your information to the Red Cross. We do our best to locate family members and to find out what happened to them."

They did not continue their card game that night. They listened to the pharmacist's grim, adventurous story and told him what had taken place at home—the innkeeper's suicide, the teacher's disappearance, and the farmer's crushed head.

After our farm had been confiscated, my mother was told to leave St. Bernhard and its district in a matter of a few days. By St. Nicholas Day,[163] she arrived with Hildegard and Reinhold in Edersleben. They stayed with our great-grandmother for six weeks. Ernst still lived at the woman's place in Gotha in order to go to high school. Hildegard went to school in Edersleben. On Christmas 1945, I was with the many relatives in Klostermansfeld while my father was with my mother, Hildegard, Reinhold, and Ernst at my great-grandmother's apartment.

My mother asked Ernst, "How did you like the bread and smoked ham I sent?"

"What bread and ham?" he asked back.

"The package I sent a week ago, just like all the other packages with food I have sent."

"I never got any of that food, Mother," Ernst said.

My mother turned to my father. "Herbert, look how skinny Ernst has gotten. We have to get him away from that woman. He will starve at her place."

My father promised that he would bring Ernst to Klostermansfeld as

---

163 St. Nicolas Day is December 6. Children put one shoe in front of their bedroom door on the night of the fifth to find it stuffed with cookies the next morning. If they had not been good, they only would find a piece of coal or a dry tree branch.

soon as it was fairly safe for him to do so. He left soon after the holidays. As long as he was hiding from the Russians under a different name, he did not dare stay in one place for long. His brother, Uncle Hans, had been arrested and was not able to escape. We suspected he was brought to the concentration camp Buchenwald, but we had no proof of it.[164] For many years, my Aunt Ida hesitated to declare that he died so she could claim the pension[165] for soldiers' widows.

In January 1946, my uncle's house saw an influx of relatives. After Uncle Martin helped Mrs. Kleefeld with her four children to get to the station so they could go back to Berlin, my mother came from Edersleben with Hildegard and Reinhold. I joined them in the two rooms Mrs. Kleefeld had occupied. Somehow, Oma had arranged for a huge double bed. It was big enough for Hildegard, my mother, little Reinhold, and me to sleep in. The other room had a sofa, some chairs, and a table. At the beginning of our stay in Klostermansfeld, we did not use it as a dining room. We ate with all the other relatives downstairs in the everyday dining room in the old farmhouse. There were sixteen people for the noontime dinner. A small table was set for the five younger children. In the evening, the toddlers ate in the kitchen and had to go to bed before we ate. There were still eleven people at the table. Soon after, we had to eat in shifts.

By January 16, 1946, Aunt Magda with her husband, Uncle Richard, and their daughter, Ingrid, came to Klostermansfeld. Their farm had fallen under the land reform.[166] They, as did my family, had to leave the district where their farm was located. Uncle Richard bred beautiful horses. The Russians who had taken over his big house tried to ride his purebred animals. His heart almost broke when he saw how these beautiful stallions and mares were treated. The Russians used neither saddles nor the most basic riding gear. A halter and a whip was all they needed.

Uncle Richard only stayed a few hours until Uncle Martin could help

---

164 After 1990, my cousin Marlis researched the Stasi documents. Years later, she found out that her father died at the concentration camp Buchenwald in 1946.

165 After the western sectors formed a new government called the Federal Republic of Germany (FRG) between 1948–49, all widows and orphans of soldiers who fought in WWII continued to receive a portion of their husband's pension, even if they had moved to other countries. After Germany was united again in 1990, my aunt declared my uncle dead and applied for this pension.

166 Originally, the four Allies concluded that all the big estates and factories had to be confiscated. It mostly only affected estates in the Russian sector. See also Chapter 9, footnote 153.

him reach the border. He crossed into the British sector successfully and from there entered the American sector to meet his brother, Uncle Willi, in Heidelberg, who helped him to secure a new position on a farm owned by Austrian nobility.

Shortly after Aunt Magda and Ingrid arrived, Aunt Lisbeth and her three young sons (about the same age as Aunt Ursel's children) needed shelter. Her husband was not with her. He left immediately for the western sectors to look for work after his farm was confiscated. Aunt Lisbeth could not go to her mother's place, since Aunt Klärchen's huge estate, located in the most fertile area of Germany, fell under the land reform. She also came to live in Klostermansfeld. They all ate in shifts, but my mother decided to bring the food upstairs to our two rooms.

In spite of the danger of being ratted on by the woman who had taken Ernst's packages, my father went to Gotha to get my brother and bring him to Klostermansfeld. Cousin Ingrid lent Ernst her bicycle so he could ride it to school. His school was located in Eisleben, about ten kilometers[167] (six miles) away. He returned late every afternoon. Once a week, he attended confirmation classes at our Protestant church.

Hildegard and I went to pre-confirmation class on Wednesday afternoons. The Russians allowed these meetings because they were called youth gatherings, a name that is without any indication of Christianity. They, like the Nazis before, wanted to indoctrinate us children against the grown-ups and win us over to the Communist ideology. They celebrated certain days of the year. One of the most elaborate was the first of May, Labor Day. Workers had to erect a huge pole near the sport field. It served as Maibaum.[168] We watched the strongest boys as they tried to climb the slippery post. Not many could reach the top to pick one of the treasures hanging from the wagon wheel. The smaller children just looked on and clapped if one succeeded. We received hot dogs and rolls with hot chocolate. For many of us, it was a treat we had not tasted for a long time. Then we marched in rows of four to eight children. All of us were ordered to form a large human square around a podium. Here, a party leader addressed us. I thought his speech would never end. Afterward, we were allowed to go home. Every celebration was the same, except for the Maibaum. Sometimes

---

167 One kilometer equals 0.621371192 miles.

168 This is a telephone-pole-like mast. It sports a wagon wheel on top from which sausages, hams, bacons, and the like are hung. Children were encouraged to climb the waxed pole. At the top, they could pick one of the delicacies and take it home.

we had to wait hours before we could march, especially during the cold winter days, but we always would get some kind of hot dog. The Communist leaders tried to drill, imbue, and implant their ideology into us children. Slowly, they tried to undermine affiliations with any church.

In 1954, they instituted an alternative for confirmations—the fourteen- to sixteen-year-old girls and boys could have a special induction ceremony instead of being confirmed. If the family chose dedication to the Communist party over confirmation, they received favors. Over the course of the forty years under Soviet control, many young Germans in the former Russian zone still prefer the Jugendweihe[169] instead of a confirmation in the Christian tradition, much to the chagrin of the West Germans. One of my professors, Dr. Rio Preisner, told me that it takes at least two generations before the influence of a dictatorship will be lessened. He knew what he was talking about. After he lectured at the university in Czechoslovakia under Soviet rule,[170] he was ousted and worked in salt mines as a political prisoner. His crime: he wanted to stay loyal to the Catholic Church.

In March 1946, my father visited again. He only wanted to stay long enough to bring Cousin Ingrid across the border into the British zone. Her father would meet them there. The Russians started to be more protective of their border with the western zones. My father was familiar with several border-crossing points where you could find cover when the Russians started to shoot. My cousin told me that they were a party of four when they left for the dangerous border crossing. When the shooting started, my father threw himself on the ground and pulled Ingrid down with him. Then they crept through the furrows of a field, but the two marine officers who were with them did not survive the Soviet bullets. My father and cousin could not help them; they would have been the next victims. They had to lie absolutely still in their furrow. During the night, they finally could move again and cross the border.

After my father brought Ernst to Klostermansfeld as he had promised, he decided that Grandma should leave St. Bernhard and join us. We divided one of our two rooms into a combined bed and living room. A big tall closet served as a separation wall, and behind it stood Ernst's bed. Reinhold's bed

---

169 To this day, in May, they celebrate it instead of a confirmation in the former Soviet-controlled states of Germany. It is not necessarily anymore a dedication to the Communist party, but an acknowledgment that the teens are now young adults.

170 In 1968, he was able to come to America via Austria during the Czech uprising.

and my bed were on one side of the closet and Grandma's and Hildegard's were on the other side. Whenever Father showed up, all of us slept and stayed in the living room, because we had to hide him in the other room.

Grandma was a great help to my mother, who often was not at home. All of my relatives said, "Paula knows how to deal with the police, with legalities, the Russians, and all the ever-changing regulations for us." Therefore, she ran errands for everyone. My mother was instrumental in helping Aunt Magda get permission to join her husband in the American zone. She even arranged for her sister to be allowed to store some of her belongings with friends until these could be transported to the little village in which her husband had found employment. He farmed for an Austrian count who owned land near Heidelberg.

Aunt Bitta and Aunt Mertens left for a nearby village where their relatives had a farm. They had to wait until the refugees and evacuees there had been ordered to go back to their hometowns, thus making room for them. Aunt Bohne was instructed to go back to Berlin. My mother made sure the old lady would receive permission to visit us often. I am positive that when my mother secured documents for my relatives, the authorities gave her the runaround. She did not get tired of it. She just wore *them* out.

She told us how she was able to get our old hope chest back, which we could not take along when we were ordered to leave St. Bernhard.

She said, "I sat stoically on the police station's steps until they got tired of me and allowed me to take possession of it again."

Aunt Lisbeth's husband and my father had the hardest time finding a place for their families to live. None of us "ousted" people were looking for a place in the Russian zone. All of us hoped for employment in the western zones.

In early summer, Uncle Martin was diagnosed with jaundice. Soon his three sons had it too, and after they were almost through with six weeks on the strictest diet, I came down with it. I laid in one of the beds in our living room/bedroom. I was only allowed to eat toasted white bread. Any fat was out of the question, along with fruits and vegetables. I had to survive on only water and bread. We had not seen white bread for ages. Oma must have used her persuasive skills (combined with a "present" of vegetables or meat) to have the baker make some loaves for our family.

Grandma did not think that this diet was a good way to get healthy again. She also knew how much I liked the lentil soup Oma had cooked for everybody. She told me, "Rosebud, you may taste some, just chew on it and then spit it out again. You may not swallow it." I took a spoonful. Now, you try to chew soup without getting any of it in your stomach! "Rosebud, you are not spitting everything out that you had in your mouth."

"Grandma, I try, but it just runs down my throat."

"Well, I have to take it away from you." She gathered my spoon and dish, but she still had pity on me.

"I'll fry some bread in a little butter for you; you have to spit it out, but it will be easier for you to get rid of." She used the last butter she had left on her ration card for this delicacy. I chewed very slowly and spewed it on the plate. I did not want any more; it had made me instantly, horribly sick. After six weeks, I was healthy again, but rather weak. Nevertheless, I had learned how to knit the most durable heels for socks, because Grandma sat at my bedside and knitted while telling stories to me. During my illness, she patiently taught me more of the art of knitting and crocheting complicated garments. Where did she get yarn for it? She unraveled worn-out socks or sweaters, wetted the yarn, and wound it around a board. After it dried, it could be reused.

Although we were under Soviet control, we were allowed to celebrate certain events—for instance the *Fasching* or "carnival"[171] season. Everybody dressed up in costumes and wore a mask. Nobody was supposed to know who the disguised person was until midnight. There were prizes for the best or most original costumes. People could behave rather differently than normal, hidden under their masks. They danced and drank a lot.

On New Year's Eve 1946, my Uncle Martin and Aunt Ursel left for a party at a friend's place. They hitched the horses to a sled, and they took warm blankets, heated foot warmers, covers for the horses, and lanterns for the nightly drive back home. Oma always smiled. She liked for all of us to have fun. She would say, "Now, Martin, don't you drink too much! You know you have to drive home!"

Uncle Martin laughed. "You know, Mother, even if I get tipsy, the horses know their way home. I do not need to do anything."

"Yes, I know. Just get into the carriage, all right? Let the reins hang loose, say *hü*, and fall asleep until the horses stop in front of our gate," she added.

With Uncle Martin and Aunt Ursel gone, Aunt Klärchen and Oma wanted us to have a nice New Year's Eve festival too. We were allowed to stay

---

171 It officially starts on 11/11 at 11:11 p.m. and lasts until Ash Wednesday. In most areas of Germany, the festivities are on weekends and really do not start until February.

up late. The younger children were asleep by nine o'clock. Intermittently, one of us checked on them. On New Year's Eve, games were allowed that supposedly foretold the future, as long as we understood this was entertainment and had nothing to do with the truth. Aunt Klärchen showed us how to melt lead and pour it into cold water. She told us, "The formed lead that you find on the bottom of the pan tells the future." I took my spoon with melted lead and poured a big blob. Could that be a baby in a cradle? Hildegard, more careful than I, gingerly let the lead flow into the water, and a delicate filigree shape emerged. "You can read anything out of this or nothing at all," Aunt Klärchen said. Then we would peel apples. "You have to start at its blossom," instructed Aunt Klärchen, "and pare down to its stem without breaking the peel. Then take the peel into your right hand and walk to the door; facing the room, throw it over your shoulder to the floor. See, it forms a letter. This is the first letter of your future husband's name." I peeled very thinly and threw the rind; it formed a *J*. Hildegard's landed in an *H*. To make sure—and really, because the apples tasted so good—we peeled another one and threw the peel again. Mine formed a *J* and Hildegard's a *D* this time.

"This really does not tell anything," my sister concluded. She had two different letters, but I thought that mine resembled a J twice. It is a funny coincidence that my husband's name is James and Hildegard's is Hans Dieter, but apple peels really do not form letters of the alphabet.

The electricity had been turned off long ago. We sat around an oil lamp with one of those pretty lampshades that Oma kept in the upper attic. Aunt Klärchen played all kinds of games with us. I never grew tired. At midnight, we were allowed to drink a little of the Glühwein[172] Aunt Klärchen had prepared. She showed us how to toast by gently clicking the Jenaer glasses[173] together. She said, "When you are older, you can drink real wine out of glasses with a stem. Then, hold the glass by its stem. The clicking sounds so much more melodious when you toast that way." She demonstrated it. She was right. Then she showed us how different a glass "sings" when half full, filled to the brim, or just a little. She wet her finger and circled around the glass rim with it until it started to hum. Now we tried it. *We are creating a real concert*, I thought. Then, it was time to go to bed. This was a much

---

172 *Glühwein* means "glowing wine." It is made from red wine mixed with water, cinnamon sticks, some cloves, and sugar. You consume it when hot or at least very warm. Sometimes they add a little rum to it.

173 In Jena, Thuringia, they produced a glass that can withstand very high temperatures. Germans like to drink tea out off these glasses.

better evening than Christmas Eve, when I had been without my siblings and parents and had to watch the toddlers who had been rather cranky.

I had so much in common with Aunt Klärchen. Both of us liked to play cards, we liked to tell stories, and we were good at bookkeeping. We loved puzzle games, crosswords, or jigsaw. We liked all kinds of social entertainment. We liked to cook. She was my favorite godmother. She soon left to live with friends in the Harz Mountains. Since she always stayed in the Russian zone and I went to the western zones in 1947, I never had the pleasure of spending time with her again.

One time, when my father came, he was covered with sores and boils because of malnutrition. He needed good food and medical care. How my mother managed to provide it, I never found out. This time, hiding Father was worse than before. I had to watch what I said even more. Again, my best friend was not allowed to visit us.

Father was cooped up in his room and bored. When he saw me drawing a picture of spring flowers for my schoolwork, he took the paper and drew a beautiful picture of snowdrops. His action created a dilemma for me. Since paper was very scarce, I only had that one piece for my homework. I turned the paper over and penciled my spring flowers on it, hoping nobody would see my father's sketch on the back of it. I kept thinking, *How can I take his drawing to school? Won't they question me about it, if I show this in class? Everybody can see that I did not draw that picture. Should I lie?* I had just learned the Ten Commandments in our pre-confirmation class, and wanted to follow those commandments.

I had made a commitment to Jesus, the only person I knew who never had changed according to the various governments. He was the same two thousand years ago. He was not like the many grown-ups and children (influenced at home) who saluted, by now, the third flag. Miss Karsdorf had made us sing and pledge to the red, white, and black swastika flag. After the Americans entered, she had us pledge to the red, white, and blue star-and-stripe one. After she was ousted by the Russians, we had to greet their red flag with hammer and sickle, holding our right fists up high. Soon Germans received new flags. In all four occupied zones these were red, black, and yellow. Later, after 1948, the DDR[174] added the hammer and sickle, but that

---

174 DDR stands for *Deutsche Demokratische Republik*; in English, "German Democratic Republic" (GDR). BRD stands for *Bundesrepublik Deutschland*; in English, "Federal Republic of Germany" (FRG). From then on, history had to deal with two German governments.

one, I never needed to respect. By then I was in the British zone and greeted the red, black, and yellow one with the eagle of the BRD.

I believed that according to the Bible lying was a sin, but so was betraying my father—and not obeying my parents was another sin.

When we had to show our homework in school, I carefully laid my paper down. I tried to hide the side on which Father drew the flowers, but my friend alongside of me saw the back page. She whispered, "You did not draw this, did you?" What was I to say? The whole morning, I had dreaded this moment and had prayed that no one would see his drawing, and now, she even asked me about it.

At the moment Klärchen had mumbled, the teacher looked at us. "Who spoke?" she asked disapprovingly. We raised our hands. "Don't speak when I try to teach!" she scolded. Good, now I was not allowed to speak, so I did not need to answer Klärchen's question.

However, I dreaded the walk home with my friend. Would she ask me again about who drew the picture? Should I lie? Should I betray my father? But this time, she looked at me and my knitted cap, which was too small for me; after all, we had lost everything and wore whatever we were given, whether it fitted or not. She said, "If you wear this hood, I am not walking with you. You look ridiculous." As painful as it was to hear my best friend talk to me in such a way, I was relieved that I did not need to walk home with her and face the dilemma of lying to her or betraying my father. The next morning, when I met my girlfriend on the way to school, she asked me again. "Who drew the picture?" and I could answer truthfully, "My father." Did I betray him? No, because that night, my father had left and crossed the Russian border successfully.

My sister and I hardly had any clothing left, since we were outgrowing the few things we had. One day, the Russian police discovered hidden materials, yarns, and all kinds of sewing goods under the floorboards of a former shop that had belonged to a Jewish family who left before I was born. These things were hauled onto a truck. The German truck driver, employed by the Soviets, drove very slowly through the village. Helga's grandma yelled, "Eh, what are you waiting for? This stuff belongs to us and is not for the Russians." She jumped on the truck and began to throw things off.

My mother stood on the curb in amazement. *This noble communist deprives her Russian comrades of that good material,* she thought. In the next moment, she heard the woman call, "Mrs. Höfer, here, take this for your girls." My mother caught several yards of first-class Scottish woolen plaid and several skeins of yarn. Oma knew a good seamstress who sewed skirts for my sister and me from the expensive material. She paid her with ham and milk.

Grandma used the yarn to knit reddish-brown jackets for us. For years, we had worn clothing made out of unraveled yarn. This reused wool scratched our skin rather badly. My sister could hardly stand it, but I clung to the old cliché, "the Spartans are tough, so am I." What did I know about the Spartans and their warmer climate, or their clothing? I pushed myself through anything that seemed unbearable with the thought of the tough Spartans.

After my great-grandmother died in the summer of 1946, we were allowed to transport some of her furniture. Oma was her only legal heir. She inherited the household goods and gave all of them to us. Uncle Martin and Ernst brought them to Klostermansfeld. Now we owned pots and pans again.

The last time my father visited us was on Ernst's confirmation on Palm Sunday in 1947. Uncle Martin, Aunt Ursel, and Oma did not spare their provisions. They prepared a feast for all of us. On Monday, my father walked downstairs, through the courtyard, and into the gentlemen's room to thank Uncle Martin for the festive dinner. Several people who knew him had seen him.

A few hours went by, and then a woman climbed upstairs to talk to my mother. "I have to speak with you, Paula," she whispered shyly. "I was at the mayor's office, and while I was there, I saw a letter on his desk. I saw that they are asking again for the whereabouts of your husband."

"Thank you for telling me," my mother said and added, knowing it was a lie, "I myself have no idea where he is. Yes, sometimes he comes, but he never stays long."

The woman left, and my mother went downstairs to catch Father before he would leave the room. "You must hide here until nightfall and then leave. They are looking for you again and suspect you are here."

He nodded. "I'll take Ernst with me. We can stay with Uncle Reinhold in Goslar."

That night, my father and my brother successfully crossed the border. Now they both were out of the Russian zone and in the British sector. Father found a place for us to live in Hamelin. Here, he could be Herbert Höfer again. He was glad to shed his false name. Now he did not need to stay under cover anymore. The days of hiding him were over for us.

Chapter 11

Hamelin

In 1947, we received permission to cross the Russian/British border and join my father and brother. In order not to stay in a cellar or camp,[175] my father contacted Mrs. Homburg, the widow of his former army major. She lived in Hamelin with her three children and her younger cousin; she already shared her five-room apartment with Major Frisch, his pregnant wife, and their five-year-old daughter, Wolftraut. Mrs. Homburg gave us one room on my father's promise to assist her in taking care of her garden located on the outskirts of town. His help was not so much in preparing the soil and sowing seeds, but rather taking turns with Cousin Kappauf in watching that nobody stole the crops. He also agreed that my mother would cook for all of us, including the uncle of the Homburg family who visited occasionally. My mother developed quite a skill in creating meals with the little food available, and with only two hours of electricity per day. We shared the kitchen with the Frisch family. They owned a stove but needed to use the sink and part of the pantry that was divided into four sections: Homburg, Frisch, Kappauf, and our family.

Hamelin had seen numerous bombing raids, especially the destruction of its station and the surrounding homes. Our five-floor apartment house, located very close to the railroad overpass, had been damaged. We lived on its second floor that was on the same level as one of the many railroad tracks. Our windows had been broken and only a few could be repaired with glass.

---

175 Usually, displaced people had to stay in a camp until they could find a place to live. Cellars were accepted as suitable living quarters.

We covered the rest with cardboard, old splintering plywood, or blankets. The balcony had lost its railing. The door leading to it could not be locked. After the Frisches' second child was born in 1947 and started to crawl, we constantly had to watch that she did not push this door open and fall from the balcony. The Frisch family lived in one bedroom adjacent to the kitchen, with bunk beds, a small chest, a coal stove, three chairs, and a card table. We had six bunk beds in the corner room, facing the railway where freight trains stopped to fill their steam engines with water. We constantly fought the soot from the locomotives' stacks.

Soon after we joined my father, he found three small wardrobes for us. They stood in the hallway. That was all the furniture we owned. We did not need more since Mrs. Homburg let us use her dining room. She, her daughter, and her youngest son occupied her former bedroom. When her older son visited, he stayed in the same room with Cousin Kappauf, either in the dining room or the living room.

At the beginning of our stay in Hamelin, my father worked for the British guards at a prison camp. He searched for food in their garbage cans, but not often, since the British had suffered food shortages during and after the war too. They hardly had leftovers and seldom threw anything edible away. They also tried to recuperate.

After the war, many Germans died of malnutrition or froze to death. Potatoes were a luxury; not many people had bread or vegetables, much less meat. Every Wednesday, my sister and I would go to a place where they slaughtered horses and boiled the meat and bones. We would stand in a long line hoping to get our little bucket filled with that broth, and when we were lucky, a bit of fat might be swimming on top. It was a welcome addition to our ration cards' food allowance. The saying prevailed: "Too little to live on, too much to die with."

Many European nations received America's help earlier than we in Germany did. It was George Marshall who voiced his concern about the war-torn nations facing famine and economic crisis in the wake of World War II. According to an account on the site of the U.S. National Archives & Records Administration:

> On June 5, 1947, in a commencement address at Harvard University, Secretary of State George C. Marshall first called for American assistance in restoring the economic infrastructure of Europe. Western Europe responded favorably, and the Truman administration proposed

legislation. The resulting Economic Cooperation Act of [April 3,] 1948 restored European agricultural and industrial productivity. Credited with preventing famine and political chaos, the plan later earned General Marshall a Nobel Peace Prize.[176]

The Stammtisch met in 1947. As usual, the farmer opened the conversation. "Does anybody know how Berliner is making out back in his hometown?"

The former mayor answered him. "Well, he did locate his wife and youngest son. He found them in a camp for people to be relocated in Berlin."

The pharmacist, who had regained his job in the local drugstore, asked, "In which sector of Berlin is he living?"

"He was lucky. He and his family were moved to the French sector," the mayor informed him. He would have liked to add aloud, "At least he is not under Communist control," but fearing somebody might denounce him, he only uttered it under his breath.

"Hush!" the farmer whispered. "You know, ever since the KPD merged with the SPD and formed the Sozialistische Einheitspartei Deutschlands,[177] we have to continually watch out. It is just like under the Nazis and their Gestapo. Now it is the Stasi.[178] Who can you trust?"

At that moment, a young pastor who had just moved to the area joined the Stammtisch members. "What's new?" he asked. "Discussing the different controls of the four Allies? Eh! I tell you, we under the Soviets have it better than the people in the American zone, where they have to fill out questionnaires to determine that they were not Nazis."[179]

---

176 "The Marshall Plan," Featured Documents, National Archives & Records Administration, http://www.archives.gov/exhibits/featured_documents/marshall_plan/.

177 SED in English stands for Social Unity Party of Germany. It was formed under the Russian-controlled merger of the Communist Party of Germany (KPD) and the Social Democratic Party of Germany (SPD) in April 1946. They adopted a programmatic document of principles and goals of the party.

178 See Chapter 10, footnote 159.

179 It is estimated that about 8.5 million Germans belonged to the Nazi party. Many of the government workers were not convinced of the Nazi program, but they would have lost their jobs if they did not join the NSDAP. By 1946, the Soviets had ousted all former NSDAP members if they fit into one of the five categories the Allies had established in January 1946. It took until the end of 1946 before the controlling government of all four sectors agreed on a consistent procedure to "cleanse" Germany of Nazis.

"Good evening, Pastor." They knocked with their fists on the table as reply to the clergy, who had disregarded the customary way of greeting.

"Sorry! I did not know you still hold to this old tradition. I heard you need a few more members for your Skat round. I thought you would not mind if I join you."

The Stammtisch members looked at each other … and then the mayor nodded and pulled a chair up for him. "You are in. Tell us where you come from."

The pastor sat down and started to shuffle the cards. Not answering the question, he said, "It is funny, you had the confiscation of many farms, even the ones that were no bigger than the 100 hectares. We in the American zone saw hardly any of this."

The farmer asked, "Well, where in the American sector—I mean, Bavaria, Hessen, and Baden Württemberg—do you find such huge estates as we had?" In his mind, he questioned the motives that led the new clergy to move to the Soviet sector. Why did he not answer the question about his hometown?

The minister replied quickly, "Wait a minute! Baden Württemberg is split into the north for the Americans, whereas South Baden Württemberg, the Saar Basin, even part of Tirol are under French control. They did experience the land reform, although to a limited degree! Usually the owners of the estates could keep the hunting rights to their forest and only the lumber became communal property. None of the owners needed to leave their homes."

"But there were bigger farms in the British zone; what happened to them?" asked the pharmacist.

"Reduced, but not all confiscated. Parceled out to poor farmworkers, cottagers, and expellees from Poland and Lithuania, just like here." The new minister seemed to know a lot about the four occupied zones in Germany.

"As far as I know, none of the Western allies dismantled and transported all of our still-functioning factories as part of the war reparations," the mayor remarked.

The farmer agreed. "Yes, I heard something to that effect too. The Brits and Americans only stripped or demolished the factories that supplied the arsenals of the German military."

The conversation became too disquieting for the pharmacist. He suspected the new clergyman to be an informer for the Stasi. He pondered, *Maybe the new pastor tries to cajole us into saying things that can be held against us.* He had reasons to be afraid of voicing an opinion that might become troublesome for him. The Stasi seemed willing to arrest anybody who said something against the newly established government under the Russian Communists' control. He switched to another topic: the ration cards, which now included restrictions on clothing, coal, and utensils.

"Ration cards!" the pharmacist complained. "They are worth as much as our money, namely nothing. They have no value. We still had stamps left for a half loaf of bread. My wife stood in a long line trying to get it, just to find out that the store was all out of bread. So she had to go on a hamster trip."[180] The pharmacist turned to the farmer, saying, "Farmer, you have it made now, with the black market thriving."

All of them chimed in with their observations.

"Your drawers must fill up with silver."

"Your wife will sport all kinds of jewelry."

"You probably received first editions of rare books."

"Do you have some paintings, maybe a masterpiece, hanging in your living room by now?"

"How many fur coats can your wife select from, when she visits her friends?"

The farmer took a deep breath and shouted, "Stop, let me get a word in edgewise. Do you think it is easy to figure out how much to give for a silver spoon? You see that poor woman on her hamster trip, peddling her last belongings for bread, vegetables, just anything to eat. I do not have it so easy either. I need to get my grain turned into flour, let the miller have part of it as payment, same with the butcher when he slaughters my animals, and the dairy when I want some butter from them—and then, there is the new government who wants most of my harvest. I have to be careful not to haggle away any of it."

"Well, farmer, I saw you unloading a centrifuge.[181] Aren't you churning your own cream now?" the pastor laughed.

The farmer's face turned red. He went to the bar and ordered schnapps. He was afraid their conversation had become too dangerous for them. Who was that minister, and what was his purpose to join them? The black market was forbidden! Why did they ever talk about it in front of this stranger? Meanwhile, the pharmacist, mayor, and clergyman smiled, silently sharing the same thought: *I know where I can bargain for some extra butter now.* Well,

---

180 So-called because people would travel with knapsacks to the country to barter with farmers for food.

181 A centrifuge is used to separate the milk from its butterfat, which then can be used for whipped cream or be churned into butter.

maybe the pastor only tried to make them believe that he was thinking about bargaining for butter.

My mother, too, bartered some of her silver flatware off for food. She had rescued our silverware several times, first from Thorn and later from the Soviets and again from the Volkspolizei[182] in the Russian zone. Since Mrs. Homburg had lived in the Hamelin area for many years, she was the one who mainly went on hamster trips. She knew the farmers who would be willing to trade for food with her.

My mother, not to be outdone, tried to stay in contact with Uncle Martin and Oma, who would share their victuals, but they lived in the Russian sector. Although a postal service between the zones was established, it often took too long for perishables to be shipped. They were spoiled before they arrived, or taken by hungry postal clerks. We had no other choice but to cross the border to bring back the goods we needed to survive.

The problem was that it became increasingly impossible to get permission to visit Oma as often as was necessary to obtain food for us all. We constantly had to find new ways to get to Klostermansfeld and arrive back in Hamelin with the essential provisions. It meant passing the border illegally on different routes.

It was not too difficult to enter into the Russian zone. The complications started when trying to get back into the western zones. The Russians would appear out of nowhere and yell, *"Stoy!"* which means "stop." We heard it on our way back into the British zone. We had walked for several miles from the train station toward the sector's border. My mother encouraged us. She pointed to a sign about twenty-five feet ahead of us.

"Look at that board! It says, 'Now you are leaving the Russian zone.' And see, there is another sign, 'British zone.' We are almost there."

At that moment, what appeared to be a tree stump in the ditch alongside of the road suddenly raised itself up. It was a Russian border guard. *"Stoy!"* he yelled and pointed the gun at us. He motioned us off the street and onto a field-path that led away from the border.

After several miles, we saw a barn and a hut. He pushed us into the shed. A tired-looking woman was already sitting there. After an hour, the guard returned and gestured for my mother and the weary woman to come with him. Our fear was great. What would the guard do to them?

---

182 *Volkspolizei* was the name for the police in the Russian zone; it means "folk police."

We waited, listening to the cold wind gust against the dirty, unsealed window. The drafty hut sent chills through us. Hildegard and I huddled down on the featherbed we had carried with us from Klostermansfeld. It did not give us much comfort; we still shivered. Ernst put on a stiff upper lip. I was sure he experienced the cold too.

My mother knew that the shed soon would be like an icebox. She found a way to persuade the guards to let her return to us and drop a few pieces of wood on the floor. She explained to us, "The Russians had a party here last night. The lady and I have to clean up the barn. Here is some wood. Ernst, kindle the fire!" The Russian motioned impatiently to her to leave. She nodded at us and said under the door, "I will be back subsequently."

Soon the little stove provided some heat. After the barn was cleaned, the guards released the exhausted woman who had been there when we arrived. We still had to stay in the shed. We awaited our fate. Finally, the guard ordered us onto another field path. There was no escape. One Russian went in front of us and another was behind us with his gun, ready to shoot. We followed. My brother and I had knapsacks filled with food supplies for the next weeks. My sister and I carried the feather comforter between us. We did not know that among its feathers Mother had hidden money that my father needed to start his insurance business. My brother lugged a cage with a female rabbit that was due to give birth soon. We wanted to keep it in the small yard of the apartment house and feed it grass and dandelions, hoping she would have many little ones. They would provide fresh meat for dinner in the future.

The Russian guards took us to a border makeshift prison and ordered us to descend into a cellar. The door was locked behind us. "Hello, welcome to our abode!" we heard, and had to get used to the dimly lit cellar room before we saw several cheerful fellow "inmates."

"How long have you been here?" my mother inquired.

One lady with a heavy Saxon accent answered, "Only two days. Every once in a while they let some of us upstairs to prepare meals for the guards, and then we have to get into the cellar again."

Suddenly, we realized Ernst was missing. I heard my mother's frightful cry. "My son! Ernst, where are you! Where is my son?"

An elderly lady answered her. "He is with the men next door. They separated us from our men. Don't worry, we have a way to contact him."

"How, where, which way?" My mother was out of control. I'd never seen her like that before.

"Wait until the guards are gone upstairs," one woman said. "Listen, some of us have been here for forty-eight hours. We will survive, just keep calm."

Another woman put her ear to the door. After a little while, she nodded, "All clear!"

The young one from Leipzig walked over to the wall and pried a brick out of it. She asked through the opening, "Is Ernst with you guys?"

"Here I am. Do you know where my mother and sisters are?"

Ernst did not quite finish his sentence when my mother stood at the wall and peeped through the hole. "Ernst, are you all right?" she shouted. The young woman pulled her back.

"Lady, don't yell! So far, the Russians have not discovered the hole we chiseled last night. Don't give our secret away."

Mother opened my knapsack, took out a sandwich, and handed it to Ernst through the hole in the wall. "Thank you, Mom!" he said. "Don't worry, I will be all right and the rabbit, too. Somebody here had some old cabbage leaves; it ate."

"Hush! I hear the guard." The brick was skillfully replaced, and the young woman stood in front of it, pretending to look at the sky that could be seen through the narrow, barred cellar window just below the ceiling. The Russian entered and selected a few women to come upstairs.

Hildegard and I sat down on our featherbed. The women revealed to us that they had bartered through the hole in the wall. "We even have some salted herring." Mother was not sure if she should share some of our food with the women, but they put her at ease. "We have enough to eat. When we help upstairs, we can get some soup or potatoes. We drop some of the food into our pockets when they are not looking, and then we share with the men in the next room." She added shrewdly, "We have a regular black market[183] going through the hole in the wall. You want to participate?"

We heard the key in the cellar door again; the guard motioned to my mother and two other women. Hildegard and I huddled together, waiting anxiously for what would happen next. I do not remember how long we had been detained before we all were ordered to come upstairs. They shoved us among lots of other people who had tried to cross the border and had been caught during the last forty-eight hours. At a border station, the guards asked my mother to pay them fifty Marks per person. Then they spurred us on to move fast among the other people. They hurried, they overtook

---

183 People caught bartering on the black market faced punishments in the form of monetary fines, losing their jobs, and often imprisonment.

us, guards bumped us with the butts of their guns. We had to watch not to get separated from each other. Finally, we saw the sign "You are entering the British zone" behind a barrier. The Russians stayed behind. The British guards lifted the pole and let us pass without checking our luggage or us.

It was late. The earliest train to Hamelin would not leave until five a.m. the next morning. Mother had to get tickets for us. She took me along, while Hildegard and Ernst sat on the featherbed and watched the knapsacks, the rabbit cage, and Mother's suitcase. The Red Cross helped mothers with small children; they were allowed to jump the line. I had to appear as tiny as possible so mother would be able to receive tickets for us before they were all sold out for the early train. We tried to sleep in the overcrowded waiting hall in the train station. My siblings succeeded taking small naps. I watched my mother fight the sleep that wanted to overtake her. I told her, "Mom, sleep, I stay awake and watch that nobody takes anything from us."

Did I see tears in her eyes? She tenderly smoothed my hair. "Yes, Rosebud, I'll take a snooze. You scream if anyone threatens us."

In the morning, we went to the platform and saw overcrowded trains coming and going. My brother told us how to jump on a slow-moving train, so we could ride on the outer step of a compartment. "Never run against the direction the train is moving, run with it to jump on it. Grab the handlebar and hold tight." I only needed to jump on a train once, but not this time. We found room inside a compartment.

Father had expected us two days earlier. He went to every train that came from Helmstedt, the little town where we crossed the border this time. When we arrived in Hamelin, Father stood at the station to help us. He saw how exhausted we were. "I wish I could go and get food from Uncle Martin," he sighed.

"Don't you even think of it," my mother broke in. "You are on their blacklist,[184] you know. I was scared enough when they separated Ernst from us. It is entirely too dangerous for you to cross the border. We just have to see how we get through the winter without hauling food from Uncle Martin's farm."

Of course, the food that three children and a woman can carry would not feed twelve people for long. Our rabbit had given birth to nine bunnies. They had just started to open their eyes when the neighbor's cat tore apart the screen of the cage. Cousin Kappauf saw it from the bathroom window. He ran, half-shaven, to rescue the rabbits, but he came too late. The cat had

---

184 This is a list of politically incriminated persons and their relatives.

killed the bunnies' mother. We tried to nurse the tiny creatures with skim milk from a doll's baby bottle, but only one survived. It never grew big or fat enough to become a roast for all of us. Soon we had no other choice but to go back to Oma and ask for food again.

My parents were always anxious about our schooling, especially for the boys. Their sons had to be prepared for the university. The problem was that in Hamelin, most of the schools had been damaged. There was simply not enough room for all the children to fit in the high school. Half of Hamelin's population was made up of refugees, fugitives, freed prisoners, and expellees from the former areas that were now controlled by the Soviet Union. My mother pleaded with the principal to let Ernst continue his education. My brother had excellent grades and no behavioral problems at his previous schools. Another plus for him was his good athletic record. He was accepted.

For Hildegard and me, it was another story. First of all, my father still had the old conviction that girls should become good housewives and raise children.[185] Yes, a certain amount of education was needed, but higher education was not essential for girls. Middle school would suffice for us. Therefore, we were allowed to enter the Wilhelm Raabe[186] School in Hamelin. Since they had not enough room for my sister in three parallel classes, they registered her in a grade below her scholastic standing, and they placed me in the same class she was in, which was above my achievements.

Now school life became miserable for Hildegard and me. The teachers constantly compared us. Hildegard learned English much faster than I. She could pronounce the *TH* and the English *R*. Our teacher called me in front of the class to teach me how to say the English *R*. I had to sound out "*Fdiede, Fdeude*," and then keep my tongue where I put it for the *D* and say, "*Friede, Freude*," which in German means "peace, joy." I just could not get the *R* right, as much as I left my tongue on the *D* spot. So much for my peace and joy! I hesitated to pronounce the *TH*. It meant putting my tongue between my teeth, practically between my lips. I thought, *That looks like I am sticking*

---

185 In Germany, the old cliché of the KKK—*Küche, Kirche, Kinder*—prevailed, meaning that women's main tasks in life are to take care of the "kitchen, church, and children."

186 Wilhelm Raabe was a nineteenth-century German novelist who depicted the middle-class life realistically. He was born near Hamelin in 1831 and died in 1910 in Braunschweig.

my tongue out at people. That was an outright nasty, offensive behavior I did not want to be accused of.

Hildegard had a beautiful soprano. I loved to sing, but I never could reach the high notes my sister sang so clearly. She was selected for the school choir. She told me, "Do not even try out for the chorus." I complied. Anyway, I needed the after-school practice time for my lessons because I still had spelling difficulties, now in German *and* English.

My mother was called into school often because of my poor grades. Sure enough, she found an old lady who would tutor me. Mother paid her with food she got from the black market. My sister had gotten supplementary rations because she was so skinny. I did not look frail; therefore I received no extra food and was always hungry. The woman dictated stories to me, which mostly had to do with delicious white buttered bread dripping with honey. My mind was fixed on the taste of these delicacies, not on the spelling of them.

In spring of 1947, the catastrophic malnourishment of children in Germany and Austria became evident. The Allies agreed to provide lunch for all schoolchildren in each of the occupied zones.[187] American care packages arrived at the churches. The ministers distributed them among the most needy. Hildegard would be confirmed soon, and I was in a confirmation class too. I had worn the hand-me-down HJ coat from my brother. The deaconess saw me in the ill-fitting garment and selected our family as a recipient of clothing from the care packages. We were given a sweater, kneesocks, and some underwear. One of the sweaters came with a note attached, with an address from Seattle. Hildegard wrote to the American family, who answered by sending packages to us personally. That was a godsend, for it became increasingly difficult to cross the border into the Russian zone and visit with Oma.

Despite the new supply of food and clothing, I sometimes fainted when the teacher called on me and I had to stand up, as was customary. I was still close to starvation, and since it soon became clear that I'd have to repeat the seventh grade, my mother decided to send me back to Klostermansfeld for a quarter of a year.[188] She thought, *There, Ilse-Rose will have enough and*

---

187 The lunch usually consisted of a cup of milk or even cocoa and a roll. In the Russian zone, the roll was dark and often under-baked, but the milk was at least 2 percent, whereas in the British zone, the milk or cacao was made from fat-free milk or water.

188 Between 1946–48, relatives, especially children living in different sectors, still could receive permission to visit each other occasionally.

better food and Uncle Große can tutor her again. She needed to wait until after Christmas before she received the necessary papers for a legal border crossing.

We tried to celebrate Christmas with Mrs. Homburg's family and the Frisches. A few days before the holy day, Hildegard, Wolftraut, Ottchen Homburg, Reinhold, and I made paper chains for a tree that my father was able to secure. With the help of one of the girls in Hildegard's and my class, I formed candles from old wax stumps we collected. We melted them and poured the semi-hot wax into wooden candle forms. After the wax solidified, we unscrewed the boxes and could lift the candles out. We had a few of them on the tree, but not having the right mixture of paraffin and wax, the candles burned down too fast.

We ate what seemed the most delicious meal. Mrs. Homburg had bartered for a can of wieners. We had not seen meat in a long time. Mother made a potato salad[189] using the last ones we grew on Mrs. Homburg's garden plot. When Mrs. Homburg played Christmas songs on the piano in the living room, my father and mother with us four, along with the Frisch family and Mrs. Homburg's children, gathered around her and sang. Ottchen, Mrs. Homburg's youngest son, had eaten his share too fast. He accompanied our singing with his hiccups; actually, it sounded like he was keeping time. My brother chuckled quietly at it. A sense of humor did not leave him even in the bleakest times. Mrs. Frisch had a Christmas present for all of us. She had drawn a board game that we children could play.

I enjoyed playing this game with Wolftraut only for a short time. The mailman delivered the permission to visit with Oma.

We arrived in Klostermansfeld in late January. My mother left shortly afterward to bring more food to Hamelin. I stayed for close to three months. I did not go to school there, since they had no middle school and the curriculum here already differed from that of the western sectors, especially in languages, geography, and history.

Uncle Große tutored me again. He did not care how I pronounced English. He used to say, "Child, if you are in Canada, they speak with a different accent than the ones in Australia, or in Great Britain. In India, they pronounce words different than in the USA, and there it depends

---

189 This salad consisted of potatoes swimming in vinegar, water, and a little oil we had extracted from beechnuts. My sister and I gathered these in the woods until one day, the forest keeper forbade us to pick them up from the ground. The wildlife needed them to survive the winter.

if you are in Texas or in Boston." Thus he combined his old-fashioned geography lessons with English. His comprehensive teaching method was avant-garde. When I was younger, he had incorporated history with literature and orthography when he dictated stories about Martin Luther to me in an attempt to improve my spelling. He put me at ease, saying, "So, do not worry about pronouncing your *R* or *TH*—but you need to spell correctly."

I went to his house only a few times during the week. Between his lessons, I needed to help alongside the farmworkers, Aunt Ursel included. Under the Soviet regime, she was regarded to be on the same level as any other worker. She still could run the household, but no longer as the privileged owner of it.

Aunt Ursel showed me and a few other young girls how to kill and prepare pigeons for dinner. She said, "Stinky Rose,"—she still called me by that name—"you hold the pigeon in your left hand. Make sure both wings are securely against its body, and then you put your right hand over its head and eyes, clasp your fingers around its neck, twist it, and pull abruptly." She demonstrated. I saw the blood spurting out of the neck. "Don't let go. Pigeons can still fly without their heads. You have to hold the bird until it relaxes in your left hand and the blood does not trickle anymore." She gave me a smaller pigeon to acquire this new skill. I learned fast. After the preparation of the birds, they were roasted in the oven. They are actually very tender and delicious when fairly young and freshly slaughtered. I remembered this, and when fifteen years later I got married, I ordered roasted pigeons for one course at my wedding dinner. I wanted to impress my American in-laws. The meal was a disaster, because the pigeons had been too old and frozen.

On another visit, in 1949, pigeons played a rather scary role in my life in Klostermansfeld. A fifteen-year-old boy harassed my nine-year-old cousin, Hermjörg. The teenager said, "Hey, you! Sell me some of your pigeons." Hermjörg had no way of catching the birds, nor would he be allowed to sell them. He was afraid to tell his father about the boy's request.

It was masquerade time again. Oma asked her seamstress to sew a chimney-sweep costume for Hermjörg and a pirate costume for me. The doctor's daughter was dressed up as a female pirate. I really was a little too old for this, but they wanted me to mind the two youngsters during the children's Fasching. When we had to walk in a circle for judging of the best costumes, some older boys and girls sat on the windowsills and watched us.

I overheard their comments about me. "That is no boy; she is a girl trying to be a pirate." We did not win a prize.

The mother of the girl pirate came and said, "We have a birthday party for my son. Hermjörg, you are invited." She turned to me, "You can stay here as long as you like." I did not want to go to the Fasching to begin with, and now … I was ready to leave and go home.

I had to walk through a narrow alley between walled-in gardens. A boy cornered me. "You better get the pigeons for me!" he shouted.

I answered, "They belong to my uncle."

"Liar! You are an Oemler, just like the rest of them. I teach you to be bigheaded." With this, he hit me on my cheek. I did not flinch, just stared in his face. Would he hit me again? What should I do? How could I get out of this remote alley where nobody seems to come and help me? Suddenly, he turned. I slipped past him and walked briskly away, expecting to be clobbered from behind. When I arrived at the courtyard gate, there he stood again, threatening me with a stick.

"What do you want now? I told you I am not an Oemler. I only live here."

"But you were a Nazi … pig."

Wasn't there anybody who would come to help me? Inside, the dog started to bark. I called, "Here Karo, come here!" The dog's growling must have scared my molester; he turned away and I had free access to the courtyard. "Karo, good dog," I whispered under tears. I knew from now on, I had to be on my guard. I took comfort in the thought that I had to leave soon for Hamelin.

It always seemed the same: it was easy to enter the Russian zone but hard to get out. When trying to get back into the British zone, I first took the train to the border and then departed and waited for the border guards to change. Generally, that was the best time to make it across[190] … or late at night, when they could not easily see people. One could find persons who would help you to pass into the western zones. They mainly lived in the border regions. They knew when the guards changed, which one of the

---

190 Until 1961, many people left the Russian sector to become part of the much better economy in West Germany. The East German government had to cope with too great a loss of skilled workers. To avoid more loss of good workers, the Berlin Wall was built, and in fifteen years, it included a five-kilometer-wide strip that was mined, had barbwire on both sides of it, was electrified in some parts, and included watch towers. All of this in the hope of keeping the people in.

guards was a bad shooter, where there was good coverage, and where there might be a hole in the barbed wire. It was dangerous to trust these persons. Some of them who pretended to help you were crooks. They stole the few things people tried to get to their families, often beating them or even killing them for the goods they carried.

When I had to repeat seventh grade, we went to Klostermansfeld without any difficulties. We had obtained legal papers to visit with my relatives, but getting back out of the Russian sector became a problem, since the conflict between the western zones and the Russian zone became part of the Cold War. Now, my permission slips and documents that I needed to go back to my parents were declared invalid. My father was on the blacklist ever since he escaped from prison. They wanted to keep me in their grasp as a possible decoy or exchange for my father.

Oma and Uncle Martin made sure that no one in the village knew I was on my way to the border. The butcher took me along in his wagon when he went to buy pigs. He let me off at a train station, where I met a man who was to take me to the border village across from the British-occupied town Vienenburg. I felt uneasy with this stranger, but when we arrived near the border at noon, he showed me the restaurant where I was to meet the former apprentice of Uncle Martin, Eberhard Fleischer. A woman who seemed to be the owner of the hotel asked me to wait in the dining room. I was supposedly to meet Eberhard at four p.m. I had five DM[191] but did not spend it on a meal for myself. I ate one of the sandwiches Oma had packed in my knapsack. I waited and waited. By six p.m., he still had not shown up.

"You have to sit in the kitchen," the woman said. "Mr. Fleischer is delayed. You cannot stay in the restaurant. The Russians have a party tonight. We have to prepare this room for them." I had to look unsuspicious, pretending to be the kitchen help.

At eleven p.m., Eberhard finally came. He had a bicycle. "Sorry, I had to wait until the Russians who are on duty were tipsy and changed with the guards. Best chance not to get shot," he told me. Pointing to the bike, he said, "Sit on the bar, put your suitcase on the carrier seat in back, and hold on to your knapsack."

I followed his orders, holding my knapsack with one hand and the

---

191 In 1948, the western zones had agreed to change the old Reichsmark into DM. To begin with, everybody received 40.00 DM. It was part of two installments, later followed by 20.00 DM for each person. The people in the Russian sector received a different currency in 1949. Thus Germany was not only politically divided but from now on also economically.

handlebar with the other. I had to be careful not to interfere with Eberhard steering the bike.

He drove through a park. Every so often, he would hiss "Duck!" to avoid a low-hanging tree branch. Apparently, he was not driving on a path but straight through the close-standing trees. Next he pedaled through a meadow, where cows lay in the grass. We came to a barbed-wire fence that stretched across a creek.

"Get off the bike," he whispered. "Crawl under the wire."

He lifted the upper strand of barbed wire, stepped on the lower strand, and I slipped through the opening he had created. He hoisted the bike over the prickly barrier. Then he waded through the creek and ducked underneath the fence where the water was shallow. I had picked up the bike and fastened the suitcase onto it again. He swung me onto the bike and started to drive like a maniac. I heard shots hissing by us. Were they shooting at us? No time to think, just hope they are too drunk, or it is too dark, or they were shooting at somebody or something else. Who knew?

Eberhard drove to the station in Vienenburg. "Stay here until your parents come. They'll pick you up around seven a.m." I wanted to give the five DM to Eberhard to pay for his help. The DM,[192] the Western currency, was the more stable money. One could buy better merchandise in the Russian zone with it—under the table, of course. However, he did not want it. He did take the American cigarettes my mother had given me in case I needed to barter or pay with them.

I sat against the wall in the station's hallway. I had to wait until morning to see my parents. Pretty soon, the station emptied; hardly anybody was left. A railroad clerk came and told me that they closed at midnight and that I needed to leave.

"But I do not know anybody here. My parents will come tomorrow morning and pick me up here. I must stay here," I explained to her.

She suggested that I buy a return ticket to Goslar, because there, the station was open all night. "Stay there and take the train back to Vienenburg at five a.m." the clerk said.

I thought, *Great. Goslar, that is where Uncle Reinhold and Aunt Anne live. If anything goes wrong, I can call on them in the morning.* I would not dare

---

192 The GDR (German Democratic Republic) currency had hardly any value on the world market, whereas the DM of the FRG (Federal Republic of Germany) was becoming a sought-after legal tender.

to call them at midnight. Remember, Oma had said, "Sleep is holy, you do not wake anybody up."

I spent the night among all kinds of unsettled people. I clutched my suitcase between my legs, put my knapsack on the table in front of me, rested my head on it, and folded my arms around it. I could hardly sleep for fear that somebody might steal my parcels.

I went back to Vienenburg the next morning. My parents met me around seven a.m. and took me back to Goslar, where they had stayed overnight. "Why didn't you call?" my Uncle Reinhold inquired.

I told him what Oma always said. "It was midnight. You were asleep. Remember, sleep is holy. You do not wake people up."

My father only shook his head and remarked, "You could have saved us a trip by calling when you arrived in Vienenburg."

Every day I went to school in Hamelin, I had to pass the police station. It was set up in a former hotel. I would hold my breath; it reeked of dead bodies. The pictures of the murdered were displayed on the wall of the building, faces marred by stab wounds, swollen up due to beatings. I had horrible nightmares from seeing these posted visages of dead bodies.[193]

Aside from these experiences, a whole new brighter world opened up for me when I repeated seventh grade. I found a new friend. She lived in our neighbor's house. Sigrid was in my class. We walked to school together. She was also in my confirmation group. Her five brothers loved to listen to my stories. Her mother was sickly. She usually lay on the sofa or was in their bedroom. Her father had worked with my father for the British garrison stationed in Hamelin. I was often at Sigrid's place, where everybody accepted me. We cleaned their kitchen together and took care of her baby brother.

In my new class, I was so well-liked that they made me the class president. With the help of our gym teacher, we put on plays, which were accomplished enough that the school let us perform them in the auditorium. We put them on not only for the girls' middle school but also for the boys' middle school.[194]

A boy from the upper class, Dieter Fischer, said to me, "Ilse-Rose Höfer

---

193 The crime rate was high not only because many of the criminals kept in prisons had been freed by the Allies, but also because people would steal and kill for food or clothing.

194 Boys and girls went to separate schools. In middle school, the pupils had a more practical education than in high school. Girls learned to cook, sew, knit, crochet, and do garden work. Boys learned wood- and metal-working.

has a nice ring to it. I can see your name on film posters. You in the lead role! You were born an actress." He was a cute boy with blond curly hair. I think he was my first crush … secretly, of course.

He came to Mrs. Homburg's apartment to play chess with me, but having played many times with our neighbor Mr. Nachtigall, I beat him. I thought I would impress him, but it did the opposite. He did not come again, although he always greeted me in a friendly manner when we chanced to see each other.

On our side of the street, the hotel converted into a police post kept a cellar pub. Here, Mr. Nachtigall, father of two girls, would look for relief from his pain. He had been severely injured in the war, losing both of his legs. Artificial limbs could not be fitted for his hips. He was confined to his wheelchair. Occasionally, when his agony became unbearable, he rolled down our street to the pub. Somebody carried him downstairs, where he met with other veterans and sometimes got drunk.

We played with his daughters in their little apartment. Usually, their mother allowed us to use their bedroom, where we acted out fairy tales. If the weather was nice, we went on long hikes together. We sang a lot and looked for secluded spots in the forest where we could act out our fantasies, forgetting the nagging hunger in our stomachs.

When Mr. Nachtigall found out that I knew how to play chess, he challenged me, showed me all kinds of neat moves, and sometimes I beat him at his own game. Whenever his suffering became so bad that he wanted to seek the pub, his wife would call my mother, asking if I would be available to come to their place to play chess with him as soon as possible. Concentrating on this game apparently had the same effect on him as did the alcohol. It was the better escape from his pain. Since by now I was in a confirmation class[195] and had learned that a good Christian helps others, I honored the request for chess with Mr. Nachtigall. It was not only out of pure Christian motives—I liked chess more than doing homework.

The Allies allowed certain dramas in the German theater as long as they did not have anything militaristic in them. In the British sector, part of our reeducation was watching their movies, which had been translated, voiced-over, and sent to Germany. I saw British films about gypsies living in the beautiful countryside of England. Instead of money, Germans sometimes

---

195 At that time, we had four years of confirmation classes before we could be accepted into the Lutheran or Reformed Protestant Church, after we passed an examination in front of the whole congregation.

paid with a lump of coal, wood, or bricks to see a performance. We listened to the music the Nazis had forbidden and loved to sing the American songs of the thirties and forties. In the school for ballroom dancing, Ernst and Hildegard learned the boogie, the jitterbug, the swing, the samba, and the rumba in addition to the traditional waltz, tango, and polka.

At many a Stammtisch in Germany, they talked about what might be in store for the members now, after they'd survived the war. The pharmacist of our group remembered how he was almost killed in Yugoslavia, either by partisans or his illness, and later when he was transported out of the new Russian areas by force. He shook his head. "Look at us! We have been spared during bombing raids, evacuation, fleeing, expelling, starvation, and freezing. I think our life should make more sense from now on. I always was and now am even more a pacifist. I say, never again war!"

"Never a fanatical ideology either! There must be a reason why we were spared," the farmer added.

The pastor concluded, "People should live in peace with each other."

The mayor had followed the development of a new German government under the rule of the Allies. He pointed out, "One thing's for sure, the Allies do not recognize the attitude we just expressed: no war! No fanatical government! Only peace! They are positive that all of us Germans are warriors and therefore need to be reeducated."

Leipziger entered the pub and joined them. He had heard the last remarks. Taking off his jacket, he commented, "The Americans would love to be able to get into the brains of all the German people and take all the Nazi ideas out of them. They still think all of us are brainwashed Nazis."

The pastor argued, "I think they might have had their concept of German people wrong right after the war. Then, they were still influenced by the lies of their media, but now, they think different. Look, who did the Western Allies call back to govern Germany again? Men who had been politically active before 1933."

The mayor, siding with the pastor, chimed in, "These are former politicians who know how to run an administration machine, having been part of the Weimar Republic. In the western zones, I would have my job as mayor back, in spite of having been in the NSDAP. They finally realized that we had to belong to this party to keep our jobs. It is different here in the Russian sector," he sighed. "Here, survivors of the concentration camps, emigrants coming back, anybody opposed to the Nazis are installed. I say 'installed'—they are not voted into their civil service. They are rewarded with jobs for having suffered under the Nazi regime. Even if they have no experience in any political or economic tasks they need to perform, they just have to claim they are Communists or at least former Socialists."

The mayor had tried to be placed in his old job again, but he was denied any political involvement. Work in the civil service was unattainable for him as long as he remained in the Russian zone. Here, by spring 1948, all professionals who held important positions in the civil service, industry, or economics, including bank personnel and lawyers, were dismissed from their work. Depending on their degree of cooperation with the Nazi party, they were shipped to Siberia, killed, tortured, or kept in local prisons. Less incriminated persons were released from prison but could not get back to their former work. They could hold blue-collar jobs in mines, on farms, in industry, or in municipalities. The mayor was allowed to be a street worker, cleaning the streets with a broom and picking up garbage, if there was any. People could use everything. Nothing was thrown away.

Leipziger remarked, "Let's face it, we like to forget the past and are willing to work on the restoration of Germany. We want better living conditions."

"You are right," the pharmacist agreed. "All of us want to live even better than before the war. My wife likes a refrigerator instead of our old icebox, and I could use one too in our drugstore."

"A washing machine would be nice," Margret, the innkeeper's daughter, mused as she brought a new round of beer to the Stammtisch members.

The minister voiced his wish by adding, "And I like to visit our neighboring parish, not with my bicycle, but with a car."

Margret added dreamingly, "A vacation trip would be awesome. I would love to travel and experience the wonders of the world on my own, not just read about them." Unfortunately, she, along with the Stammtisch members living in the Russian zone, would experience ever more stringent travel restrictions instead of seeing the wonders of the world personally. Relatives who lived on the five–kilometer-wide border strip created by the Soviets were denied visitors. Eventually, everyone who occupied a home there had to leave it. During the almost forty years of Soviet-controlled rule, these border areas became desolate. They reached from the Baltic Sea all the way to Hungary. Five kilometers where no human being interfered, where wildlife could roam freely; birds nested undisturbed, and the fauna and flora reestablished itself. A "green belt" grew out of harsh political and inhumane harassment of the people living in the Russian zone. That is the flipside of the Russian border.

The treatment of the western people stood in stark contrast to that of their relatives in the east. Under the more and more relaxed rule of the British and Americans, the West German government worked toward rebuilding the cities, infrastructure, factories, and international trade, which resulted in the Wirtschaftswunder.[196]

It was the beginning of the remarkable recovery in the western sectors that prompted my Aunt Ursel to assign a rather daring task to me.

In 1950, my younger brother and I had obtained a visa from the Russian authorities to cross the border so we could spend our summer vacation with my relatives in Klostermansfeld. We had legal papers to take a bus trip from Hannover into a town in the Russian sector. When the time came to go back to Hamelin, my Aunt Ursel said, "Take Hermjörg with you; he has his school vacation now. He would like to eat some good chocolate, we cannot get it over here." She did not listen to my reservations about her plan. She just packed his suitcase. I was not sure how I would get him across the border without the legal documents.

The bus driver hardly looked at our papers. He might have thought, *They are kids, why bother?* The trouble emerged at the border when the Russian guards searched our luggage. They questioned me about two boys, whereas my documents only showed one boy. I told them that I received permission for two people to cross, apparently for two adults. I explained, "The two boys take only one seat on the bus like one adult would. That makes one adult seat for them and the other for me. I am even not really an adult, since I am only fourteen years old." I do not know if they let me pass with Hermjörg and Reinhold because I was so young or if they were impressed by my "clever" answer. This was the last trip I was able to make to Klostermansfeld. One year later, we moved to Mülheim on the Ruhr.

I was not allowed to see the place I grew up in until 1992 when I showed it to my husband, but only for a short visit. It was too painful to see the old farmhouse and stables converted into apartments. Where formerly the Victorian garden house stood, ugly garages blocked off what had been the garden. I could not enter the courtyard. My husband and I left disappointed.

---

196 Translated, *Wirtschaftswunder* means "Wonder of economic recovery." Universally, the fast recovery of West Germany was called an economic miracle.

After my Uncle Martin died, the Treuhand [197] granted my cousins Hermjörg, Lutz, Jochen, and Martin Jr. the inheritance rights to the farm. In 2009, Hermjörg took us inside the old farmhouse. I could not show the former layout of its rooms to my husband; all of them had become part of the apartments. However, we walked up the steep stairs to where the two rooms had been that we occupied when we had to hide my father—and wouldn't you know it, the old key to the door leading to the roof still hung on its nail. But access to the barn across the gate had been torn down. I declined to walk over the roof again as I had done so often as a child.

---

197 The *Treuhand* was created in Germany after 1990. It is the administration of restoring lost property to the original owners. It came into existence when the states belonging to the Russian zone were incorporated into the Federal Republik of Germany.

Chapter 12

From Hamelin to
Mülheim on the Ruhr

Between 1948 and 1949, occupied Germany became politically divided. The three western zones were combined to form a new democratic government under the guidance of the Americans, British, and French. The Russians declined to join them; in fact, they opposed the capitalistic Federal Republic of Germany (FRG) by promptly setting a communistic regime against the west. It was called the German Democratic Republic (GDR) under Moscow's management. In the forty years that followed, the two separated German states drifted further and further apart—politically, economically, and culturally.

One thing became clear to all Germans: in the west, you could travel freely, choose your profession, establish your own business, and rebuild the destroyed factories and cities. In the east, although the word "freedom" dominated the Communist propaganda, people were restricted in travel, had to give up privately owned firms, factories, even small shops, and had hardly any choice of careers. They had to go where jobs needed to be filled. The control of the Russians over the GDR continued well into the 1970s.

The East German police followed the Soviets' command to monitor all meetings of the civilians in the GDR. Nevertheless, the Stammtisch continued their get-together for Skat, beer, and discussion. However, their numbers dwindled, because the allure of the western zones was too strong for the less-privileged East Germans. They could not and did not want to resist the appeal of the unfolding Wirtschaftswunder[198] across the border.

One evening, the mayor was missing. The farmer asked, "Why is the mayor not coming? Does anybody know?"

The pharmacist, looking rather thoughtful, remarked, "Maybe he will not come anymore."

"At all?" cried the farmer in simulated surprise. "Tell me, why? Did they incarcerate him again?"

The pharmacist leaned over the table and whispered, "I think he left for the western zones. He could not get employed here in his capacity, always had to fear to be arrested once more." At that moment, the minister entered and the pharmacist waved to him cheerfully. "Hello, pastor. How are you?"

"Fine, thank you." He looked at the farmer and inquired, "Why are you so gloomy? Our pharmacist is friendly enough."

"I am afraid we will never see our mayor again. He might be shipped to Siberia by now," the farmer replied.

The minister shook his head, exclaiming, "Siberia!? Don't be so sure about this. He might just be detained again so he can inform about people here who committed crimes during the Nazi time or, on a too familiar but newer scale, they hope he can tell about those people in our village who have relatives or associates in the west and might plot against the GDR regime."

"Or most likely, he is getting tired of being picked up by the police," the farmer proposed. "They know where to find him, namely here on Thursday nights at eight o'clock. He probably wanted to avoid being booked in front of us."

Margret came to their table to bring their usual round of beer. She had overheard their conversation and remarked, "He took some vacation."

"From what?" asked the pharmacist. "Ever since the Red Cross had to let him go, he could not get any suitable position anywhere. I would not blame him for leaving. All he was allowed to do was clean our streets and pretend to be happy about it."

The farmer grew tired of their speculation. He suggested, "Let's not puzzle over reasons, why the mayor hasn't shown up tonight. We have enough people to play a good round of Skat." Actually, the farmer felt uneasy. He knew that their Stammtisch member had left for good. The

---

198 For *Wirtschaftswunder*, see Chapter 11 footnote 196.

mayor had confided in him and asked him to plow under a few documents that could cause trouble for his friends in the village. He had tried to get permission to move to the west but was denied. The authorities were not willing to let him go. As the minister suspected, the Stasi hoped to press him for more information on former Nazi affiliates and, increasingly, about people with connections to the FRG.

No wonder the minister nodded at the farmer and continued, "You know one thing! We have to be aware of the Socialist Communist movement in the GDR. Now we belong to the so-called Worker and Farmer State of Germany. The Soviet government controls us. Differences between blue-collar or white-collar workers must disappear. We should act united for the common interest of the entire Communist nations." He paused, searching in their faces if any of them could not be trustworthy. Silently he stipulated, *Farmer is too down-to-earth to get politically involved, and he still barters on occasion with people desperate for food. Secretly, of course. Pharmacist? He is cunning. Didn't I hear about his escape from the partisans in Yugoslavia and how he made it to Poland through enemy lines?* True to his profession as minister, he instructed them, "From now on it would be better to belong to one of the many government-controlled organizations if we want to gather for card games."

"Unless," the pharmacist interjected, "we meet privately in one of our homes."

The farmer added, "But we cannot meet regularly. That would be suspicious. Before you know it, our homes are bugged and our conversation is overheard by the secret police. We would need to gather at different times, days, and places."

Regardless, the Stammtisch members decided to continue to meet as usual until some authority would ask them to join one of the many manipulated new groups that had been established. They played their card game and drank their beer. But from then on, they abstained from discussing any political, economic, or even cultural issues. They never knew who would listen in on their conversation, or worse, if one of their members might be a Stasi informer.

At the end, in the 1950s, our Stammtisch ceased to exist in the "green heart" of Germany. On a small scale, it reflected the political impact on the German people from the 1920s to the 1950s. You remember that the first one to leave was the shopkeeper, Mr. Schumann. He left in 1934 before the Nazi Nuremberg laws came into effect, since his wife was of Jewish ancestry.

His family went to France, and then to Spain, and finally to America, where he could find a job in a clothing factory. He worked his way up the ladder and pretty soon became their best salesman.

The pastor and pharmacist were drafted. The first lost his life at the Russian front; the other was missing in action when left by his unit to die in Yugoslavia. But he did survive and came back in the late fall of 1945. He had been forced with millions of expellees from Eastern bloc countries[199] to settle in the Russian zone.

The teacher and later headmaster fled to Chile[200] early on in 1945, even before Germany had been divided into the four Allied occupied zones with distinct borders.

In the course of relocation, Hamburger, Berliner, and Leipziger—as evacuees—had been ordered back to their respective hometowns in 1946. Hamburger was old enough to retire and, being handicapped, received a pension after 1948.

Berliner worked at a post office. Although he had bad eyesight, he could handle the new currency because all of the new German DM coins and paper notes were cut into different sizes according to their value. The five DM bill was the smallest, and 500 the largest.[201] A blind person could tell the value of a bank note by feeling it. Stamps were filed in categories, so a blind clerk could sell them without looking at them. This was one measure by the FRG to take care of the many injured soldiers and get them back into the workforce.

Although Leipziger had an amputated leg, his well-designed artificial limb allowed him to travel. He secured a job at the Leipzig Gewandhaus.[202] He loved his new position, since it gave him permission to go to the west with the world-renowned Gewandhaus Orchestra. He stayed in the Russian zone to the end. He took part in the peaceful, quiet revolution of 1989. The

---

199 Eastern bloc countries, the Communist bloc, or Soviet bloc were terms used to denote groupings of states aligned with the Soviet Union, even states outside Central and Eastern Europe.

200 Countries of South America and Egypt became a refuge for former Nazis.

201 Coins came in one, two, five, ten, and fifty-penny pieces, followed by 1.00, 2.00, and 5.00 DM coins. Each was, according to its value, bigger and heavier than the lesser one. The paper money followed the same pattern. It came in 5.00, 10.00, 20,00, 50.00, 100.00 and 500.00 bills. When the Euro was introduced in 1999, the European Union agreed to keep this manner of sizing for coins and paper money.

202 The Gewandhaus Orchestra has existed for over 250 years.

leader and conductor, Kurt Masur, had opened the Gewandhaus building for discussions about reforms and the future of the GDR. These conversations, opposing the politics of the GDR, were one more strike against the closed borders between the GDR and FRG and the hated travel restrictions for the East Germans.

As for the mayor, by 1950, his mind was made up. He had to leave in secret without his family and cross the border into one of the western zones illegally. His wife, daughter, and son would have liked to accompany him, but the police were already spying on them. His family would have been forcefully stopped in any of their moves. He and his wife had plans to meet at Berliner's apartment in the French sector of Berlin. The mother did not reveal anything to their children; she only hinted that they might go on a trip during their summer vacation. She intended to file for permission to visit the GDR's capital. The chance to receive the coveted stamp of approval to travel to Berlin grew dramatically for the East Germans if they declared they wanted to experience the excitement at international meetings of Eastern bloc countries staged there with the spectacle of Russian military parades that usually accompanied these political ceremonies—or if applicants stated they wished to see major sport or cultural events. The mayor met his family at Berliner's place, but they could not stay in the tiny apartment. They had to live in a barrack of the overcrowded reception camps in Berlin. The subhuman conditions there, void of all decent privacy, became too much for the son. One day he declared that he wanted to go back to their village, because he loved Margret, the innkeeper. Reluctantly, his parents let him go. Their daughter stayed with them until the mayor found a job in his old profession as burgomaster[203] in a small town near Munich. Here their daughter was able to enter the university and study chemistry, an opportunity that had been denied her in the Russian zone.

The farmer had no choice; he had to leave his farm behind in 1953. He had been unable to supply the demanded pork, beef, chickens, eggs, milk, and produce, and he could not substitute for it. He had no money. He went under the pretense to visit Berliner in the GDR capital. At this time, one still could travel from the east to the west inside of Berlin. His one-eyed friend, Berliner, gave him shelter until the farmer could secure an airplane ticket to Hamburg. Here he looked up Hamburger, who helped him find a job in the Lüneburger Heide (Luneburg Heath), trucking farm goods,

---

203 *Burgomaster* is another term for mayor used frequently in Bavaria.

including livestock, especially the Heidschnucken.[204] He never farmed again. His family was allowed to join him later.

The last one to leave was the pharmacist. He decided too late to flee by night into the American zone. By the late 1950s, the borders had been more secured by the Soviet-controlled German government. A border guard spotted him from a watchtower and shot him. He was left to bleed to death in the five-kilometer-wide strip between the double-fortified border of the Russian zone called the *Niemandsland* (no-man's-land).

Margret stayed. She married the mayor's son. He had been a leader for the Junge Pioniere[205] and became a seemingly convinced Communist, knowing his decision for the SED party would open the future for his children. Both continued to run the pub as well as they could under the political circumstances.

The new minister was allowed to preach as long as he supported Communism and condoned the Jugendweihe[206] that was established in 1954. He too took part in the peaceful revolution by starting meetings for young people in the church as early as 1981.[207]

On a small scale, the Stammtisch exemplifies the flight of many East Germans to the west in the 1950s. Life became unbearable in the eastern zone. At that time, we started to be glad that our farm had fallen under the land reform, although only for political reasons. We had been forced to manage an existence in the British zone. Until 1948, our life was tough, but gradually it became easier for us all.

After the first two years of our stay in the crowded apartment in Hamelin, the Frisch family had moved upstairs into the converted living quarters in the attic. Mrs. Homburg's living room served as Father's office

---

204 The *Heidschnucke* is a collective term for moorland sheep in northern Germany.

205 Translated as "young pioneers." This political organization for young children was patterned in 1954 after the Leninpioniers of the Soviet Union. Its goal was to train children according to the socialistic ideology of the GDR. First through third graders wore blue scarves; from fourth grade on, members wore red scarves on white shirts or blouses. Approximately 98 percent of all schoolchildren belonged to this organization in 1989.

206 *Jugendweihe*: see footnote 169 in Chapter 10.

207 Dr. Horst Strohbusch describes the early peaceful revolution starting with gatherings of young people in the churches in his book *Das Licht kam aus der Kirche: die Wende in Meiningen, 1989–1990.* The book is not translated; the title means "The Light Penetrated Out of the Church: The Turn in Meiningen, 1989–1990." Meiningen is a town in Thuringia.

during the daytime and as my parents' bedroom at night. My father had designed bed boxes that looked like sofas. We children slept in the room that had been occupied by Frisches before. Now the corner room, void of the sold bunk beds, housed the filing cabinets, typewriter, and desks for the bookkeeper and the secretary.

By 1951, my father needed more room for his business. He had applied for a larger office and better location. No matter how hard he tried to convince the town fathers of Hamelin to let him move, they refused to accommodate him, thinking that the available bureau spaces should be given first to the original firms of their town. They were just as immovable when we asked to rent an apartment. They said. "First we accommodate our people, and then come the displaced people." Since half of Hamelin's occupants were refugees, evacuees, or expellees, we had hardly any chance to receive suitable living quarters.[208]

My father looked for other towns that were more hospitable. In the southwest of the largest, most densely settled industrial district in Germany he found Mülheim on the Ruhr. This city had been bombed more extensively than Hamelin, but its town fathers saw potential growth for their city by encouraging new businesses to settle there. They gave the whole upper floor of the Commerce Bank to Father for his offices and found an apartment for us in a partially repaired house across from the bank.

A few weeks before the movers came to haul our meager belongings to the Ruhr-district, Hertha Homburg and my mother reminisced about their life together since 1947.

"Mrs. Homburg," my mother said.[209] "Now you will finally have the whole apartment to yourself."

Our landlady, who looked forward to being the sole occupant again, concluded, "Yes, it will be nice not sharing my bedroom with my two children; each of them can have their own room now. We will have the living room again and can roll the piano out of the dining room. The landlord will even send a contractor to fix the balcony."

"It was better for us when Frisch family moved upstairs. We did not need

---

208 Housing all the people created headaches for the German authorities even into the 21st century. Germans still need to apply for apartments or for building permits on their own properties.

209 Although Hertha Homburg shared her apartment for over four years with us, living in tighter quarters than relatives usually do, the two ladies did not address each other by their first names. In Germany, it takes a long time before older people are on a first-name basis.

to share the kitchen anymore. And what is best, we finally have electricity almost all the time."

"Remember when my Cousin Kappauf moved out after he married?"

"That was the time Herbert extended his office. He got rid of the bunk beds and designed a kind of sofa bed. In the morning, we put two boxes on top of each other, stuffed the bedding into it, and covered them with one mattress."

Mrs. Homburg chimed in, "I remember! Every day before going to school, your kids turned one mattress on its side to act as a sofa's backing." She had to laugh. "Your husband's clients never knew they were sitting on beds."

My mother joined her cheerfulness and said, "Luckily we found material to cover them, so that each of them would look like a couch."

"Are you taking all of them with you?"

"Yes, we need them in Mülheim. We have only Herbert's big desk, these box beds, and the wardrobes."

"What will you do for chairs and a table?"

"Herbert's secretary, Miss Siepermann, is moving with us. She'll bring all of her furniture. She will have one room in our apartment. We'll divide the biggest room with her hutch and our closets. In front of this partition will be our dining area, and behind it the children will sleep. Herbert and I will have our own bedroom. I shall cook for Miss Siepermann in return for her letting us use her furniture. She does not need to pay rent for her one room, and I will do her laundry as well."

Mrs. Homburg thought, *This woman never stops cooking for others. Her husband is fortunate that she always agrees to his arrangements.*

My mother took a sip of her coffee. Did it ever occur to her that she again was the cook and now even the laundry woman for somebody else?

My father had hired a cleaning woman,[210] Lisel, after Mrs. Homburg's living room became his office during the day and my parents' bedroom at night. Lisel lived in the country near Hamelin. Once a week she took the train to come and help us. In the beginning of our stay with Mrs. Homburg, Hildegard and I, under Mother's supervision, had taken turns with the Frisches in cleaning the kitchen, hallway, bathroom, steps to the apartment, and stairs leading to the cellar. These were especially crummy, since everybody in the house used coal stoves to heat each individual room.

---

210 At that time in Germany, it was still customary that the middle-class people had servants. My parents hired help as soon as they could afford it.

The coal dust from carrying the briquettes or the egg-shaped coke upstairs was tough to get rid of. We needed several pails of water to wipe everything clean. After Lisel came, we could devote more time to our schoolwork and friends.

My mother continued her chat with Mrs. Homburg. "Remember 1948, when we received the DM?"

"It was amazing how we suddenly were able to get bread, butter, sugar, all the basic food, and that without ration cards." She chuckled. "Good-bye hamster trips!"

"But just think what the new western currency meant for divided Berlin. The Soviets were offended. They blocked all traffic in and out of Berlin."

"Only they could not stop air traffic," Mrs. Homburg added. "If it would not have been for the American and British pilots flying everything into the western sectors of Berlin, the people of the French, British, and American districts would have starved or frozen to death."

"Already in 1946, Churchill had called the border between the Russian and the western zones the Iron Curtain," my mother stated, contemplating the divided Germany. "The Cold War started then. The Russian zone received its independent government."

Mrs. Homburg took up the train of thought, saying, "That means now, politically, we are separated."

"They have a different currency."

"So, economically we are separated."

"Communism is taught like a religion to the young people."

"So, culturally we are becoming separated as well." My mother sighed long and deep, saying, "And visiting my mother and brother emerges as an unsolved problem."

Mrs. Homburg nodded and voiced her opinion about the former trips to the Russian zone. "I have to tell you how amazed I was that you allowed your daughter to cross the border in 1949 to stay a quarter of a year with your mother."

My mother became uneasy about discussing those border crossings. She changed the subject, saying, "Herbert worked for several insurance companies. First he just sold truck-and-car insurance. Remember how he went to his clients!"

"Oh my! He took the one bike all of us shared. It was a lady's bicycle. He did not care. Nobody cared, and now—he owns a nice VW."

"When he added life insurance to his agency, he needed a car. That's when our business took off. He hired Uncle Reinhold and several others as sale representatives. Mr. Venator and Miss Siepermann took care of the office here. She can take shorthand faster than anybody I know and holds a speed record in typing."

"And your bookkeeper, Bob Venator, is fantastic. Didn't he work for German ship companies before the war?"

"Yes. All of our employees were glad to have a job with Herbert."

"When will you leave?" our landlady asked.

"We will move in early summer. First we'll observe Ilse-Rose's confirmation on Palm Sunday.[211] We will not celebrate it here in the Ratskeller,[212] as we did with Hildegard's confirmation. We will rent a special room in a hotel in Bad Pyrmont."

"Bad Pyrmont! The spa for the misunderstood women!" Mrs. Homburg exclaimed.

At that moment, the doorbell rang. My mother got up and opened the door, expecting one of Herbert's clients. She looked at the pale, tall man and then, in sudden recognition, she clasped her hand in front of her mouth, shouting, "Major Conn! Is it really you? What brings you here? Come in! Come in! How did you find us?"

He took both of her hands and shook them heartily. Entering, he followed Mother into the dining room and greeted Mrs. Homburg as my mother introduced him. He finally answered her question, "Well, I work in Hamburg with somebody who has connections to Herbert's business. When I heard Roselett is going to be confirmed soon, I wanted to talk to her. May I?"

"Of course you may," my mother told him.

Uncle Conn visited with mother and Mrs. Homburg until school was out. I hardly recognized him. Six years of imprisonment and work in the lead mines in Siberia had left their mark on him. He invited me to a little café not far from the Hamelin Munster, a beautiful church resting on a Romanesque foundation. It had been expanded in the thirteenth century into a big Gothic cathedral. Our family belonged to its congregation.

Major Conn told me about his daughter and what advice he had given her. Now he wanted to relate it to me. "Roselett," he said, still using the diminutive of my name as he had called me in Thorn, "whenever you feel

---

211 Palm Sunday is traditionally the day for confirmation in the Protestant Church in Germany.

212 Usually the town halls in Germany have a restaurant located in the cellar of the building. Here, the town fathers like to take a break during their meetings. The Ratskellers are known for excellent food and service.

something for a man and might even think you love him, look at that fellow closely. Always consider if you would like to have him as the father of your children, before you get into a relationship with him."

I listened, wondering why he would tell me this. I did not even have a boyfriend. Hildegard did, but not me. He continued counseling. I felt a little awkward but also very important that he took the time to discuss guidelines for my future life. I have no idea how much Uncle Conn knew about my father and the changes he had gone through because of the war and its aftermath. I cannot explain what happened to him. But so much was true: Father had little time for us children. He worked hard and found his relaxation away from Mrs. Homburg's crowded apartment. Therefore it was especially meaningful for me that Major Conn talked to me in a way none of the grown-ups ever had before.

I told him about my four years of confirmation classes. How I had learned many Bible verses and hymns. I especially loved the Easter song "O Haupt voll Blut und Wunden";[213] I had memorized it while kneeling in front of the hymnal. When I mentioned this to Uncle Conn, he could not relate to my religious attitude. I kept quiet from then on. I did not tell him that I would have liked to enter the deaconess's school. What hindered me? I needed parental permission to access the institution. My father did not like my decision and had threatened to abandon me. If he threw me out on the streets, I had no place to go. I could not find refuge at Oma's in the Russian zone, because they were secretly thinking of leaving their farm.

I must have stated to Uncle Conn, "It does not matter to which denomination I belong, as long as I go to a Christian church." At the end, Uncle Conn gave me a small package to be opened on the day of my confirmation. It contained the third edition of Theodor Storm's *Meisternovellen* (master novellas).[214] The Georg Westermann Publishing Company had reissued the 1918 version of the book, keeping the gothic script of the original publication. When I opened the little volume, I found a dedication on the flyleaf. Major Conn had written it in Sütterlin letters.[215] I never had learned to write these archaic characters, but I was able to read them because Oma used a mixture of Latin and Sütterlin script in her letters to me.

---

213 In American hymnals, you would find this song by Paul Gerhardt (1607–1676) under the title, "O Sacred Head, Now Wounded."

214 Theodor Storm was born in 1817 and died in 1888 in Husum. He is considered one of the great masters of the novella.

215 Sütterlin: see Chapter 4, footnote 62.

For a long time I did not understand the meaning of Uncle Conn's inscription. Years later, after I had studied German literature, had learned about Storm's attitude toward religion, and had read about the difficulties for postwar authors[216] to overcome the Nazi language, I realized that the major still used the jargon of the Nazi time and expressed his Christian belief mingled with heathen undertones, so prevalent in the Nazi ideology.

When we left Hamelin, our household helper, Lisel, went with us to Mülheim. By now she was part of our family; nevertheless, she was rather shy when it came to running errands. I told her that I too had to get used to the big city. As an example, I related to her my encounter with the blind clerk selling stamps at the first window in the post office. I said to her, "I greeted him politely, but he would not answer. He probably did not know if the voice he heard was directed toward him. I wished I would know his name, and then I could call on him directly, but so, I said louder than necessary, 'Could I please have a stamp for a letter to St. Bernhard?' He promptly said, 'You do not need to shout, girly, I am not deaf.' And then he asked if St. Bernhard is in the Russian zone. After I told him that it was close to Hildburghausen, he asked for the envelope. He took it, felt its size, weighed it, and gave me the correct postage."

Lisel listened patiently and suggested, "Could you, please, always buy the stamps for me?"

Lisel never got used to Mülheim. She only stayed a short time with us. One day she asked my mother if her sister Annie would be allowed to take her place. "The many steps to your apartment on the fourth floor are too much for me," she claimed. "My sister likes to come and clean for you while I go back to my parents. Anyway, I am tired of washing Miss Siepermann's clothing. I never do it good enough for her."

My mother had noticed how pale Lisel had become since she lived with us in the big city. She said. "Well, Lisel, I think you might be homesick. Call your sister, she can stay here and share your sleeping accommodation when she visits."

---

216 Wolfdietrich Schnurre said about the German language that it was terribly hard to use after 1945. In K. Wagenbach's edition *Das Atelier* 1963, page 149, he writes: "The Nazi and war years had contaminated the language. Painstakingly, the author has to knock off the dust (mud) from each word, before it can be used." The Nazi propaganda and ideology alongside the military jargon had changed the meaning of the words. Many of the postwar authors experienced this phenomenon.

Lisel's face flushed as she shyly said, "No, Mrs. Höfer, let me go home and let her come after I left. She will be all right." My mother agreed to this arrangement.

Soon our young helper left and her older sister arrived subsequently. Annie was much stronger than Lisel but had been working on a farm and knew practically nothing about a city household. Mother sighed often. After a few weeks, Annie received a letter from home and broke down in tears. We stood around her wondering what made her cry so hard. Sobbing and wiping her eyes, she told us that Lisel had died.

My mother went to the funeral and found out, that Lisel had contracted syphilis when she had been raped. Now we understood why Lisel did not want to share her bed with her sister, because she knew she was contagious and did not want to infect her or us. Her parents wanted to keep Annie at home. My mother did not object. I think my mother was actually glad that Annie wanted to get back to her family near Hamelin and work on a farm again. My mother was rightfully anxious about infections. She did not want us to be harmed in any way, let alone by a venereal disease. From now on, she made sure we did not share our living quarters with any household helpers again.

My mother found a cleaning lady to come twice each week and a washwoman for the large laundry when it was our turn to use the wash kitchen open for all renters in our apartment complex. Both women lived in Mülheim. They helped us until my father decided to buy a house in the Westerwald region of Germany.

I entered the middle school in Mülheim in September. The school's curriculum was geared to practical applications for life. I chose shorthand, typing, garden work, cooking, and sewing, along with algebra, bookkeeping, biology, geography, English (mandatory in the British zone), and French. Somehow the latter language suited me much better, but since my grades in English were poor, I had to drop French. I thought, *Too bad we are not living in the French zone, then it would be compulsory instead of English.* Every Wednesday morning our teachers separated Catholics and Protestants to go to our respective church services. Religion was another subject we had to attend.

We had moved from Victoria Street and the bomb-damaged house. It was too dangerous to live in the dilapidated building. The town fathers decided to tear it down. It had to make room for a commercial building in the city center. We were allotted an apartment in the beautiful area of the Ruhr River Park. From our new location, I could walk in a few minutes to a privately owned school for ballroom dancing. In 1953, I had reached the age when in the evening, teenage girls and boys received training in the right steps of popular dances along with a thorough education in proper social behavior. Since the school system still believed it best to separate boys and girls in our schools, it was here that we had a chance to meet the opposite sex.

In the same year, Uncle Martin and his family joined us in Mülheim. They escaped in stages to the west. First Oma and Jochen came to Berlin. Then Uncle Martin, Aunt Ursel, and their other sons Hermjörg and Lutz followed. They were spared the barracks of the overcrowded reception camps in Berlin. They had enough money to stay in a hotel room in West Berlin. They lived there until they received permission to come to Mülheim on the Ruhr, where we could help them. Now we were finally able to repay the kindness they had shown us ever since we had lost everything. We remembered very well that without their continuous help, we would have starved to death.

Political regulations forced them to leave the land and house that had been in the family since 1525. My uncle saw no future for his sons under the Soviet-controlled government of the GDR. Although his farm had not been confiscated, the demands to deliver goods became too much to fulfill. And since they did not withdraw from the church, his sons most likely would be denied a high-school education; they certainly would not be allowed to study at a university. He and Aunt Ursel saw no future for their children, no freedom to choose a profession.

As soon as we found an apartment for Uncle Martin and his family, we gave our box beds to them. Oma slept on the low mattress. She had a hard time getting up from it, but she never complained.

My grandmother was a remarkable woman. Let me take the liberty of inserting here a translation of a recent article from the *Mansfelder Zeitung* (Mansfelder newspaper). Under their regular heading "100 years ago," they choose for January 19, 2012 a report from January 15, 1912[217]. A little shortened, it reads:

> 100 years ago two bolting horses created some anxious
> moments. They galloped through the streets constantly
> being driven on by a broken sled runner. A young servant

---

217 The Mansfelder Zeitung is a local newspaper printed by the Mitteldeutsche Druck- und Verlagshaus GmbH & Co KG in Halle on the Saale. The entire article from 1912 was reprinted without the name of its author.

grabbed the reins and with the help of a few other servants he could calm the animals, and free them of the broken sleigh. The sled belongs to a landowner in Klostermansfeld [none other than my grandfather]. One runner of the sleigh split off when turning the vehicle over the tracks of the electric narrow-gauge railway causing the horses to bolt. The courageous lady in the sleigh did not let go of the reins until she was thrown off. Fortunately she did not suffer any injuries.

That fearless lady was my Oma. She must have been in her early thirties then. Now in her seventies, she did not succumb to her fate. She let us know that it hurt to leave her home, but she softened her pain by relating to us, "I have lost my homeland, my possessions, I may not tend to my husband's grave anymore, but I'll get over it. Didn't God grant me to be with my son and now with *all* of my twelve grandchildren?"

My father employed Uncle Martin briefly until a farming position could be found for him. Aunt Hilde's husband, Uncle Richard, had connections to the nobility. A baron in the Heidelberg area was looking for an experienced former landowner to farm his estate. The Oemler family—it always included Oma—moved into a converted hunting mansion on the outskirts of a little village. Old worn-out stone steps led from the large courtyard to the entrance hall. On either side of it were two huge rooms. They held grain, stored there for fermentation. When the grain reached the desired ripening phase, the farm helpers poured it into huge kettles to be heated. From there it was filtered and the liquid brought to a distillery located on the right wing of the main house. The remnants of the fermented grain served as pig and cow fodder. Every month a government agent came to oversee the loading and delivery of the high-alcohol product.

My father sensed the ever more stringent rules and danger for crossing the border between the Russian zone and the West. He wished his mother would join us. Having no telephone connections to her, he relied on friends to convey his message to Grandma: She should meet him at the northern border between the American and Russian zones near Hof. She crossed the border there without any interference by the border guards. We assumed the police did not stop her because she was old and of no more use for the workforce in the Russian zone. From then on, Grandma took turns living in Goslar with her youngest son, Uncle Horst, and with my parents in Mülheim.

I had graduated from middle school and had several months of leisure before I needed to leave for Coburg, where I intended to become a physical-education teacher. In May, I visited with the Oemler family in their little village.

Uncle Martin had found a new Stammtisch. One day, he took me to the inn where the members met regularly. They were short of men for their beloved Skat. I acted as the fourth "man." Why were they short? Some of their members celebrated Father's Day. In Germany, it falls on Ascension Day, the Thursday thirty-nine days after Easter. The Stammtisch brothers lamented about too many holidays that Germany had acquired by now. Uncle Martin said, "This morning my helper milked the cows early so he could join his bowling-club members. They'll travel to a beer-garden. Tonight my sons and I'll have to tend to the cows."

"Yes, my son is one in their party," one grey-haired member chimed in. He continued as I shuffled the cards. "We have too many holidays. We just celebrated International Worker's Day on May first, now Ascension Day, in ten days we have Pentecost with Monday off, and a month ago we just had the Holy Week with Good Friday and Easter Monday off."

Uncle Martin put his cards in the order he liked to play from and mumbled, "And now we get a new holiday, the 17th of June, the day of freedom to commemorate the rebellion of the GDR workers in Berlin. Do you remember the picture in the papers with one man standing in front of a Russian tank? His only defense against the Soviet army was a stone in his hand.[218] I was glad we'd left Berlin before the uprising took place."

"Well, Uncle Martin, as always, Lutz and Hermjörg will fill in for the farmworkers who want those days off," I remarked, picking up my own stack of cards and sorting them according to the jacks and colors of the decks.

"Yeah! You have sons who can help out," complained the butcher. "I am all by myself. Okay, my shop is closed on holidays, but the smokehouse, the machines, all have to be looked after. My wife and I really do not get any days off. Here in Baden Württemberg,[219] we even celebrate Corpus Christi on a Thursday in June. That is sixty days after Easter."

---

218 The 17th of June commemorating the Workers' Uprising of 1953 was first observed in 1954. It was also known as the Day of German Unity, but only in the FRG. It was canceled in 1990 and replaced with the Day of German Unity on October 6. The East German national day to commemorate the founding of the DDR in 1949 on October 7 was also dropped.

219 Württemberg is one of the sixteen states of the Federal Republic of Germany.

"At least during harvest time, we can work uninterrupted," Uncle Martin pointed out. He played his hand against the butcher and me. He tried to pull our trumps out by opening the game with the lowest jack, the jack of diamonds.

I answered with one of my two trumps, the queen of spades, and kept the jack of clubs, the highest trump in Skat. Although only worth two points, it could overtrump the ace of spades. I wanted to show off my knowledge about the many holidays they keep in southern Germany. "In Bavaria, you have Epiphany off."

"So do we," both of my Skat partners said simultaneously.

"But do you have August 15, Assumption Day, as a holiday?"

Uncle Martin shook his head. "You would know this, going to study in Bavaria, but only the schools are closed that day. Employees have to show up for work on Assumption Day."

I was determined to continue. "Still, it is a free day, and if I would study in Augsburg, there they celebrate the Peace Festival on August 8."

Uncle Martin grinned. "Augsburg is a big town, they do not need to consider the harvest season." At the same time, he collected his seventh trick and now played his last trump, saying, "There! Now you have to give me your aces you kept for the last trick." He won that hand.

The butcher pointed out, "Did you notice that most of these holidays are Catholic? There is still All Saints Day, November 1, for us."

I counted our points and pushed the stack of cards to my left for Uncle Martin to shuffle. He dealt me a good hand. He felt he needed to mention that there were Protestant holidays, too. "Don't forget the Reformation Day October 31 and the Day of Repentance and Prayer on Wednesday before the last Sunday, Death Sunday, in the church year."

I replied, "That's the Prussian Calvinistic influence! Typically for their working ethics, the Protestants put their holidays at a time when the farmers have a period of rest anyway, namely at the end of the fall season."

"All right!" the butcher said, getting tired of holiday talk, but he added, "Then there are still the two days for Christmas on December 25 and 26, and one week later, the first of January. But of course, these are observed by everybody, no matter if Christian or nonbeliever."

Uncle Martin laughed. "That's the type of conversation you get when you bring a young women to the Skat table!" Tongue in cheek, he continued, "Now all that's missing is that you tell us about all the customs and traditions the individual states keep alive." I was not taken aback; nevertheless, I just listened to their remarks about prices of pork and beef, eggs and corn and whatever. I concentrated on the game and thought about the many age-old costumes and traditions that had survived for centuries, most recently during the Nazi regime, and now during the Allied occupation. Hopefully they would be still observed for many years to come.

Selected Bibliography

Complete Fairy Tales of the Brothers Grimm. Translated by Jack Zipes. Expanded ed. New York: Bantam Books, 2002.

Draeger, Hans, PhD. *Der Vertrag von Versailles (The Versailles Treaty).* Berlin: Heinrich Beeken Verlag, 1933.

"France Sends Roma Gypsies Back to Romania." BBC Television, August 20, 2010.

Goethe, Johann Wolfgang von. *Goethe's Poems.* Selected by James Boyd, PhD. 10th impression. Oxford: Basil Blackwell, 1965.

Hamberger, Wolfgang. *America—My Fascination: Biography of a Friendship from the Nazi Era to the Present.* Translated by Joan Clough-Lamb. Fulda: Impressum, 2009.

National Archives & Records Administration. "The Marshall Plan." Featured Documents, General Records of the United States Government, Record Group 11. Accessed August 2010. http://www.archives.gov/exhibits/featured_documents/marshall_plan/.

Reitsch, Hanna. *Fliegen—Mein Leben.* Stuttgart: Deutsche Verlags-Anstalt GmbH. no date

Schnurre, Wolfdietrich. "Swalinka." Unpublished manuscript. Deposited in Das Deutsche Literaturarchiv, Marbach, Germany.

Strohbusch, Horst. *Das Licht kam aus der Kirche: die Wende in Meiningen, 1989–1990.* 2nd ed. Meiningen: Verlag Börner PR, 2009.

"Vor hundert Jahren." *Mitteldeutsche Zeitung*, Mansfelder edition. Heimatgeschichte sec., January 19, 2012. author unknown. Mitteldeutsches Druck- und Verlagshaus GmbH & Co Kb. Halle an der Saale.

Wagenbach, Klaus, ed. *Das Atelier: Zeitgenössische deutsche Prosa*. Frankfurt: Fischer Bücherei, 1963.

Selected List of Works Consulted

Arnold, John H. *History: A Very Short Introduction*. New York: Oxford University Press, 2000.

Detwiler, Donald S. *Germany: a Short History*. 3rd rev. ed. Carbondale: Southern Illinois University Press, 1999.

Elton, Geoffrey. *Political History: Principles and Practice*. New York: Cambridge Basic Books, 1970.

Ewen, David. *Encyclopedia of Concert Music*. New York: Hill and Wang, 1959.

Frenzel, Herbert A. and Elisabeth Frenzel. *Daten deutscher Dichtung: Chronologischer Abriß der deutschen Literaturgeschichte*. München: deutscher Taschenbuch Verlag, 1990.

Fulbrook, Mary. *A Concise History of Germany*. In the series *Cambridge Concise Histories*.1. vol. 2nd ed. Cambridge: Cambridge University Press, 2004.

Hagen, William W. *German History in Modern Times: Four Lives of the Nation*. New York: Cambridge University Press, 2012.

Kettenacker, Lothar. *Germany 1989: In the Aftermath of the Cold War*. Harlow, England: Pearson Education Limited, 2009.

Kitchen, Martin. *A History of Modern Germany: 1800 to the Present*. Chister, West Sussex: Wiley-Blackwell, 2012.

Koeltzsch, Hans. *Der neue Opernführer*. Stuttgart: Verlag Deutsche Volksbücher, 1961.

Lixl-Purcell, Andreas. *Stimmen eines Jahrhunderts 1888–1990: Deutsche Autobiographien, Tagebücher, Bilder und Briefe*. Boston: Thomson, Heinle, 1990.

Pothorn, Herbert. *Baustile: die Anfänge, die grossen Epochen, die Gegenwart*. München: Südwest Verlag, 1968.

Reinhardt, Kurt F. *Germany: 2000 Years*. 4th rev. ed. New York: Ungar Publishing Co., 1965.

Schulze, Hagen. *Germany: A New History*. Translated by Deborah Lucas Schneider. London: Harvard University Press, 1998.

von Wilpert, Gero. *Deutsches Dichterlexikon: Biographisch-bibliographisches Handwörterbuch zur deutschen Literaturgeschichte*. 3rd rev. ed. Stuttgart: Alfred Kröner Verlag, 1988.

Index

CPSIA information can be obtained at www.ICGtesting.com
Printed in the USA
LVOW11s2348281215

468193LV00001B/47/P